"*The American Statesmen Series was a pathbreaking venture in its time; and the best proof of its continuing vitality for our time lies in the testimony of the introductory essays written by eminent scholars for the volumes of the Chelsea House edition—essays that not only explain the abiding value of the texts but in many cases represent significant scholarly contributions on their own.*

"*Chelsea House is contributing vitally to the scholarly resources of the country—and, at the same time, helping us all to understand and repossess our national heritage.*"

—*Professor Arthur M. Schlesinger, jr.*

John Jay

American Statesmen Series

The Home of John Jay

Other titles in this Chelsea House series:

CHARLES FRANCIS ADAMS, *Charles Francis Adams, Jr.*
JOHN ADAMS, *John Quincy Adams and Charles Francis Adams*
JOHN QUINCY ADAMS, *John T. Morse, Jr.*
SAMUEL ADAMS, *James K. Hosmer*
JUDAH P. BENJAMIN, *Pierce Butler*
JOHN C. CALHOUN, *Hermann E. von Holst*
LEWIS CASS, *Andrew C. McLaughlin*
SALMON P. CHASE, *Albert Bushnell Hart*
HENRY CLAY, *Carl Schurz*
ALBERT GALLATIN, *Henry Adams*
ALEXANDER HAMILTON, *Henry Cabot Lodge*
PATRICK HENRY, *Moses Coit Tyler*
ANDREW JACKSON, *William Graham Sumner*
THOMAS JEFFERSON, *John T. Morse, Jr.*
JAMES MADISON, *Sydney Howard Gay*
JOHN MARSHALL, *Albert J. Beveridge*
JAMES MONROE, *Daniel Coit Gilman*
GOUVERNEUR MORRIS, *Theodore Roosevelt*
JOHN RANDOLPH, *Henry Adams*
CHARLES SUMNER, *Moorfield Storey*
MARTIN VAN BUREN, *Edward M. Shepard*
GEORGE WASHINGTON, *John Marshall*
DANIEL WEBSTER, *Henry Cabot Lodge*

Forthcoming titles in this Chelsea House series:

JOHN P. ALTGELD, *Harry Barnard*
THOMAS HART BENTON, *Theodore Roosevelt*
JAMES G. BLAINE, *Edward Stanwood*
DANIEL BOONE, *Reuben G. Thwaites*
WILLIAM JENNINGS BRYAN, *M. R. Werner*
AARON BURR, *James Parton*
PETER COOPER, *R. W. Raymond*
STEPHEN A. DOUGLAS, *Allen Johnson*
DAVID FARRAGUT, *Alfred Thayer Mahan*
ULYSSES S. GRANT, *Louis A. Coolidge*
NATHANIEL GREENE, *Francis Vinton Greene*
MARCUS ALONZO HANNA, *Herbert D. Croly*
SAM HOUSTON, *Marquis James*
HENRY KNOX, *Noah Brooks*
LUTHER MARTIN, *Paul S. Clarkson and R. Samuel Jett*
ROBERT MORRIS, *Ellis Paxson Oberholtzer*
FRANKLIN PIERCE, *Nathaniel Hawthorne*
WILLIAM H. SEWARD, *Thornton K. Lothrop*
JOHN SHERMAN, *Theodore E. Burton*
WILLIAM T. SHERMAN, *B. H. Liddell Hart*
THADDEUS STEVENS, *Samuel W. McCall*
ROGER B. TANEY, *Carl Swisher*
TECUMSEH, *Glenn Tucker*
THURLOW WEED, *Glyndon G. VanDeusen*

JOHN JAY
GEORGE PELLEW

INTRODUCTION BY
RICHARD B. MORRIS

American Statesmen Series

GENERAL EDITOR
ARTHUR M. SCHLESINGER, JR.
ALBERT SCHWEITZER PROFESSOR OF THE HUMANITIES
THE CITY UNIVERSITY OF NEW YORK

CHELSEA HOUSE
NEW YORK, LONDON
1980

Cover design by Zimmerman Foyster Design

Copyright © 1980 by Chelsea House Publishers, a division of
Chelsea House Educational Communications, Inc.
Printed and bound in the United States of America

Library of Congress Cataloging in Publication Data

Pellew, George, 1859-1892.
    John Jay.

    (American statesmen)
    Reprint of the 1898 ed. published by Houghton
Mifflin, Boston.
    Includes index.
    1. Jay, John, 1745-1829. 2. United States--
Politics and government--Revolution--1775-1783.
3. United States--Politics and government--1783-
1809. 4. Statesmen--United States--Biography.
5. Judge--United States--Biography.   I. Series:
American statesmen (New York)
[E302.6.J4P3 1980]   973.3'092'4 [B]   80-19992
ISBN 0-87754-193-0

Chelsea House Publishers
Harold Steinberg, Chairman & Publisher
Andrew E. Norman, President
Susan Lusk, Vice President
A Division of Chelsea House Educational Communications, Inc.
70 West 40 Street, New York 10018

CONTENTS

ILLUSTRATIONS
FOLLOWING PAGE 148

General Introduction

BLAZING THE WAY
Arthur M. Schlesinger, jr.

THE ORIGINAL AMERICAN STATESMEN SERIES
consisted of thirty-four titles published between
1882 and 1916. Handsomely printed and widely read, the Series made a notable contribution
to the popular appreciation of American history. Its creator was John Torrey Morse, Jr.,
born in Boston in 1840, graduated from Harvard
in 1860 and for nearly twenty restless years
thereafter a Boston lawyer. In his thirties he
had begun to dabble in writing and editing; and
about 1880, reading a volume in John Morley's
English Men of Letters Series, he was seized by
the idea of a comparable set of compact, lucid
and authoritative lives of American statesmen.

It was an unfashionable thought. The celebrated New York publisher Henry Holt turned
the project down, telling Morse, "Who ever
wants to read American history?" Houghton,
Mifflin in Boston proved more receptive, and
Morse plunged ahead. His intention was that
the American Statesmen Series, when com-

plete, "should present such a picture of the development of the country that the reader who had faithfully read all the volumes would have a full and fair view of the history of the United States told through the medium of the efforts of the men who had shaped our national career. The actors were to develop the drama."

In choosing his authors, Morse relied heavily on the counsel of his cousin Henry Cabot Lodge. Between them, they enlisted an impressive array of talent. Henry Adams, William Graham Sumner, Moses Coit Tyler, Hermann von Holst, Moorfield Storey and Albert Bushnell Hart were all in their early forties when their volumes were published; Lodge, E. M. Shepard and Andrew C. McLaughlin in their thirties; Theodore Roosevelt in his twenties. Lodge took on Washington, Hamilton and Webster, and Morse himself wrote five volumes. He offered the authors a choice of $500 flat or a royalty of 12.5¢ on each volume sold. Most, luckily for themselves, chose the royalties.

Like many editors, Morse found the experience exasperating. "How I waded among the fragments of broken engagements, shattered pledges! I never really knew when I could count upon getting anything from anybody." Carl Schurz infuriated him by sending in a two-volume life of Henry Clay on a take-it-or-leave-it basis. Morse, who had confined Jefferson, John Adams, Webster and Calhoun to single volumes, was tempted to leave it. But Schurz threatened to publish his work simultaneously if Morse commissioned another life of Clay for the Series; so Morse reluctantly surrendered.

When a former Confederate colonel, Allan B. Magruder, offered to do John Marshall, Morse, hoping for "a good Virginia atmosphere," gave him a chance. The volume turned out to have been borrowed in embarrassing measure from Henry Flanders's *Lives and Times of the Chief Justices.* For this reason, Magruder's *Marshall* is not included in the Chelsea House reissue of the Series; Albert J. Beveridge's famous biography appears in its stead. Other classic biographies will replace occasional Series volumes: John Marshall's *Life of George Washington* in place of Morse's biography; essays on John Adams by John Quincy Adams and Charles Francis Adams, also substituting for a Morse volume; and Henry Adams's *Life of Albert Gallatin* instead of the Series volume by John Austin Stevens.

"I think that only one real blunder was made," Morse recalled in 1931, "and that was in allotting [John] Randolph to Henry Adams." Half a century earlier, however, Morse had professed himself pleased with Adams's

Randolph. Adams, responding with characteristic self-deprecation, thought the "acidity" of his account "much too decided" but blamed the "excess of acid" on the acidulous subject. The book was indeed hostile but nonetheless stylish. Adams also wrote a life of Aaron Burr, presumably for the Series. But Morse thought Burr no statesman, and on his advice, to Adams's extreme irritation, Henry Houghton of Houghton, Mifflin rejected the manuscript. "Not bad that for a damned bookseller!" said Adams. "He should live for a while at Washington and know our *real* statesmen." Adams eventually destroyed the work, and a fascinating book was lost to history.

The definition of who was or was not a "statesman" caused recurrent problems. Lodge told Morse one day that their young friend Theodore Roosevelt wanted to do Gouverneur Morris. "But, Cabot," Morse said, "you surely don't expect Morris to be in the Series! He doesn't belong there." Lodge replied, "Theodore . . . *needs the money,*" and Morse relented. No one objected to Thomas Hart Benton, Roosevelt's other contribution to the Series. Roosevelt turned out the biography in an astonishing four months while punching cows and chasing horse thieves in the Badlands. Begging Lodge to send more material from

Boston, he wrote that he had been "mainly evolving [Benton] from my inner consciousness; but when he leaves the Senate in 1850 I have nothing whatever to go by. ... I hesitate to give him a wholly fictitious date of death and to invent all the work of his later years." In fact, T.R. had done more research than he pretended; and for all its defects, his *Benton* has valuable qualities of vitality and sympathy.

Morse, who would chat to Lodge about "the aristocratic upper crust in which you & I are imbedded," had a fastidious sense of language. Many years later, in the age of Warren G. Harding, he recommended to Lodge that the new President find someone "who can clothe for him his 'ideas' in the language customarily used by educated men." At dinner in a Boston club, a guest commented on the dilemma of the French ambassador who could not speak English. "Neither can Mr. Harding," Morse said. But if patrician prejudice improved Morse's literary taste, it also impaired his political understanding. He was not altogether kidding when he wrote Lodge as the Series was getting under way, "Let the Jeffersonians & the Jacksonians beware! I will poison the popular mind!!"

Still, for all its fidelity to establishment

values, the American Statesmen Series had distinct virtues. The authors were mostly from outside the academy, and they wrote with the confidence of men of affairs. Their books are generally crisp, intelligent, spirited and readable. The Series has long been in demand in secondhand bookstores. Most of its volumes are eminently worth republication today, on their merits as well as for the vigorous expression they give to an influential view of the American past.

Born during the Presidency of Martin Van Buren, John Torrey Morse, Jr., died shortly after the second inauguration of Franklin D. Roosevelt in 1937. A few years before his death he could claim with considerable justice that his Series had done "a little something in blazing the way" for the revival of American historical writing in the years to come.

New York
May, 1980

INTRODUCTION
TO THE
CHELSEA HOUSE EDITION

Richard B. Morris

John Adams called John Jay "a Roman," comparing him to the ancient hero Cato the Elder, renowned for his simplicity of manners, integrity, and courage. That traditional image of Jay was preserved for posterity in Giuseppe Ceracchi's marble bust and in Gilbert Stuart's portrait of the robed Chief Justice. It is the special virtue of George Pellew's biography that it was the first to paint a balanced portrait of Jay, to show his human side as well as his public presence.

Pellew had advantages denied to previous biographers. Nephew of Jay's grandson, John Jay II, he not only had access to the family papers, but, as a good oral historian, he recorded reminiscences and anecdotal material that carry the hallmark of authenticity. Back in 1833 Jay's son William, the noted antislavery leader, had published a two-volume edition of his father's life and letters, volumes stressing his public career. Therein Jay appears stately, virtuous, dignified, prim, and bloodless. Those of his father's letters that the son published conformed to that portrait, and even then he carefully excised evidence of ribaldry or taints of impropriety on the part of Jay family members or other correspondents.

As Pellew's biography reveals, and more recent publications of the papers of John Jay confirm, Jay was a complex personality. Beloved and admired by family, friends, and colleagues of the standing of Franklin, John Adams, and Lafayette, he was also dreaded by others, including certain diplomats of the Spanish and French courts and the opponents of the Jay Treaty of 1794. He could be affectionate, compassionate, eloquent, fun-loving, and even ribald on occasion and in the appropriate surroundings; but to those less favored by this side of his nature, he seemed irritable, obstinate, and a stickler for the letter of the law. In dealing with foreign diplomats, he scrupulously perused their formal written powers and, for himself, acted only on receipt of authenticated official instructions from Congress. Nevertheless, when in his judgment the national interest dictated violating such instructions, he could display an initiative, not to say audacity, in the conduct of his negotiations belied by his circumspect lawyerlike exterior.

What is especially appealing in the Pellew biography is not the analysis of Jay the public man, statesman, and diplomat, so much as the intimate and affectionate profile of Jay the family man. Pellew drew upon hitherto unused family papers, as well as the recollections of members of the family. We see here John Jay, the devoted son, loving husband, and totally responsible brother, often, even in times of public crisis, preoccupied with his blind brother and sister, both maimed by smallpox in infancy, and with another troubled sister deserted by her Tory preacher husband, for whose son, Peter Jay Munro, Jay assumed full responsibility.

Pellew gives us intriguing glimpses of the lifelong romance between John Jay and his wife, Sarah Van Brugh Livingston, the daughter of the renowned Whig Governor of New Jersey, William Livingston. Sally, who possessed beauty and charm and could flutter like a socialite of her day, shared with John the hardships and dangers of a wartime crossing of the Atlantic and the arduous journey across the Pyrenees from Spain to Paris, as well as the responsibilities of running a home in France and rearing two young daughters abroad. A distinct social asset to her husband, she proved a good diplo-

mat as well as a rock of support in troubled
times.

In this biography the author captures flashes
of Jay's taciturn Yorker humor. When General
Horatio Gates, victor at Saratoga, rode over to
Fishkill to try to persuade John Jay that the
lenient surrender terms he had given General
Burgoyne were justified, he was unable to
budge his listener. "Do you not think the Saratoga convention a good convention?" Gates
asked. "Unquestionably, my dear general,"
countered Jay, "*provided* you could not have
made a better." The disappointed general
turned to a companion and said, "Come, it is
time for us to go." Years later, when the irre-
pressible Gouverneur Morris was reminiscing at
Bedford, Jay's retirement estate, Morris remarked about the old days at the Second Continental Congress, "Jay, what a set of damned
scoundrels we had in that second Congress."
"Yes," said Jay, "that we had," as he knocked
the ashes from his long clay pipe.

As might be expected of a very proper nine-
teenth-century biographer, there is a side to
Jay and the Jay family about which Pellew is
silent. We find here no rattling of family skele-
tons, no references to the personal controversies in which Jay managed to get himself involved. From the passing allusions to Jay's

elder brother, one would never realize what an embarrassment James proved to John and the rest of the family. Sir James, knighted for his clouded efforts to raise money for King's College, ever managed to show up at the wrong time, at the wrong place, and, so far as the rest of the family saw it, on the wrong side. His fund-raising for Columbia's predecessor involved years of litigation, to the chagrin of the family, before the college got the money. James also lined up with opponents of John in the New York legislature. After joining a faction in the New York State Senate that took a hard line toward the Loyalists—a position John Jay deplored—James managed to get himself captured by the British and shipped to England. At the very time when John was engaged in sensitive peace negotiations for his country, Sir James was trying to sell a naval invention to the British and to score a triumph over his brother by pressing his own unauthorized peace plan. No mention of this in Pellew, nor of James's postwar career, when he set up housekeeping in New Jersey with a liberated married woman and sired offspring from whom was descended Alfred Thayer Mahan, America's most famous naval strategist and geopolitician.

Nor can one learn from Pellew that Jay,

while eminently successful in dealing with his peers, with a Washington, a Franklin, or a John Adams, encountered enormous problems in handling subordinates, including his young brother-in-law Brockholst Livingston, who was his personal secretary in Spain, and William Carmichael, the official secretary of the Spanish mission, whom Jay suspected of systematic intrigue to undermine his authority. Most surprising is the complete omission of the name of Lewis Littlepage, that foppish teenage Virginian whom Jay had agreed in a generous moment to sponsor in Spain, and who proved insolent and ungrateful. Jay and Littlepage participated in a literary duel in the postwar years, culminating in a lawsuit in which Jay recovered the money he had advanced Littlepage abroad. Jay's commanding reputation survived the scandal. Jefferson, never an intimate of Jay, summed up the notorious affair admirably: "In truth, it is affliction that a man who has passed his life in serving the public, who had served them in every of the highest stations with universal approbation, who though poor, has never permitted himself to make a shilling in the public employ, should yet be liable to have his peace of mind so much disturbed."

Aside from his intimate glimpses of the first Chief Justice, Pellew had a more serious purpose. He sought to counter the partisan critics of Jay and the High Federalists, critics who gave less than a charitable interpretation of three of the more controversial events in which John Jay participated—the negotiations of the peace with Great Britain in 1782-83, Jay's proposal to Congress to yield temporarily the right to the free navigation of the Mississippi in return for major concessions from Spain, and last, but not least in the eyes of the Jeffersonian Republicans, his negotiations with Great Britain in 1794, culminating in the treaty that bears Jay's name.

Although Pellew did not have access to foreign archives, his defense of Jay's role in engaging in separate and secret negotiations with Great Britain has been bolstered by subsequent revelations. British Foreign Office archives and private papers abroad document French efforts to limit America's westward territorial aspirations in order to placate the French King's Spanish ally, as well as French reluctance to admit the United States to the Grand Bank fisheries, which England and France had traditionally divided. As regards Jay's proposal in the 1780s to forgo free navigation on the Mississippi for a limited number of years, Pellew frankly concedes that Jay did not take into account the rapid settlement of the western territories, which was a post-Revolutionary phenomenon. "An error of judgment" on Jay's part, Pellew writes, but at least one actuated by national, not sectional, motives. "A fair treaty" is Pellew's verdict on the compact of 1794 with Great Britain, although its disclosure created the greatest partisan storm of the Washington administration and indubitably damaged Jay's reputation in national politics. Historians, after damning the treaty for almost two centuries, are now inclined to accept Pellew's estimate as realistic. Circumstances had made it possible for Jay to be a tough negotiator in 1782-83. He no longer held a strong hand in 1794 and was forced to make the best of his weak situation, to the detriment, as Pellew points out, of his own national career. The author quotes Jay's response to his attackers: "Calumny is seldom durable. It will in time yield to truth." Time, beginning perhaps with Pellew's book, has contributed to a more constructive estimate of Jay's accomplishments in putting his signature to the treaty of 1794.

In bold strokes Pellew draws a portrait of Jay as a nationalist statesman. His experiences as wartime President of the Continental Congress and postwar Secretary for Foreign Affairs had persuaded him of the inadequacy of the Articles of Confederation. He advocated a strong chief executive, the separation of powers, a system of checks and balances, and, with the possible exception of Alexander Hamilton, held the most advanced views of anyone on centralization and the subordination of the states. While Jay's strong Federalist views prevented his being named a delegate to the Constitutional Convention in Philadelphia, he became a leading champion of ratification once the Constitution's text was disclosed.

With Hamilton and James Madison he collaborated on the famous *Federalist* letters, writing numbers two through five as well as sixty-four, the last with its implication that the making and ending of treaties was a joint responsibility of the President *and* the Senate. Perhaps Jay's most effective pamphlet was his "Address to the People of the State of New York," whose reasoning Pellew praised as "eminently practical and cogent," and whose warnings to its readers helped counter the strong anti-Federalist sentiment upstate. "Our distresses are accumulating like compound interest," Jay warned, adding that were the Constitution to be rejected, "every band of union would be severed." At the New York Ratifying Convention's deliberations in Poughkeepsie, Jay, along with Hamilton and Robert R. Livingston, was one of the three undisputed leaders of the pro-Constitution party. Couching his arguments in palatable, even conciliatory language, keeping his temper under control, and working tirelessly among delegates both on and off the floor, Jay finally brought about the compromise whereby the convention resolved unanimously to circularize state legislatures recommending a general convention to consider amendments. That event did not occur, however, because the second-convention movement was aborted by the adoption of the Bill of Rights.

As first Chief Justice of the United States Jay insisted that the Supreme Court abstain from taking a political stance or rendering advisory opinions that might be construed as interfering with the legislative powers of Congress. However, as Pellew shows, the Chief Justice, an activist by temperament, remained much involved in politics. He stumped the country on foreign policy issues, using the charge to the grand jury on circuit as the medium for his views; he drafted a proclamation of neutrality (although not the one Washington finally issued) and entertained no doubts about the President's constitutional power to proclaim neutrality unilaterally.

Far from feeling that such comments were improper, Jay and his colleagues on the High

Court regarded it as incumbent upon the Court to instruct the public in the essence of the constitutional system, in whose construction they themselves had labored so strenuously, and to warn of events that might threaten the newly formed union. It took courage on Jay's part to tell an audience of French sympathizers that they should be neutral in their behavior or to tell Southern debtors that they were honor bound under the Treaty of 1783 to pay their debts to British creditors. But Jay had the backbone of older-fashioned statesmen. He did not take a national poll before expressing his views but told the country what he thought was best for it, even if the advice was unpopular. That was leadership of a kind sorely missed in more recent years.

Finally, it was the measure of the man, as Pellew shows, that Jay, in his two-term governorship of his state, put nation above party, and principle above partisanship. When urged to replace an inherited officeholder with a man from his own party, he rejoined, "And do you, sir, advise me to sell a friend that I may buy an enemy?" Nor would he support a candidate from his own party who possessed an objectionable private character. "Adherence to party has its limits" was his reply.

Jay's principled conduct is perhaps best

exemplified by his behavior during the presidential election contest of 1800. In the spring of that year the Jeffersonian Democratic-Republicans had won control of the New York legislature, which meant that New York's twelve electoral votes would go to Jefferson and Burr. A frenzied Alexander Hamilton now urged Jay to call the adjourned lame-duck Federalist legislature into special session and have it pass an act redistricting the state and choosing presidential electors by popular ballot. Had Jay done so, the Federalists might have picked up five and possibly six of the electors—enough to elect a Federalist President. "In times like these in which we live, it will not do to be overscrupulous," Hamilton wrote Jay. Governor Jay did not lose his head. He recognized that the will of the people had been expressed in the April elections that had returned the Democratic-Republican legislature. Was it fair to change the rules in the middle of the game? Taking up Hamilton's letter, he turned it over and thus endorsed it: "Proposing a measure for *party* purposes, which I think it would not become me to adopt." It was in character for Jay to permit his party to go down to defeat rather than to win dishonorably.

Finally, it seems consistent with John Jay's long opposition to slavery that the bill for gradual emancipation enacted in New York in 1799 bore his signature as Governor. "I wish to see all unjust and unnecessary discriminations everywhere abolished," Jay wrote in 1785, "and that the time may come when all our inhabitants of every color and discrimination shall be free and equal partakers of our political liberty." That time was still distant, but the Founding Father so intimately portrayed by George Pellew did as much as any of his American contemporaries to bridge the gap between his own time and a more egalitarian era.

New York, New York
June, 1980

BIBLIOGRAPHICAL NOTE

A small portion of Jay's writings first appeared in excised form in the biography written by his son, William Jay, *The Life of John Jay*, 2 vols. (New York, 1833). Some half-century later a four-volume edition of his papers appeared under the editorship of Henry P. Johnston, *The Correspondence and Public Papers of John Jay* (New York, 1893). Incomplete, inaccurate, and also excised, the Johnston edition is currently being supplemented by Richard B. Morris's projected four-volume edition of Jay's unpublished papers. Published to date: *John Jay: The Making of a Revolutionary* (New York, 1975) and *John Jay: The Winning of the Peace* (New York, 1980). Jay's central role in the peacemaking has been treated by Morris, *The Peacemakers: The Great Powers and American Independence* (New York, 1965), and his controversial treaty with Great Britain in the classic monograph by Samuel Flagg Bemis, *Jay's Treaty: A Study in Commerce and Diplomacy* (New Haven, 1923), and more recently in Jerald A. Combs, *The Jay Treaty* (Berkeley, 1970). The constitutional and judicial aspects of Jay's career are evaluated by Morris, *John Jay, The Nation, and The Court* (Boston, 1967). More recent than Pellew's is Frank Monaghan's biography, *John Jay* (New York, 1935).

PREFACE TO THE 1898 EDITION

IN preparing this new edition of the American Statesmen series, it has not been found necessary to make any alteration in the life of Jay. Since the book was written, the author, Mr. Pellew, has unfortunately died. But he had performed his work so thoroughly that it is not likely that, if he had lived, he would have desired to amend it in any particular. The upright character and open career of Jay left no opportunity for posterity to make discovery of unsuspected schemes or intrigues, ambitions or failures, such as often give rise to surprise and discussion in the cases of many men in public life. From the beginning to the end, all which he did lay open to inspection in broad daylight. His biographers find nothing to explain, nothing to dispute over, nothing to place in new lights. The only matter of debate concerns the famous treaty which he negotiated with England. Whether this was as favorable as it should have been for the United States was a question disputed between the two political parties at the time, and which has continued to cause some disagreement between historical writers since then. Opinion is gradually taking the shape that he obtained all that was possible, if not all that was desirable. But whatever may be held by different authorities upon this point, it is not likely that any new facts can ever be adduced to add to or to change the views and arguments heretofore so fully expressed.

The works of Mr. Jay are in process of publication. But it is not supposable that they will give occasion for any change in this volume. Mr. Pellew was a descendant of Mr. Jay; he had the advice and assistance of the Hon. John Jay, who was the head of the family when this biography was in preparation; and he had the free use of all the papers and manuscripts from which the published Works are only a selection. Nothing, therefore, is coming to light in the way of unexplored material.

THE EDITOR.

January, 1898.

AUTHOR'S PREFACE
TO THE
1890 EDITION

THE public life of John Jay was so active and varied that it is almost impossible to compress the essential facts into small compass without losing much of their interest and suggestiveness. Moreover, he was by disposition so reticent and unimpulsive, so completely self-controlled, that there is scarcely any material for constructing a history of his inner private life. He was singularly free from those faults which, trivial or serious, attract men's love by exciting their sympathy or pity. Conscientious, upright, just, and wise, John Jay, like Washington, survives in the popular imagination as an abstract type of propriety; and his fair fame has been a conspicuous mark for all who are offended by hearing an Aristides always called the Just, or who, from an *a priori* notion of history, believe that statesmen have always been as corrupt, civic virtue as tainted, and politics as demoralizing, as they are in our time. In this belief there is undoubtedly much truth, — but there are exceptions to most rules, or rather what is true of a generation in the average is never true of every individual comprised in it, — and a careful study confirms the contemporary opinion that the character of Jay was, unfortunately for mankind, exceptional.

Any life of John Jay must, of course, be based on the two volumes of his Life and Letters by his son, Judge William Jay; but an undue sense of the sanctity of domestic life prevented then the publication of anything not clearly of a public, almost of an official, nature. Subsequently, as the Works and Letters appeared of Washington, John Adams, Madison, Jefferson, Fisher Ames, and the other Revolutionary patriots, and the gleanings of Sparks and others from the government papers, more light was thrown on the motives and movements of the time, and Jay's life was rewritten by Flanders, who dispelled, almost for the first time, the odium, begotten by partisanship of ignorance, that so long assailed the memory of the early Federalists. Certain popular prejudices still survived from the days when blind devotion to France, a veritable "love frenzy," was a test of party fealty, and these prejudices obscured any clear view of the peace negotiations of 1782. Sparks, editing official documents, interjected with misleading positiveness a note that Jay's suspicions of France were unfounded, — and this suggestion, itself unfounded, has until recently been followed implicitly by historians, even by Mr. Bancroft. A hundred years after the event, papers from the French archives published by De Circourt, the correspondence between Vergennes and Luzerne, Fitzherbert and Fox, Oswald and Shelburne, in the "Stevens MSS.," and the revelations in Fitzmaurice's "Life of Shelburne," enabled the Honorable John Jay to prove the absolute correctness of his grandfather's convictions, and the consequent necessity of the course of action he adopted. This new information has not yet been incorporated into any life of Jay.

Within the last year the third volume has been published of Doniol's "La participation de la France dans l'établissement de l'indépendance des Etas-Unis," which contains the official documents relating to the treaty of Aranjuez, elucidating with extreme fullness the relations between the courts of Paris and Madrid in the critical years of 1778, 1779. The "Jay MSS.," from which a selection is now preparing for publication, and an elaborate digest, with quotations, of the "Stevens MSS.," have also been studied with minute care; and to these sources, and to the constant valuable suggestions and criticisms of my uncle, the Honorable John Jay, is due whatever of new or original may be found here.

GEORGE PELLEW.

New York, March 1, 1890.

JOHN JAY

CHAPTER I

YOUTH

1745-1774

JOHN JAY, the eighth child and sixth son of Peter Jay and Mary, the daughter of Jacobus Van Cortlandt, was born in the city of New York, on the 12th of December, 1745. His father was a wealthy merchant, who retired from business at the age of forty to live at a country house and farm at Rye in Westchester County. The family was of French descent; the great grandfather, Pierre Jay, a Huguenot merchant of La Rochelle, left France on the revocation of the Edict of Nantes, when the greater part of his property was confiscated, and died in England. The grandfather, Augustus, after many hazardous adventures, settled in New York in 1686, where he married Anna Maria Bayard, a descendant of a Protestant professor of theology at Paris, who had likewise chosen to leave his country for religion's sake, making his home in Holland. Through his wife's relations, the Bayards and Stuyvesants, and his brother-in-law, Stephen Peloquin, a merchant of Bristol, England, Augustus Jay soon formed a large business connection. From Bristol came invoices of kerseys and mohairs, hats, gloves, and beer; to the Barbadoes he shipped flour, bread, pork, and hams, receiving in return cargoes of sugar and rum; and occasionally his ships made adventures to Surinam. Peter Jay soon became a partner with his father; in 1740 his name appears as one of the aldermen of the city of New York; and the family was allied with the manorial families of Van Cortlandt and Philipse, to which was soon to be added the most influential of all, the family of Livingston.

From Peter Jay, who seems to have been a typical New York merchant of the last century, "a gentleman of opulence, character, and reputation," [1] his son John inherited many marked traits of character, as is testified by the now yellowing pages of the old merchant's letter book. In letters to his son James,[2] in England, even in the brief business-like notices of the death of relations, is shown the piety of the man and of the family: " Let us endeavor to adhere to the worship of God, and, observing his holy ordinances as the rule of our lives, let us disregard the wicked insinuations of

---

[1] Jones, *History of New York*, ii. 223.

[2] Afterwards knighted for his success in raising funds in England for King's College, now Columbia College, a member of the New York Senate, and a physician of distinction in New York.

libertines, who not only deride our most Holy Religion and the professors of it, but also endeavor to gain prosilites to their detestable notions, and so rob the Almighty of the honour and adoration that is due to him from his creatures." [1]

Now and then a casual sentence opens a tiny chink through the shutters that close so tightly round that little family circle. " When you come home," his father reminds James, " don't forget to bring me Bishop Patrick's Devout Christian, a book you doubtless well remember, as it contains the family prayers we always use." [2] " I desire you," he says a few months later, " to make me a present . . . of a box with five or six groce of neat long pipes, but not very long and weighty, and to your mother an oval tortoise shell snuff box, with a joint to the lid, the length of the box not exceeding six inches." [3] One wonders whether James, when he returned after many years, did remember that snuff box so minutely described, and whether it was the recollection of those " neat long pipes" that made John Jay always so fond of long " Church wardens."

Occasionally politics are mentioned. There is, however, nothing but loyal enthusiasm for the success of the troops during the French war, honest regard for the successive governors, and regret for their mistakes and mischances, especially for the

---

[1] To James Jay, December 7, 1751, *Letter Book of Peter Jay*, iii.

[2] September 2, 1754. [3] November 26, 1754.

fate of Sir Danvers Osborne, " our late new governor," who " very unhappily committed a violence upon himself, and was found in a melancholy
situation fastened with his handkerchief." [1] But
from the date of the Stamp Act, and the measures
restrictive of trade that were passed simultaneously
with its repeal, the tone gradually changed. " Our
colonists cannot digest the hard measure they are
dealt with in Parliament at home, when at the
same time they think the sugar islands are greatly
indulg'd to their prejudice. . . . The political
views of the great, in measures in disfavour of the
Colonyes, are to me impenetrable ; they may, for
aught I can conceive, tend to very satisfactory
ends, but they are considered here by the most
judicious in a very different light, as the unhappy
occasion of making very bad impressions on the
minds of the people, and the laying a foundation
for much trouble, that will sooner or later be the
inevitable consequence of too harsh usage. In my
situation in life, the measures complained of can
very inconsiderably affect me, and thus far they
give me no concern, but nevertheless I can't help
having a feeling for the great numbers who are
likely to suffer by them." [2] The hard times that
followed are noticed briefly : " The reasonableness
of a general complaint of the difficult times in
these Colonyes by the great restrictions lay'd on
trade, etc., begins to manifest itself by frequent

[1] To David Peloquin, October 24, 1753.
[2] To same, May 7, 1765.

failures, and by a shocking general bad pay among the people;"[1] and as the year advances to its close, the language becomes stronger, and the keen-eyed merchant begins to see pretty clearly the meaning of what is taking place. "The general and spirited resentment that prevails in the Colonyes," he writes on November 25, 1765, "gives reason to expect that the enforcing the Stamp Act will be opposed at all events, and then England as well as the Colonyes may both have reason to curse the first promoters of it, who by this impolitick act have effectually united the several Colonyes into the strongest tyes of mutual interest and friendship, which political measures of former Ministrys, we always thought, tended to prevent."[2]

Peter Jay, then, was a sound Whig from the beginning, and his son naturally took the same independent stand. When the final appeal to arms came, Peter Jay remained true to his Whig principles, though no extremist. "God grant," he wrote to John in the spring of 1776, "that all attempts of the ministerial troops may be frustrated, and be the means of a happy reconciliation,"[3] a curiously illogical wish, but one that reflected closely the Whig popular opinion of a few months earlier, and which was, even then, the wish of both father and son, and of a majority of the Congress.

One letter more may be quoted, full of character, and of character that did not die with the

[1] To David Peloquin, June 4, 1765. [2] To same.
[3] April 18, 1776, *Jay MSS.*

writer. It was written in 1771, to his son John, and is about a dispute with a neighbor, in itself unimportant: —

" DEAR JOHNNY, — Your brother tells me Mr. Bayard and you have agreed about the road. The settlement of our lott never was an object to me, and had that gentleman condescended to ask me for a road as a matter of favour he should have had it. His attempt to draw me into the measure by regard to my own interest, was a little piece of art which I was determined should not succeed. . . . Design is not his talent, he had better act with candor and openness. His threats of an Act of Assembly and an Application to the Corporation, were better calculated to excite ridicule than fear. I have nothing to ask or fear from any man, and will not be compelled into measures. The truth of his former pretences appears now from his consenting to pay so dearly for a road; tell him he may have his land and a road too." [1]

Piety, independence, and a keen sense of justice were natural birthrights in the Jay family; to these, several generations of successful business men had added the more worldly virtues of prudence and perseverance; while from his father John Jay seems to have inherited a firmness of character which, in excess, would have been obstinacy, and a strength of feeling seldom suspected because united with unusual self-control. It is also noticeable that of Jay's great grandparents not one was English, three were French and five Dutch, so that

[1] To John Jay, 1771, *Jay MSS.*

he was one of the few men of the Revolution who could say, as he did in 1796, "Not being of British descent, I cannot be influenced by that tendency towards their national character, nor that partiality for it, which might otherwise be supposed to be not unnatural." This fact in itself, combined with the hatred of interference traditional among merchants, may have had no little influence in making John Jay a leader in the American Revolution without his ceasing to be, or rather because he was, a conservative.

The year of his birth he was taken to Rye, and there his early childhood was passed in the old Jay house, which at that time was " a long low building, but one room deep," extended, as the family increased, by some eighty feet in length.[1] After surviving an attack of sore throat, of which a younger sister died, and escaping the dreaded small-pox that left his brother Peter and his sister Nancy totally blind, he was taught by his mother " the rudiments of English, and the Latin grammar." " Johnny is of a very grave disposition and takes to learning exceedingly well," wrote his father, when the boy was nearly seven years old ; " he will be soon fit to go to a grammar school ; "[2] and to a grammar school he accordingly went the next year. "My Johnny gives me a very pleasing prospect," wrote Mr. Jay again in the autumn ; " he seems to be endowed with a very good ca-

[1] Scharf, *Hist. of Westchester Co.* ii. 672.
[2] To James Jay, July 3, 1752.

pacity, is very reserved and quite of his brother
James's disposition for books." [1]   The school was
kept by the Rev. Peter Stoope, the pastor of the
French Huguenot church, then lately joined to the
Episcopal communion, at New Rochelle. He was
by birth a Swiss, an eccentric man, very absent-
minded, and wholly devoted to mathematics, so
that the parsonage was allowed to fall into decay,
and the boys were half-starved under the management of his wife, " who was as penurious as he
was careless."   To keep the snow off his bed in
winter, John used to stuff the broken panes of his
window with bits of wood. But the plain food
agreed with him, his health was excellent, and he
used to recall afterwards the pleasure he had in
the woods picking nuts, which "he carried home
in his stockings."   French was spoken generally
at the parsonage and by the people of the village,
who were, as its name suggests, chiefly descend-
ants of French refugees ; thus he easily and early
learned the language that was to prove so useful
to him.   At New Rochelle he stayed for three
years, when he was taken home to Rye, and prepared for college by a tutor, Mr. George Murray.

Jay entered King's (now Columbia) College in
1760, when he was but a little over fourteen years
old.   For admission he was required to read " the
first three of Tully's orations, and the six first books
of Virgil's Æneid into English, and the ten first
chapters of St. John's Gospel into Latin," to be

[1] To Messrs. D. & L. Peloquin, October 24, 1753.

well versed in Latin grammar, and to be "expert
in Arithmetick as far as Reduction." At that time
the college was under its first president, the learned
and pious Dr. Samuel Johnson, an old friend of
Mr. Peter Jay, whose eldest son Augustus had
studied reading and writing at the doctor's parsonage at Stratford. Dr. Johnson was a gentle, studious man, who had been one of the first graduates
of Yale College to desert Congregationalism for
the Church of England. Single-handed at first,
then with one and afterwards two assistants, he
instructed the few students of King's College, and
was just gaining some success, when he resigned
on the death of his wife of the small-pox, which for
some years had been epidemic in New York, and
for fear of which he scarcely ever ventured out of
doors.[1] Young Jay early won his regard, and on
Dr. Johnson's resignation in 1763 he learned from
his father that the doctor wished to hear from him.
"I would have you gratify him with a letter, which
he has a right to expect from you, and, although I
believe things go well in the college now," Mr. Jay
suggested with characteristic caution, "yet I would
not have you write more than may be communicated out of college."[2] The boy wrote accordingly,
and the late president answered promptly, incidentally showing how early, with its unfamiliar strains
of wild romance, McPherson's bombastic Ossian
charmed the fancy even in America: "I gave

[1] Baird, *Life of Dr. Samuel Johnson.*
[2] August, 1763, *Jay MSS.*

Brooks a much better and more correct copy of
what I had added to Ossian's Address to the Sun
than what you had before, from which I wish you
and all of them would exactly transcribe for the
future." [1]

Of Jay's college life little is known. During
the first two years he lodged at the house of Lawrence Romer, a painter, at "the corner of Verlet-
tenburgh Hill and Broadway," and the last two
years he had rooms in the college. He set himself
at once, of his own accord, to curing certain defects
of utterance and rapid reading, and he made an
enthusiastic study of English composition, a study
that bore fruit in the graceful and easy, but at the
same time often laconic, style for which he was
noted, and which in the first Continental Congress
at once placed him in "the little aristocracy of
talents and letters " with William Livingston and
Dickinson.[2] "My son John has now been two
years at college," wrote Mr. Jay in 1765, "where
he prosecutes his studyes to satisfaction. He is
indued with very good natural parts, and is bent
upon a learned profession. I believe it will be the
law." [3] In his last year at college, Jay, then " a
youth remarkably sedate and well-disposed," [4] as
his father called him, determined on the law as his
profession, and is said to have begun his prepara-

---

[1] From Rev. Dr. S. Johnson, October 27, 1763, *Jay MSS.*
[2] John Adams's *Works*, x. 79.
[3] *Ibid.*, April 14, 1763.
[4] To David Peloquin, *Letter Book*, May 16, 1763.

tion for it by carefully reading through Grotius
" De Jure Belli et Pacis," and its discussion of
international law and so-called natural rights may
have seemed to have a bearing on the perplexing
and pressing problems of the day. His decision to
study law was apparently the result of thought and
deliberation, as Mr. Jay wrote to him on hearing
of it: "Your observations on the study of the law
I believe are very just, and as it's your inclination
to be of that profession, I hope you'll closely attend to it, with a firm resolution that no difficulties
in prosecuting that study shall discourage you from
applying very close to it, and, if possible, from
taking a delight in it." [1]

In 1763 Dr. Johnson was succeeded as president by Dr. Myles Cooper, "a wit and a scholar,"
said Verplanck, "whose learning and accomplishments gave him personal popularity and respect
with his pupils, and of course added authority to
his opinions, and those were the opinions and prejudices of the high-toned English University Tory
of the last century." [2] Twelve years later, to escape a mob, this good gentleman was forced to leap
over the college fence with an undignified precipitation little befitting a poet and a Fellow of Ox-
ford, and he sailed forthwith for England; but at
this earlier time he was not unpopular, and he was
always spoken of respectfully by Jay, who might

[1] August 23, 1763, *Jay MSS.*
[2] Gulian Verplanck, *Address before College Societies*, August 2,
1830.

naturally have resented what he then deemed a most unjust punishment in the following matter. One day a number of students in the College Hall began to break the table, — such at least is the traditional description of their nefarious enterprise. The president heard the noise, went in, and asked one student after another, "Did you break the table?" "Do you know who did?" All answered "No," until he came to Jay, who was the last but one. To the first question Jay answered like the others; to the second question, "Yes, sir." "Who was it?" asked Dr. Cooper. "I do not choose to tell you, sir," was the sturdy reply; and the next and last boy answered as Jay did. These two were called before the professors, when Jay argued ingeniously and reasonably enough that, as information against fellow students was not required by the college statutes, they were not technically guilty of disobedience in not informing; but the professors were unconvinced, and Jay was rusticated only a short time before he was to graduate. His term of suspension over, he returned to college, and at the Commencement held in May, 1764, in the presence of General Gage, his majesty's council, and other notables, delivered a dissertation on the blessings of peace, and received his bachelor's degree.

Two weeks after leaving college, Jay entered, as a student, the office of Benjamin Kissam, a barrister " eminent in the profession," [1] binding himself

[1] *Letter Book*, May 15, 1764.

an apprentice, on the payment of £200, to serve
for five years, with liberty to apply the last two
years to the study of the law, and to visit the sessions with only occasional attendance then at the
office. This arrangement was a happy ending of
much anxiety on the part of Mr. Peter Jay, for the
lawyers of New York had a few years before made
an agreement to take no one as clerk who proposed
to enter the profession, and a new and more liberal agreement " under such restrictions," however,
" as will greatly impede the lower class of the people from creeping in," [1] was made only in time to
prevent Jay from starting for England to get a
professional education there.

" The office duties of clerks at that period," according to Peter Van Schaack, who three years
later was studying under William Smith of the
same bar, " were immensely laborious ; everything
was written, and the drudgery of copying was
oppressive. Printed blank forms, which are now
used by the profession with so much economy of
time and labor, were then unknown. Even the
argument of questions of law before the Supreme
Court was conducted in writing." [2] The law books
of the time were the ponderous tomes of reports
and digests that preceded Blackstone's Commentaries, which did not reach America till the third
year of Jay's apprenticeship. In this drudgery

[1] *Letter Book*, May 15, 1764.
[2] *Life of Peter Van Schaack*, by Henry Van Schaack, pp.
6, 7.

Jay had as companion for a while Lindley Murray, afterwards the famous grammarian, who was soon struck by the unusual qualities of his fellow student, qualities which, as he then noted them, were characteristic of Jay throughout a long life. " He was remarkable," said Murray, " for strong reasoning powers, comprehensive views, indefatigable application, and uncommon firmness of mind." [1] With Mr. Kissam, Jay, though very young and only a clerk, was before long on terms of intimacy. Many years afterwards, he had the pleasure of introducing Kissam's son to John Adams, with the remark that the father was " one of the best men I have ever known, as well as one of the best friends I have ever had." [2]

In the sixties the must of the Revolution was already fermenting, but politics were apparently ignored by both master and clerk except so far as concerned their legal business. In April, 1766, Mr. Kissam proposes going " on a jaunt" to Philadelphia, if the news of the repeal of the Stamp Act does not arrive in the mean time; for as, he writes, " on the Repeal of the Stamp Act we shall doubtless have a luxuriant harvest of law, I would not willingly, after the long famine we have had, miss reaping my part of the harvest. . . . As soon as it reaches you, I beg you 'll come down, and be ready to receive all business that offers." [3] Kis-

---

[1] *Autobiography of Lindley Murray.*
[2] To John Adams, February 16, 1788, *Jay MSS.*
[3] To John Jay, April 25, 1766, *Jay MSS.*

sam, while absent, wrote to ask about the conduct of the office, and Jay replied in a letter that was, as he expressed it, "free enough in all conscience:" "If by wanting to know how matters go on in the office, you intend I shall tell you how often your clerks go into it, give me leave to remind you of the old law maxim, that a man's own evidence is not to be admitted in his own cause. Why? Because 't is ten to one he does violence to his conscience. If I should tell you that I am all the day in your office, and as attentive to your interest as I would be to my own, I suspect you would think it such an impeachment of my modesty as would not operate very powerfully in favor of my veracity. And if, on the other hand, I should tell you that I make hay while the sun shines, and say unto my soul, 'Soul, take thy rest, thy lord is journeying in a far country,' I should be much mistaken if you did not think that the confession looked too honest to be true." [1] The fun of a lawyer of twenty-one in 1766 does not, perhaps, bear quoting, but it shows the familiar, pleasant relationship he had already established with his "master," and the boyish gayety that was so soon, perforce, concealed by an acquired or natural gravity. It was about this time, too, that Jay by a diplomatic, though not insincere, reply got his father's leave to keep a horse. "John, why do you want a horse?" "That I may have the means, sir, of visiting you frequently." The fact was that

[1] Jay, *Life of John Jay*, i. 18.

then, as in after years, Jay suffered from ill health, especially from dyspepsia, and found his best medicine in regular exercise.

In 1768 he was admitted to the bar, and became almost immediately successful, forming at first a temporary partnership with Robert R. Livingston, afterwards chancellor of the State and secretary for foreign affairs. Benjamin Kissam, when unable to attend to his own business, would often ask Jay to act for him, and a letter of his shows the nature of the cases: "One is about a horse race, in which I suppose there is some cheat; another is about an eloped wife; another of them also appertains unto horse flesh. . . . There is also one writ of Inquiry."

The practice of a country lawyer to-day could scarcely be less interesting. Indeed, before the Revolution, so far as can be gathered, the chief law business, even in New York, consisted in suing out writs of ejectment, and in collecting debts due to English merchants. It was seldom that a case arose like that of Zenger, involving principles of constitutional law, and establishing the reputation of the victorious counsel. One cause only of some consequence is mentioned, in which Jay was engaged, that of a contested election in Westchester County, in which the right of suffrage was discussed, and questions of evidence of more than usual intricacy arose. On this occasion Jay was opposed by his friend Gouverneur Morris. In 1770 Jay speaks of going to Fairfield to try two

causes;[1] and in 1774 he is addressing a jury at
Albany. His practice, then, was varied, though he
was engaged in no great cases, and was at no time
noted for brilliant or "magnetic" oratory. In
after years his "quiet, limpid style, without ges-
ture," attracted the attention of the younger Hamilton during the great debates on the ratification
of the Constitution in the New York Convention,
and, as a young lawyer, he must have been unusually clear-headed and tactful. "All the causes
you have hitherto tried," wrote Kissam in 1769,
"have been by a kind of inspiration."[2] These
two still continued great friends, though sometimes
engaged on opposite sides. On one such occasion
Kissam, in a moment of embarrassment, complained
that he had brought up a bird to peck out his own
eyes. "Oh, no," retorted Jay, "not to peck out
but to open your eyes."

In November, 1770, a number of lawyers in New
York formed "The Moot," a club that met the
first Friday of every month for the discussion of
disputed points of law. Jay was one of the younger
members, together with his college friends, Egbert
Benson, in due time judge of the New York Supreme Court; Robert R. Livingston, Jr.; James
Duane, Jay's colleague in the Continental Congress,
and first mayor of New York after the Revolution;
Gouverneur Morris, as yet without that wooden leg
which he brandished with such happy effect in the

[1] To Dr. Kissam, March 1, 1770, *Jay MSS.*
[2] From Benjamin Kissam, November 6, 1769, *Jay MSS.*

face of a Paris mob; and Peter Van Schaack,
whom Jay was to exile from the State, but who
loved him to the end, and wrote an epitaph on him;
while among the older lawyers, who attended occasionally, were William Smith, who later became
chief justice of Canada, after having been confined
in Livingston Manor, and banished as a Tory sym-
pathizer; Samuel Jones, the chief justice, whose
office was to be the training school of De Witt
Clinton; John Morin Scott, the popular orator
of the Liberty Boys, lawyer, patriot, and general;
William Livingston, and Benjamin Kissam. The
decision of the club on a matter of practice is said
to have been followed by the Superior Court; and
its sessions must have been invaluable to the
younger members. Party politics of the province
were a forbidden topic at the meetings, which were
long remembered with delight; "a recollection,"
wrote Van Schaack to Jay before many years had
passed, " of those happy scenes, of our clubs, our
moots, and our Broadway evenings, fills me with
pleasing melancholy reflections, — *fuimus Troes,
fuit Ilium.*" [1]

In the mean time the young lawyer's practice
steadily increased, and in the autumn of 1771 he
was able to write to Dr. Samuel Kissam, a college
friend in business at Surinam: " With respect to
business I am as well circumstanced as I have a
right to expect; my old friends contribute much to
my happiness, and upon the whole I have reason

[1] *Life of Peter Van Schaack*, p. 100.

to be satisfied with my share of the attention of Providence." [1] Not many lawyers of twenty-six can say so much to-day. Two years later his official or public life began with his appointment, February 17, 1773, as secretary to the royal commission to determine the disputed boundary between New York and Connecticut. The following year, April 28, 1774, at patriotically named "Liberty Hall," Elizabeth, New Jersey, he married "the beautiful Sarah Livingston," the youngest daughter of William Livingston, soon to be the famous Revolutionary governor of New Jersey, and already well known for countless literary and political poems, letters, and essays. In the notices of the wedding, Jay, young as he was, could be described as "an eminent barrister," [2] — the same phrase that was applied to him a month or two later by Lieutenant-Governor Colden.

With this spring closes the first third of Jay's life, of which, as curiously happened, the second third of twenty-eight years was spent wholly in the public service, and the last third wholly in retirement. So far as can be gathered from the meagre records extant, his twenty-ninth year found him a studious, quiet lawyer, devoted to his profession and but little excited by the politics of the day. As a boy he was not precocious; no brilliant-winged creature like Hamilton, but a lad "remarkably sedate." His college life won him no

[1] August 27, 1771, *Jay MSS.*
[2] *New York Gazette*, May 9, 1774.

sudden reputation like that of so many English statesmen from Pitt to Gladstone, but it did win him the love and esteem of many friends that continued till his death. Carefully and well nurtured, in the comfortable society of honorable relations and friends, occupied in the profession of his choice, successful in the love of his heart, he was now a slender, graceful man, with refined, handsome, serious face; whose slowly matured character had ripened to well-balanced wisdom unconsciously and apparently unsuspected. By family traditions he was independent of England, and a Whig; and now by marriage he was connected with the great Whig family of Livingston, which had for generations contested the province with the Tory De Lanceys.

CHAPTER II

CONSERVATIVE WHIG LEADER

1774–1776

" THROUGHOUT America the constitutions favored individuality. Under the careless rule of Great Britain, habits of personal liberty had taken root, which showed themselves in the tenacity wherewith the people clung to their habits of self-government; and so long as those usages were respected, under which they had always lived, and which they believed to be as well established as Magna Charta, there were not in all the king's dominions more loyal subjects than Washington, Jefferson, and Jay." [1] In 1773 Jay was as loyal as any man " in all the king's dominions;" in 1776, as chairman of a secret committee, he was punishing with imprisonment and exile many men whose only crime was retaining the opinions he himself had held three years before. Yet, in the mean while, Jay's principles of conduct and his mental attitude were unchanged. How such could be the case is worth inquiry; especially as Jay, rather than impulsive men like Adams, or quick-

[1] Brooks Adams, *The Emancipation of Massachusetts*, pp. 316, 317.

witted men like Hamilton, was typical of the generation that fought the Revolution.

In 1773 the tax on tea was imposed. On October 22 the Mohawks of New York, a band of the Sons of Liberty, were ordered by their old leaders to be on the watch for the tea-ships; [1] and it was merely the chances of time and tide that gave the opportunity of fame first to the Mohawks of Boston. December 15, soon after the Boston tea-party, there was revived the old organization of the Sons of Liberty, which had first been formed to put down the Stamp Act, holding together after the repeal of that measure to oppose such acts of Parliament as the Mutiny Bill, and which, as late as 1770, established a committee to enforce non-importation. [2] An "association" was now circulated for signatures, engaging to boycott, "not deal with, or employ, or have any connection with," any persons who should aid in landing, or " selling, or buying tea, so long as it is subject to a duty by Parliament;" [3] and December 17 a meeting of the subscribers was held, and a committee of fifteen chosen as a Committee of Correspondence that was soon known as the Vigilance Committee. Letters also were exchanged between the speakers of many of the houses of assembly in the different provinces; and January 20, 1774, the New York Assembly, which had been out of touch

[1] Leake, *Life of John Lamb*, p. 76.
[2] *Ibid.* pp. 2, 69.
[3] *New York Journal*, December 16, 1773.

with the people ever since the Stamp Act was passed in the year after its election, appointed their speaker, with twelve others, a standing Committee of Correspondence and Enquiry, a proof that the interest of all classes was now excited. April 15 the Nancy with a cargo of tea arrived off Sandy Hook, followed shortly by the London. The Committee of Vigilance assembled, and as soon as Captain Lockyier of the Nancy landed in spite of their warning, escorted him to a pilot boat and set him on board again, while the flag flew from the liberty pole, and cannon thundered from the "Fields." April 23 the Nancy stood out to sea without landing her cargo, and with her carried Captain Chambers of the London, from which the evening before eighteen chests of tea had been emptied into the sea by the Liberty Boys.[1]

The bill closing the port of Boston was enacted March 31, and a copy of the act reached New York by the ship Samson on the 12th. Two days later the Committee of Vigilance wrote to the Boston committee recommending vigorous measures as the most effectual, and assuring them that their course would be heartily supported by their brethren in New York.[2] So rapid had been the march of events that not till now did the merchants and responsible citizens of New York take alarm. Without their concurrence or even knowledge they were being rapidly compromised by the unauthor-

[1] Leake, *Life of John Lamb*, pp. 81–84.
[2] *Ibid.* p. 87.

ized action of an irresponsible committee, composed
of men who for the most part were noted more for
enthusiasm than judgment, and many of whom had
been not unconcerned in petty riots and demon-
strations condemned by the better part of the com-
munity. The one weapon in which the Sons of
Liberty trusted was " Non-importation," a prohibition of trade with England, and this was a measure
which injured the merchants of New York more
than any others, and had been abandoned in 1770
as a failure. " The men who at that time called
themselves the Committee," wrote Lieutenant-Governor Colden the next month, " who dictated and
acted in the name of the people, were many of them
of the lower ranks, and all the warmest zealots of
those called the Sons of Liberty. The more considerable merchants and citizens seldom or never
appeared among them. . . . The principal inhabitants, being now afraid that these hot-headed men
might now run the city into dangerous measures,
appeared in a considerable body at the first meeting of the people after the Boston Port Act was
published here." [1] This meeting, convoked by
advertisement, was held May 16, at the house of
Samuel Francis, " to consult on the measures proper to be pursued." It was proposed to nominate
a new committee to supersede the Committee of
Vigilance, authorized to represent the citizens. A
committee of fifty, Jay among them, instead of one
of twenty-five as at first suggested, was nominated

[1] *Am. Archives*, 4th Series, i. 372.

"for the approbation of the public," "to correspond with our sister colonies on all matters of moment." Three days later these nominations were
confirmed by a public meeting held at the Coffee House, but not until a fifty-first member was
added, Francis Lewis, as a representative of the
radical party, which had been as much as possible
ignored. The chagrin of the Sons of Liberty at
the conservative composition of the committee was
intensified by the exultation, unfounded though it
proved, of the Tories. "You may rest assured,"
wrote Rivington, the editor of the Tory newspaper,
to Knox, then a bookseller in Boston and afterwards secretary for war, "no non-im- nor non-ex-
portation will be agreed upon, either here or at
Philadelphia. The power over our crowd is no
longer in the hands of Sears, Lamb, and such
unimportant persons who have for six years past
been the demagogues of a very turbulent faction
in this city; but their power and mischievous capacity expired instantly upon the election of the
Committee of Fifty-one, in which there is a majority of inflexibly honest, loyal, and prudent
citizens."

At the Coffee House again, on May 23, the
Committee of Fifty-one met and organized; they
repudiated the letter to Boston from the Committee of Vigilance as unofficial; [1] a letter from Philadelphia was read; Paul Revere, the "express" or
confidential messenger from Boston, attended with

[1] Leake, *Life of John Lamb*, p. 88.

a letter dated May 13, requesting concurrence with
the resolves of the Boston town meeting of that
day ordering non-importation from Great Britain
and discontinuance of trade with the West India
Islands; and McDougall, Low, Duane, and Jay
were appointed a sub-committee to report the same
evening a draft of an answer to this last. The
draft, as reported, is believed to be by Jay. It
urged that " a Congress of deputies from the colonies in general is of the utmost moment," to form
" some unanimous resolutions . . . not only respecting your [Boston's] deplorable circumstances,
but for the security of our common rights; " and
that the advisability of a non-importation agreement should be left to the Congress. This report
was unanimously agreed to; a copy was delivered
to Paul Revere, and another copy to a messenger
for Philadelphia.[1] The importance of this letter
can hardly be exaggerated, for it was the first serious authoritative suggestion of a general congress
to consider " the common rights " of the colonies
in general. The people of Boston in the indignation of the moment were preoccupied wholly with
their private local wrongs, for which they were
ready to involve the continent in a war of commercial restrictions. The Sons of Liberty in New
York and elsewhere were equally incapable of any
broader views. The resolutions about the same
date, some a day or two earlier, some a day or two

---

[1] *New York Journal*, May 26, 1774. In Leake's *Life of Lamb*,
p. 88, the date of this meeting is erroneously given as May 26.

later, of meetings in Providence and Philadelphia, and of the Burgesses of Virginia, were all deficient either in being unofficial or as limiting the object of the congress to the quarrel of Boston.[1] It was the conservative merchants of New York alone who were at the time calm, clear-headed, and far-sighted enough to urge the postponement of violent measures, which would then almost certainly have been only sporadic and abortive, to the discretion of a congress concerned with the welfare of all. The advice of New York was followed gradually by the other colonies; but even before a Continental Congress was a certainty, the Committee of Fifty-one, with singular confidence, resolved that delegates to it should be chosen, and called a meeting for that purpose for July 19.

Meantime the Committee of Vigilance was dying hard. It still tried to enforce the Boston resolutions by a system of espionage and threats. The

[1] " The first, or one of the first, to claim that the particular grievances of Boston were not the only ones to be considered — though the committee of Philadelphia, in the letter forwarded with this to Boston, had adopted somewhat the same tone — and the first to propose a convention of all the colonies to take concerted action on all their grievances; for the recommendation of the town of Providence, May 17, only requested their delegates in the approaching General Assembly to use their efforts to that end, and the committee of Philadelphia, May 21, merely mentioned the suggestion without urging it." The Committee of Correspondence of Connecticut concurred with the New York recommendation, June 4; the General Assembly of Rhode Island, June 15; the General Court of Massachusetts, June 17; and Philadelphia at a meeting of the citizens, June 18. Dawson, *Westchester Co. during the Revolution*, p. 18.

chairman of a committee of merchants complained
to the Fifty-one of these persons inquiring "into
their private business," and the Fifty-one promptly
denounced them. This was more than Lamb, the
leader of the old committee, could stand. In the
words of his biographer: "Satisfied of the intentions of the Fifty-one to paralyze the energies of
the people, . . . they resolved to frustrate their
designs," [1] and by an unsigned advertisement
called for the evening of July 6 what was afterwards known as the "Great meeting in the Fields,"
now City Hall Park. Alexander McDougall pre-
sided, and strong resolutions were passed and
pledges made in favor of non-importation. These
proceedings were promptly disavowed the next day
by the regular committee as "evidently calculated
. . . to excite groundless . . . suspicions, . . . as
well as disunion among our fellow citizens;" and
a sub-committee on resolutions was chosen, — Low,
Lewis, Moore, Sears, Remsen, Shaw, McDougall.
McDougall and others refusing to attend, a new
committee was appointed, July 13, — Low, Jay,
Thurman, Curtenius, Moore, Shaw, and Bache, who
reported resolutions: "That it is our greatest Happiness and Glory to have been born British Subjects, and that we wish nothing more ardently than
to live and die as such;" that "the Act for Block-
ing up the port of Boston is . . . subversive of
every idea of British Liberty;" and that it should
be left to the proposed congress to determine the

[1] Leake, *Life of Lamb*, p. 92.

question of non-importation, which would be justified only by " dire necessity." [1]

The resolutions were adopted, and Philip Livingston, John Alsop, Isaac Low, James Duane,
and John Jay were nominated as delegates to be
submitted to the public meeting July 19. The
people met accordingly at the Coffee House, and
after a stormy debate elected the committee's candidates in spite of a strong effort to substitute for
Jay, McDougall, the hero of the Liberty Boys
since his imprisonment in 1769 for libel on the
Tory Assembly. But they rejected the proposed
resolutions, which had been violently denounced
by Lamb, that brave but turbulent spirit, for humility, ambiguity, inconsistency, and aversion to
non-importation. Jay, with fourteen others, was
directed to draft amendments. On motion of Jay,
too, a committee was appointed to relieve the distress of Boston. The next day Livingston, Alsop,
Low, and Jay refused to accept their election, on
the grounds that the meeting was not representative, and that they agreed in the main with the rejected resolutions, so determined were they, even
in such quasi-revolutionary proceedings, that nothing should be done except decently and in order.
It is known that the popular party wished to have
the nominations referred for approval to the Committee of Mechanics, a trade organization which
now, like every other, began to take part in politics, and which professed to represent, and to some

[1] *New York Journal*, July 14, 1774.

extent was the sole representative of, the unen-
franchised and, as ever in times of excitement and
in cities, extremely radical masses ; while the majority of the Committee of Fifty-one wished the
nominations submitted to the freeholders and freemen, as at ordinary elections.[1] A compromise was
happily effected. Polls were ordered by the committee to be opened July 28 for the election of
delegates in each ward under the superintendency
of the aldermen and members of the Committee of
Fifty-one and of the Mechanics' Committee.[2] In
answer to letters from the latter, the candidates
stated that they believed at the moment in the propriety of non-importation, but were determined to
hold themselves free to act, if elected, as should
seem best in the Congress. In this concession the
mechanics, meeting at the house of Mr. Mariner,
acquiesced.[3] At the election Jay and his colleagues
received a unanimous vote.

Thus, fortunately, at the very inception of the
Revolution, before the faintest clatter of arms,
the popular movement was placed in charge of the
Patricians, as they were called, rather than of the
Tribunes, as respectively represented by Jay and
McDougall. " The former were composed of the
merchants and gentry, and the latter mostly of
mechanics. The latter were radicals, and the former joined with the loyalists in attempts to check

[1] Leake, *Life of Lamb*, p. 94.
[2] Rivington's *Gazette*, July 28, 1774.
[3] *New York Journal*, August 4, 1774.

the influences of the zealous democrats." [1] At the meeting on May 19, which ratified the election of the Committee of Fifty-one, Gouverneur Morris was present, and remarked with uneasiness the successful attempt of the minority to control the more numerous but less skillful party, for at the moment a reaction seemed imminent; and the next day he wrote with some bitterness: "I see, and I see it with fear and trembling, that if the disputes with Britain continue, we shall be under the worst of all possible dominions. We shall be under the domination of a riotous mob." [2] As it happened, the *Tribunes* succeeded in modifying to suit themselves the resolutions adopted, and the *Patricians* succeeded in sending the delegates of their choice unpledged to the Congress.

On Monday, August 29, Jay set off for Philadelphia alone, and without announcing his departure, though he joined his father-in-law, William Livingston, at Elizabeth, thus avoiding the complimentary farewell with which the people speeded his fellow delegates. "Mr. Jay is a young gentleman of the law, of about twenty-six [in fact, twenty-nine], Mr. Scott says, a hard student and a good speaker," is the entry in the diary of John Adams, jotted down a few days earlier, as he, too, was riding on to Philadelphia. [3]

[1] Lossing, *Hist. of N. Y. City*, i. 32.
[2] Gouverneur Morris to Penn, May 20, 1774, Sparks, *G. Morris*, i. 25.
[3] John Adams's *Works*, ii. 350.

There the Congress met at Carpenters' Hall, on
September 5, and the delegates sat steadily day
after day, for six weeks, from eleven till four
o'clock.[1] Here for the first time were gathered together from the different colonies representative
men of every shade of opinion, whose reputations
and very names were as yet for the most part unknown to one another. " To draw the character
of all of them," wrote John Adams after the lapse
of half a century, " would require a volume, and
would now be considered a caricature print, — one
part blind Tories, another Whigs, and the rest
mongrels." [2] It was natural enough that such
should be the case, for the Congress was not a revolutionary body in the sense in which the phrase
could be applied to the provincial congresses and
conventions of the next few years. In its origin
and organization it usurped no illegal authority,
but was a purely consultative assembly, like those
that had met occasionally in times of emergency
earlier in the century. " The powers of Congress
at first were indeed little more than advisory," said
Judge Iredell of the United States Supreme Court;
" but, in proportion as the danger increased, their
powers were gradually enlarged." [3] So great was
Jay's sense of the diversity of opinion that, when it
was moved to open the first meeting with prayer,
he objected, though as devout a man as any pre-

[1] Sparks, *Gouverneur Morris*, i. 217.
[2] John Adams's *Works*, x. 78, 79.
[3] 3 Dall. 91.

sent, " because," said Adams, " we were so divided in religious sentiments."[1]   Still, in spite of this caution, a chaplain was appointed, whose prayers, though he afterwards joined the royalists, excited no dissension.

The first regular business of Congress was to appoint a committee "to state the rights of the colonies in general." Jay was a member of the committee, and, when a debate arose on the source of the rights of the colonies, he stated the views that finally prevailed. " It is necessary," he said, " to recur to the law of nature and the British Constitution to ascertain our rights. The ' Constitution ' of Great Britain will not apply to some of the charter rights."[2]   In this reference to " the law of nature " may be detected a suggestion of revolutionary methods, which at the moment was doubtless not traced to its logical conclusion. The discussion, on the contrary, was practical rather than theoretical, and " the great state papers of American liberty," of which Jay wrote so many, " were all predicated on the abuse of chartered, not of abstract rights."[3]   This was indeed the chief distinction between the beginnings of the American and the French revolutions, and was one cause, and not the least efficient, for the permanent results of the first.

[1] John Adams's *Works*, x. 79.

[2] *Ibid.* ii. 370.

[3] Gibbs, *History of the Administrations of Washington and Adams*, i. 3.

The question of voting in Congress had next to be determined. Patrick Henry, urging voting by delegates without regard to the State as a unit, made the famous speech in which he declared, " I am not a Virginian, but an American. . . . I go upon the supposition that government is at an end. All distinctions are thrown down. All America is thrown into one mass." "Could I suppose," Jay replied, "that we came to frame an American constitution, instead of endeavoring to correct the faults in an old one, I can't yet think that all government is at an end. *The measure of arbitrary power is not yet full, and I think it must run over, before we undertake to frame a new constitution.*"[1] In this last sentence is found the principle of Jay's conduct throughout the early Revolutionary period, before the Declaration of Independence. It was at once the path of duty and of prudence; for only in this way could the people be compelled by the logic of facts as well as of argument into something like unanimity. In the matter of voting, Jay's party prevailed, and it was decided that each colony should have one vote, but that this decision should not be made a precedent. When the discussion arose which ended in the adoption of the non-importation resolution on September 27, Jay also expressed the opinion of the majority, unwisely according to nineteenth century notions of political economy, but most wisely in the light of those days and in the political emergency of the moment.

[1] John Adams's *Works*, ii. 367, 368.

"Negotiation, suspension of commerce, and war," he said, "are the only three things. War is, by general consent, to be waived at present. I am for negotiation and suspension of commerce."[1] On September 28 a motion was introduced that proved the extreme conservatism of the Congress. Joseph Galloway of Pennsylvania made a proposition which Adams condensed as follows: "The plan, two classes of laws: 1. Laws of internal policy. 2. Laws in which more than one colony is concerned — raising money for war. No one act can be done without the assent of Great Britain. No one without the assent of America. A British-American legislature." In other words, all affairs in which more than one colony was interested, or which affected Great Britain and the colonies, were to be regulated by a president general appointed by the crown, and by a grand council of delegates from the various assemblies. The motion was defeated only by vote of six colonies to five, though it was afterwards ordered expunged from the minutes; but Jay spoke for it. "I am led to adopt this plan," he said. "It is objected that this plan will alter our constitution, and therefore cannot be adopted without consulting constituents. Does this plan give up any one liberty, or interfere with any one right?"[2]

Jay was then placed on a committee to draft an address to the people of Great Britain, and a me-

---

[1] John Adams's *Works*, ii. 385.
[2] *Ibid.* ii. 389.

morial to the people of British America; and the former was assigned to him.   The keynote of the address was: "We consider ourselves, and do insist that we are and ought to be, as free as our fellow subjects in Britain, and that no power on earth has a right to take our property from us without our consent. . . . You have been told that we are seditious, impatient of government, and desirous of independence.   Be assured that these are not facts, but calumnies. . . . Place us in the same situation that we were at the close of the last war [1763], and our former harmony will be restored."   Jay shut himself up in a room in a tavern to write the address.   It was at once reported favorably by the committee and adopted by Congress, and Jefferson, while still ignorant of the authorship, declared it "a production certainly of the finest pen in America."[1]   After a session of some six weeks, Congress dissolved, recommending the appointment of local committees to carry out the non-importation association.

The action of the Congress won popular favor, and the New York delegates on their return were presented by their former critics, the Committee of Mechanics, with an address acknowledging their "readiness in accepting and fidelity in executing the high and important trust" reposed in them; and in their answer the delegates showed themselves equally free from partisanship: "Let us all, with one heart and voice, endeavor to cultivate and

[1] Jefferson's *Writings*, i. 8.

cherish a spirit of unanimity and mutual benevolence, and to promote that internal tranquillity which can alone give weight to our laudable efforts for the preservation of our freedom, and crown them with success." [1] Jay was at once elected one of a committee of sixty, called a Committee of Inspection, that superseded the old Committee of Fifty-one, and that was specially charged with promoting non-importation. It is not surprising that in this familiar business the Committee of Mechanics coöperated heartily. [2] The committee for the relief of Boston, of which Jay was also a member, was likewise not unoccupied. On one day, December 23, for instance, they received "for Boston, from the people of Hanover, twelve barrels of fine, eight of common, and five of cornel flour, and £17 17s. in cash, and from the precinct of Shengonk, thirteen barrels of flour and three of corn." [3] The Committee of Inspection was variously engaged, searching ships for imported goods, examining captains and boatmen, selling confiscated property at public vendue, warning the people of, for instance, the scarcity of nails, and recommending that none should be exported, or contradicting false statements published by the loyalist editor, Rivington. [4]

The time now came for the election of delegates

[1] *Jay MSS.*
[2] Leake, *Life of John Lamb*, p. 95.
[3] *New York Journal*, December 29, 1774.
[4] *Ibid.* March 23, April 13, 1775.

to the second Continental Congress, which was to
meet May 10, 1775. The Committee of Inspection ordered that delegates should be chosen by
the counties, to meet in New York city, and select from among themselves representatives for the
province. A meeting of the citizens of New York,
called for the purpose, marched to the Exchange.
" Two Standard Bearers carried a large Union
flag, with a Blue Field, on which were the following inscriptions: On one side ' George III. Rex,
and the Liberties of America. No Popery.' On
the other, ' The Union of the Colonies, and the
Measures of Congress.' " [1] This time, instead of
confusion being created by the radicals or " Tribunes," the meeting was interrupted, but ineffec-
tively, by Tories, who had purposely met the same
morning at the house of the Widow de la Mon-
taigne, and adjourned the hour of the meeting to
the Exchange, where, with clubs, they got for a
time the better of the argument until the Whigs
plundered a neighboring cooper's yard, and drove
them off the ground with pieces of hoop sticks.[2]

Many of the councilors and assemblymen, including the speaker,[3] attended the meeting at the
Exchange, a further proof of the march of public
opinion. There Jay was elected to the Provincial
Convention, as it was called, though its functions
were purely electoral and it sat only a few days.

[1] *New York Journal*, March 9, 1775.
[2] Gordon, *Hist. of N. Y.* i. 306.
[3] Memorandum in *Jay MSS.*

By this body he was chosen, with his former associates (except Low who declined and subsequently turned royalist), and five others, a delegate to the second Continental Congress. To their delegates the people now granted authority incomparably greater than that legitimately possessed by the first Congress, intrusting specifically "full power to them or any five of them to concert and determine upon such measures as shall be judged most effectual for the preservation and establishment of American rights and privileges, and for the restoration of harmony between Great Britain and the colonies."[1]

Meantime, as the confusion of the country increased, while all regular constitutional government had practically ceased to exist, the Committee of Inspection found their powers too limited; they therefore recommended the election of a committee of one hundred, with authority adequate to the emergency, to conduct the government, to enforce the association, and to elect deputies to a provincial congress to meet in New York, May 22. The old Colonial Assembly dissolved on April 3, 1775, never to meet again; and on April 28 the new committee was elected, usually known as the Committee of Observation, but in reality a revolutionary committee of safety. Jay and his next younger brother, Frederick, were members. The new committee at once drew up for general circulation an association engaging to obey the committees and

[1] *Journals of Prov. Congress*, etc. i. 22, 75.

Congress, and to oppose every attempt by Parliament to enforce taxation. They had the streets patrolled at night to prevent the exportation of provisions, and called on the citizens to arm. May 5, a letter to "The Lord Mayor and Magistrates of London," drafted by Jay, was signed by him and eighty-eight members of the committee. "This city," the letter ran, "is as one man in the cause of Liberty. . . . While the whole continent are ardently wishing for peace on such terms as can be acceded to by Englishmen, they are indefatigable in preparing for the last appeal;"[1] a brave statement to publish, when the committee knew that the city was absolutely defenseless, and that troops had already been ordered thither and were on their way. On May 10 the second Continental Congress assembled at Philadelphia. The shot had been fired at Lexington. The measures before Congress were of necessity warlike. An address to the inhabitants of Canada was drafted by Jay, reported from a committee in which he was associated with Samuel Adams and Silas Deane, and on adoption was ordered to be translated into French for circulation across the border. The address warned the Canadians that the measures urged against the Americans may be turned against them, and concluded: "As our concern for your welfare entitles us to your friendship, we presume you will not, by doing us an injury, reduce us to the disagreeable necessity of treating you as ene-

---

[1] *New York Journal*, May 25, 1775.

mies." Jay was a member of the committee which
prepared the Declaration, published July 6, "setting forth the causes and necessity of their taking
arms." "Against violence actually offered, we
have taken up arms. We shall lay them down
when hostilities shall cease on the part of the ag-
gressors, and all danger of their being renewed
shall be removed, and not before."

In spite of strong opposition, Jay persuaded
Congress of the propriety of a loyal and respectful
second petition to the king. A committee including himself was appointed to draft it, but it was
actually written by Dickinson, and on July 8 the
petition was signed by the members of Congress
individually. It was necessary, to quote Jay's
words of a year before, " that the measure of arbitrary power . . . must run over." An address to
the people of Jamaica and Ireland was also agreed
to by Congress, and was written by Jay, at the
request of William Livingston. "Though vilified
as wanting spirit, we are determined to behave like
men; though insulted and abused, we wish for reconciliation; though defamed as seditious, we are
ready to obey the laws, and though charged with
rebellion, will cheerfully bleed in defense of our
sovereign in a righteous cause;" but the main
object of the address was to explain and excuse, as
unavoidable, the cessation of trade. "I never be-
stowed much attention to any of those addresses,"
wrote rugged old John Adams to Jefferson toward
the close of his life, " which were all but repetitions

of the same things; the same facts and arguments; dress and ornaments, rather than body, soul, or substance. . . . I was in great error, no doubt, and am ashamed to confess it, for these things were necessary to give popularity to the cause, both at home and abroad." [1]

Jay's position in urging the second petition to the king becomes still more clear when we listen to his speech to the Assembly of New Jersey in December, when Congress sent him with two others to dissuade them from a similar petition. He argued, said a member present, that " we had nothing to expect from the mercy or the justice of Britain. That petitions were not now the means; vigor and unanimity the only means. That the petition of United America, presented by Congress, ought to be relied on; others unnecessary; and hoped the House would not think otherwise." [2] " Before this time," wrote Jay in 1821, " I never did hear any American of any class, or of any description, express a wish for the independence of the colonies," and this statement was confirmed by Jefferson and Adams. Indeed, in a paper, undated, but written probably at this time, the autumn of 1775, Jay quotes paragraph after paragraph [3] from the Journal of Congress to prove " the malice and falsity " of the " ungenerous and groundless charge of their

[1] John Adams's *Works*, x. 80.

[2] Hare, *Archives*, 4th Ser. iv. 1874, 1875.

[3] The MS. pages cited are pages 59, 63, 64, 84, 87, 149, 150, 155, 163, 165, 172, etc., *Jay MSS.*

aiming at independence, or a total separation from Great Britain." "From these testimonies," Jay concludes, "it appears extremely evident that to charge the Congress· with aiming at a separation of these colonies from Great Britain, is to charge them falsely and without a single spark of evidence to support the accusation. . . . It is much to be wished that the people would read the proceedings of the Congress and consult their own judgments, and not suffer themselves to be duped by men who are paid for deceiving them." It was, then, the rejection of the petition, as events showed, which, as much as anything, suggested and justified the idea of independence to the minds of the people.

Jay was one of a committee of four which reported upon a request from Massachusetts for advice, and recommended the semi-revolutionary step of electing a new Assembly, but according to the customary manner. He was also one of a committee of five which drafted the declaration for Washington to publish on his arrival before Boston. In many of the debates in Congress he took part, and not always on the popular side. It was proposed to close the custom-houses throughout the country, so as to place New York, North Carolina, and Georgia on the same footing as the other provinces. "Because the enemy has burnt Charlestown," said Jay, "would gentlemen have us burn New York? . . . The question is, whether we shall have trade or not? And this is to introduce a . . . scheme which will drive away all your sailors, and lay up all your ships to rot at the wharves." In November Jay was appointed with Franklin, Harrison, Johnson, and Dickinson a secret committee to correspond "with our friends in Great Britain, Ireland, *and other parts of the world.*" [1] In this capacity Jay had more than one promising but fruitless interview with the first of the secret emissaries of the French court, Bonvouloir, and these apparently harmless interviews were conducted with almost fantastic mystery. "Each comes to the place indicated in the dark," wrote Bonvouloir, in one of his reports, "by different roads. They have given me their confidence as a friendly individual." [2] In the autumn the committee sent Silas Deane to France, who, until his recall, held frequent correspondence with Jay by fictitious letters with the wide margins written upon with invisible ink.

Queens County, New York, having refused formally to send delegates to the Provincial Congress, William Livingston, Jay, and Samuel Adams were appointed a committee to consider the present state of the colony. The report, which Jay is said to have drawn, urged the arrest of certain disaffected persons, and that those who had voted against sending delegates should be prohibited from leaving the country. The New York Congress had applied for soldiery to disarm the latter unfortunate persons,

[1] *Journals of Congress*, 1775, pp. 272, 273.
[2] Durant, *New Materials for History of American Rev.* 1, 5.

and, the committee assenting, the disarmament was
effected forthwith by Colonel Nathaniel Heard and
Lord Stirling's battalion.

Jay was also placed on a committee to draw up
a declaration justifying the determination of Congress to fit out privateers against the commerce of
England. He was on committees to devise means
for supplying medicines for the army; to inquire
into the dispute between Pennsylvania and Connecticut; to examine into the qualifications of generals; to purchase powder for the troops besieging
Boston; to recommend the proper disposition of
the tea then in the colonies; and to ascertain the
truth of a report that Governor Tryon of New
York had made "the passengers in the late packet
swear not to disclose anything relative to American affairs except to the ministry." His time, then,
was fully occupied in anxious and laborious work.
But even the Continental Congress sometimes enjoyed a holiday. "The Congress spent yesterday
in festivity," wrote Jay to his wife, September 29,
1775.[1] "The Committee of Safety were so polite
as to invite them to make a little voyage in their
Gondolas as far as the fort, which is about twelve
miles from the city. Each Galley had its company,
and each company entertained with variety of
music, etc. We proceeded six or eight miles down
the river, when, the tide being spent and the wind
unfavorable, we backed about and with a fine
breeze returned, passed the city, and landed six

[1] *Jay MSS.*

miles above the town at a pretty little place called
Paris Villa. . . . I wished you and a few select
friends had been with me. This idea, though
amidst much noise and mirth, made me much
alone. Adieu, my beloved."

At first there was some difficulty in getting the
colonies to make any provision for the delegates.
New York finally allowed them four dollars per
day, though " the allowance," says Jay, "does by
no means equal the loss." As Christmas ap-
proached, Jay asked for leave of absence, but was
refused, since, with two of the five New York delegates away on leave, the province would otherwise
be unrepresented. " Don't you pity me, my dear
Sally?" writes the young husband. " It is, however, some consolation that, should the Congress
not adjourn in less than ten days, I have determined to stay with you till ——, and, depend upon
it, nothing but actual imprisonment will be able to
keep me from you." [1]

In the mean time Jay was not unobservant of
events in New York. In November the press of
Rivington, the Tory printer, had been destroyed
by a party of light horsemen from Connecticut,
who also seized Bishop Seabury and others who
had protested against the doings of the Congress.
Jay's comments show a rather complicated state
of mind. "For my part I do not approve of the
feat, and think it neither argues much wisdom nor
much bravery; at any rate, if it was to have been

[1] To Mrs. Jay, December 23, 1775, *Jay MSS.*

done, I wish our own people, and not strangers, had taken the liberty of doing it. I confess I am not a little jealous of the honor of the province, and am persuaded that its reputation cannot be maintained without some little spirit being mingled with its prudence." [1] To Alexander McDougall, in the New York Convention, he writes, urging them " to impose light taxes rather with a view to precedent than profit." McDougall now had become an intimate friend. A month earlier he had been the means of Jay's making the only application for office he ever made in his life. McDougall wrote, complaining of the reluctance of men of position to take commands in the provincial militia, and at once Jay applied for appointment, and was appointed colonel of the second regiment, New York City Militia.[2] For the next year or two his name appears as Colonel Jay in the Journal of the New York Congress and conventions. Jay was also urged by Hamilton, the astutest politician of nineteen years that ever lived, to frustrate the Tory scheme to issue writs for a new Assembly, by becoming, with Livingston, Alsop, and Lewis, a candidate for New York County. "The minds of all our friends will naturally tend to these," he added, " and the opposition will of course be weak and contemptible; for the Whigs, I doubt not, constitute a large majority of the people." [3]

[1] To Colonel Woodhull, November 26, 1775, *Jay MSS.*
[2] October 27, 1775.
[3] From Alexander Hamilton, December 31, 1775, *Jay MSS.*

In April, 1776, Jay had been elected a delegate
to the New York Provincial Congress, which met
at the city hall on May 14.   Four days before
the day of meeting, the Continental Congress had
passed a resolution recommending the colonies " to
adopt such government as shall, in the opinion of
the representatives of the people, best conduce to
the happiness and safety of their constituents in
particular, and America in general."   Jay was at
once summoned to lend his counsel in the emergency, without vacating his seat in the Continental
Congress, though the New York Provincial Congress forbade his leaving "without further orders."
For this reason it was that Jay's name is not among
those of the signers of the Declaration of Independence.   Obedient to the call of his colony, Jay
mounted horse and started forthwith for New
York, where he was sworn in and took his seat in
the local congress on May 25.   He was at once
placed on one committee to draft a law relating to
the peril the colony is exposed to by " its intestine
dangers," [1] and on another to frame into resolutions
the report of the committee on the recommendation
by Congress of a new form of government.[2]   Accordingly, on June 11, certain important resolutions on the subject of independence were moved
by Jay and agreed to: " That the good people of
this colony have not, in the opinion of this congress, authorized this congress, or the delegates of
this colony in the Continental Congress, to declare

[1] *Journals of Prov. Cong.* i. 461.   [2] *Ibid.* i. 402.

this colony to be and continue independent of the crown of Great Britain."

This action of Jay's was not due to any doubt in his own mind as to the necessity of the proposed change, but simply to his conservative adherence to constitutional methods. Duane, his colleague in Congress, wrote urging delay: "The orators of Virginia with Colonel Henry at their head are against a change of government. . . . The late election of deputies for the convention of New York sufficiently proves that those who assumed excessive fervor and gave laws even to the convention and committees were unsupported by the people. There seems, therefore, no reason that one colony should be too precipitate in changing the present mode of government. I would first be well assured of the opinion of the inhabitants at large. Let them be rather followed than driven on an occasion of such moment."[1] "So great are the inconveniences," replied Jay, "resulting from the present mode of government, that I believe our convention will almost unanimously agree to institute a better, to continue until a peace with Great Britain may render it unnecessary."[2] Further reflection, however, convinced him that the unmistakable assent of the people was the only safe foundation for a new government, and perhaps, too, that the existing convention was less republican than he supposed. "Our convention," he wrote to Livingston, "will,

[1] From James Duane, May 18, 1776.
[2] To Duane, May 29, 1776.

I believe, institute a better government than the present, which, in my opinion, will no longer work anything but mischief; and although the measure of obtaining authority by instructions may have its advocates, I have reason to think that such a resolution will be taken as will open a door to the election of new or additional members." [1] It should be remembered, too, that only the preceding December the last Provincial Congress had resolved "that it is the opinion of this congress, that none of the people of this colony have withdrawn their allegiance from his majesty." [2] Such being the case in December, it was surely prudent in June to refer again to the people before announcing their independence.

The Declaration of Independence, that was now signing at Philadelphia, was a turning-point in Jay's public life. In the Committee of Fifty-one he was apparently the representative of the well-to-do merchants who had confidence in the son of Mr. Peter Jay. Judicious and prudent, rather than emotional, Jay's disposition was at the time eminently conservative. With the example of Boston before them, with excited Sons of Liberty declaiming in every tavern, ringing bells, parading with banners, and threatening loyal business men with letters signed "Committee on Tar and Feathers," there was grave danger that order might be destroyed by mob violence, and trade ruined by ill-

[1] To R. R. Livingston, May 29, 1776, *Jay MSS.*
[2] *New York Journal*, December 21, 1775.

considered restrictions. The only safety was in
deliberation and caution. The colonies, as yet,
were united neither by sentiment nor interest, and
in every colony, especially in New York, the parties
of Whig and Tory, the radicals and conservatives,
were, in aggregate wealth and influence, nearly
equally divided. Of Jay, and of every man of that
day like him, it may be said, though in a different
sense from that of the old Roman, that *cunctando
restituit rem*, by delay he created a nation. Conservative though not Tory, he saw that the struggle
was to preserve and continue liberty they had always possessed, rather than to win liberty. The
Revolution, as he was fond of saying, found us free
as our fathers always were; therefore it is false to
suggest that we were ever emancipated. For this
reason was the result of the war to be permanent,
since it was the work of evolution, rather than of
revolution. It is often said that the action of Jay
and Dickinson, in promoting petition after petition
to the king in terms of almost undignified conciliation, lost the opportunity for successful action and
protracted the war. It is forgotten, perhaps, that
at that early period the only action possible would
have been spasmodic, and far from unanimous; and
that, even if successful, a sudden and short war
would have left unchanged the disposition of half
the people, which even the long years of the Revolution changed but slowly. The reaction which
followed in the distracted days of the Confederation, and which nearly wrecked the infant state,

would otherwise surely have resulted in thirteen
jealous and disunited colonies, instead of one great
nation.

To this end did the work of Jay tend, consciously
or unconsciously. To this end was the long succession of state papers that he prepared as drafts-
man, so to speak, of the Continental Congress. To
this end was his work in New York, reconciling
the conservative merchants and the radical mechanics, keeping the favor of the less bigoted royalists,
and winning gradually the confidence of the Sons
of Liberty.

Time soon decided the matter. The old government was dead beyond resuscitation. Anarchy
threatened, the Revolutionary committees were essentially local and temporary expedients. The war
might last for years, and a more stable government
was essential. "I see the want of government in
many instances," wrote McDougall. "I fear liberty is in danger from the licentiousness of the
people on the one hand, and the army on the other.
The former feel their own liberty in the extreme." [1]
A significant admission from the old Son of Liberty. It was the course of wisdom to establish a
new form of government, and it was only the circumstances of the moment that required it to be
based on a Declaration of Independence.

[1] From Alex. McDougall, March 20, 1776, *Jay MSS.*

CHAPTER III

THE new Provincial Congress of New York met at White Plains on July 9, and at once referred to a committee a copy of the Declaration of Independence, just received from Philadelphia. From this committee, on the same afternoon, Jay, as chairman, reported a resolution of his own drafting, which was unanimously adopted: " That the reasons assigned by the Continental Congress for declaring the United Colonies free and independent States are cogent and conclusive; and that while we lament the cruel necessity which has rendered that measure unavoidable, we approve the same, and will, at the risk of our lives and fortunes, join with the other colonies in supporting it." [1] The New York delegates in Congress were accordingly authorized to sign the Declaration, which they had hitherto refrained from doing on the ground of lack of power. The next day the style of the House was changed to the " Convention of the Representatives of the State of New York." British

[1] *Journals of Provincial Congress*, p. 518.

ships of war were at this moment at Tarrytown,
within six miles of White Plains.

Jay had been a member of the committee that
reported to the old convention, June 6, a purely
formal acknowledgment of the Virginia resolutions of independence; a report which the convention agreed to keep secret till after the elections
of delegates "to establish a new form of government."   But his course in moving the declaration
of July 9 was not therefore inconsistent, "most
refined deceit," as it is termed by one writer.[1]
For the old convention was not authorized to commit itself upon the question, while the new convention was so authorized specifically.   His action of
June 6 and 11 was identical in spirit with that of
Duane at Philadelphia, who pledged New York to
independence, at the same time declaring that he
could not legally vote on the question until further
instructions were received from his constituents.[2]
Of the wisdom of the measure, even with regard
to its effect on European politicians, Jay was now
thoroughly convinced; and it was on this ground
that the opposition rested in Congress.   "This
most certainly," he wrote to Lewis Morris, "will
not be the last campaign, and in my opinion Lord
Howe's operations cannot be so successful and decisive as greatly to lessen the ideas which foreign
nations have conceived of our importance.   I am
rather inclined to think that our declaring inde-

---

[1] Dawson, *Westchester Co. in the Am. Rev.* pp. 186, 187, 196, 197.
[2] Lamb, *Hist. of N. Y.* ii. 83.

pendence in the face of so powerful a fleet and
army will impress them with an opinion of our
strength and spirit; and when they are informed
how little our country is in the enemy's possession,
they will unite in declaring us invincible by the
arms of Britain." [1]

Almost immediately a short but sharp dissension arose between the convention and Congress.
The latter body issued a colonel's commission to a
major in the New York militia, who had distinguished himself in the Canadian campaign, and
ordered him to raise and officer in New York a
battalion for the Continental service.   Though Jay
had urged at Philadelphia in the spring the wisdom of removing from colonial control all the
militia so soon as they were ordered out on active
duty, the contrary practice still prevailed; and
this sudden discrimination in the case of New
York filled him and the convention with indignation, as an arbitrary exercise of power; and in a
sharp report, which the convention moderated, he
condemned the excuse of " the necessity of the
case," as a fruitful mother of tyranny.

New York city was now occupied by the enemy,
and the British fleet in the bay was daily expected
up the river.   Warned by Washington of the danger of the passes being seized between the Hudson
and Albany, the convention appointed Jay with
five others a secret military committee " to devise
and carry into execution such measures as to them

[1] September, 1776, *Jay MSS.*

shall appear most effectual for obstructing the channel of Hudson's River, or annoying the enemy's ships ; " and the next day authorized them to impress " boats, . . . wagons, horses, and drivers . . . as well as to call out the militia, if occasion should require." [1] The committee held its first meeting at the house of Mr. Van Kleeck, at Poughkeepsie, and at once sent Jay to the Salisbury Iron Works in Connecticut for cannon and shot. He found himself obliged to obtain permission from Governor Trumbull at Lebanon, and the governor had to consult his council; but finally Jay procured several small cannon, which he transported safely to Hoffman's Landing and thence to Fort Montgomery. [2]

Jay was not a man of war ; his duties as colonel were apparently purely formal ; but from his connection with the secret committee and other military committees he was in constant communication with the generals at headquarters, with McDougall and Troup, and later with Washington, Clinton, and Schuyler. To Jay, McDougall commended his son, a prisoner in Canada, " lest he should in the exchange of those prisoners be forgot. . . . If I should do otherwise than well, I pray remember this boy." [3] "You always were my benefactor," wrote Troup, " and I hope will continue so as long as I walk in the line of prudence, and prove my-

[1] *Journals of Provincial Congress*, i. 526.
[2] Report by Jay, August 7 (?), *Jay MSS.*
[3] From General McDougall, December 2, 1776, *Jay MSS.*

self a lover of American liberty." [1] And it was
to Jay that Schuyler, embittered by the partisan
charges that were provoked by the evacuation of
Ticonderoga, intrusted the defense of his reputation. On the eve of an expected engagement with
the British troops he wrote sadly: " I may possibly
get rid of the cares of this life, or fall into their
hands; in either case I entreat you to rescue my
memory from that load of calumny that ever follows the unfortunate." [2] Of the details of the war
Jay kept himself unusually well informed, and his
private agents were reputed as being, with those of
Generals Clinton and Heath, and Governor Livingston, among the most intelligent in that service.[3]
His opinions, then, on the military measures that
should have been adopted are worth noting, though
they were not followed, and are quoted by Mahon
merely on account of their severity. He believed,[4]
and urged in vain,[5] that the city of New York and
the whole of the State below the mountains should
be desolated, the Hudson shallowed at Fort Montgomery, the southern passes fortified, and the army
stationed in the mountains on the east of the river
with a large detachment on the west. Thus, he
added, " the State would be absolutely impregna-
ble against all the world on the sea side, and would

[1] From General Troup, July 22, 1777, *Jay MSS.*

[2] From General Schuyler, July 27, 1777, *Jay MSS.*

[3] *Mag. Am. Hist.* xi. 59.

[4] Force, *Am. Archives*, 5th Ser. ii. 951. To G. Morris, October
6, 1776.

[5] To General Schuyler, December 11, 1776, *Jay MSS.* ii. 17.

have nothing to fear except from the way of the lake."

In view of the dangers menacing the State, the consideration of a new form of government was postponed till August 1, when, on motion of Gouverneur Morris, seconded by Mr. Duer, the convention appointed a committee to prepare and report a plan for the organization of a new form of government. Jay was made chairman, and his associates included men of eminent ability: Gouverneur Morris, Robert R. Livingston, William Duer, Abraham and Robert Yates, General Scott, Colonel Broome, Mr. Hobart, Colonel De Witt, Samuel Townsend, William Smith, and Mr. Wisner. The committee was directed to report on August 16. The convention notified Jay and two of his associates on the secret military committee of their new appointment, and commanded their attendance. Jay was still occupied in fortifying West Point, and on the 12th the convention summoned them still more imperatively unless they were "absolutely necessary in the secret committee." But General Clinton refused to let them go. Towards the end of the month the increasing danger from excursions of the enemy forced the convention to move from White Plains to Harlem, where they sat in the church, afterward meeting successively at Kingsbridge, at Odell's, in Philipse's Manor, then at Fishkill, Poughkeepsie, and Kingston.

Outside of the city of New York there was no overwhelming popular sentiment for independence

in that State.   A local aristocracy had been founded
by the Dutch East India Company, and had been
fostered by the English governors.   Many of the
first families of the province were ardent royalists,
connected by blood or long association with England; on the large manorial estates, the tenant
farmers inclined to be either indifferent to politics or adherents of their landlords; while, with
an English army in the city and an English fleet
on the river, there were thousands who naturally
deemed neutrality to be the only wisdom.   The
upper part of the State was already cut off from
the lower, and but little organized treachery would
have sufficed to place the whole State at the mercy
of the British.   Meantime the fate of the continent
seemed for the moment to hinge upon New York;
and to the patriotic convention it appeared essential to the common welfare to rid the State, still
within their control, of the disaffected, and of all
who were secretly but none the less actively hostile.
On motion of Jay, the convention had already, on
June 16, declared guilty of treason, with the penalty
of death, all persons inhabiting or passing through
the State who should give aid or comfort to the
enemy;[1] a resolution which, in spite of its harsh-
ness, was almost identical with that adopted about
a week later by the Continental Congress.   Fortunately the law may be said to have been "merely
buncombe, meaning nothing;"[2] but it may have

[1] *Journals of Provincial Congress*, i. 526.
[2] Dawson, *Westchester Co. in the Am. Rev.* p. 210.

been none the less a useful bit of policy. In the middle of June, when Forbes, the gunsmith, was charged with conspiring against the life of Washington,[1] the late convention had in great haste appointed Livingston, Jay, and Gouverneur Morris as a secret committee to examine disaffected persons. When, after ten days' labor, their sessions were interrupted by the panic that was caused by Lord Howe's arrival, there were twenty-seven prisoners in the city hall, and forty-three (including the mayor) in the new jail.[2] How many, like Thomas Jones, the historian, were examined and banished for disaffection, is unknown.[3] This was the last that is heard of what was known as the committee to examine disaffected persons.

The new convention found itself fallen upon days still more evil. Governor Tryon, from his refuge on board ship, seemed as active and omnipresent as the Prince of Evil; "so various, and, I may add, successful have been the arts of Governor Tryon and his adherents," wrote Jay, "to spread the seeds of disaffection among us, that I cannot at present obtain permission to return to Congress." [4] On September 26 a secret committee was appointed, on motion of Duer, consisting of Jay and three, subsequently six, others. It was termed "a committee for inquiring into, detecting, and defeat-

[1] Force, *Am. Archives*, 4th Ser. †ix. 1178.
[2] Dawson, *Westchester Co. in the Am. Rev.* p. 171, note.
[3] Jones, *Hist. of New York*, ii. 295.
[4] To R. Morris, October 6, 1776, *Jay MSS.*

ing conspiracies . . . against the liberties of America," and was empowered " to send for persons and papers, to call out detachments of the militia in different counties for suppressing insurrections, to apprehend, secure, or remove persons whom they might judge dangerous to the safety of the State, to make drafts on the treasury, to enjoin secrecy upon their members and the persons they employed, and to raise and officer two hundred and twenty men, and to employ them as they saw fit." This committee organized, October 8, at Conner's tavern at Fishkill, with Duer in the chair. Their minutes for 1776 are in the handwriting of Jay, who, besides acting as secretary, after the first few meetings sat permanently as chairman. Day after day the local county committees of safety sent to Fishkill batches of prisoners under guard, men, women, and girls, upon charges of receiving protection from the enemy, corresponding with the enemy, refusing to sign the association or oath of allegiance to the Congress, or simply with disaffection to the cause. Those who subscribed to the association were usually dismissed ; but all who refused were subjected to punishment, confinement in jail, transportation to another town or colony, residence at Fishkill under parole " to remain within three miles of the stone church," or, in less serious cases, to residence at home under parole not to go six miles away. Peter Van Schaack, Jay's friend and classmate, was sent with his brother David to Boston, " under the care of a discreet officer," at " their

own expense . . . there to remain on their parole
of honor," because they " have long maintained an
equivocal neutrality in the present struggles and
are in general supposed unfriendly to the American cause." [1]   One lot of prisoners was sent to New
Hampshire, and the committee wrote at the same
time to the New Hampshire legislature, desiring
that such as were not directed to be confined, and
not in circumstances to maintain themselves, be
put to labor and compelled to earn their subsistence.[2]   One James McLaughlin, for being "notoriously disaffected," was ordered to be " sent to
Captain Hodges of the ship of war Montgomery,
at Kingston," and Captain Hodges was directed
" to keep him aboard the said ship, put him to such
labor as he may be fit for, and pay him as much as
he may earn." [3]   These sentences were often ingenious, but, however painless, they were unquestionably severe to people of position ; for all were so
worded as to be indefinite in duration, " till further
orders from this committee, or the convention, or
future legislature of this State."   Sometimes Jay
and Morris were the only members present, but the
committee did not on that account neglect its business.   On February 27, 1777, it was dissolved by
order of the convention, and in its stead commissioners were appointed under instructions drawn
by their predecessors.

[1] *Minutes*, December 21, 1776.
[2] To the General Court of New Hampshire, October 31, 1776,
Jay MSS.
[3] *Minutes*, January 4, 1777.

It is, perhaps, not surprising that Jay's conspicuous position on this extra-legal despotic tribunal should have excited against him the bitter enmity and vituperation of the royalists. "In imitation of the infamous Dudley," said the "Royal Gazette," he "had formed and enforced statutes that destroyed every species of private property and repose." [1] But the times demanded prompt and stern measures; under military rule, in days of civil war, which the Revolution was in New York, suspected traitors are generally shot with short shrift; and if any man less cool-headed and humane than Jay had been in control, it may be doubted whether imprisonment would have been substituted for death. "Can we subsist, did any state ever subsist, without exterminating traitors?" wrote Major Hawley of the Massachusetts Provincial Congress to Elbridge Gerry. "It is amazingly wonderful that, having no capital punishment for our intestine enemies, we have not been utterly exterminated before now. For God's sake, let us not run such risks a day longer." [2] In New York the times were even more critical than in Massachusetts.

Jay's official conduct towards the royalists was throughout inspired by a sense of duty and by rigid impartiality. "In the course of the present troubles," he said, referring to his action on the secret committee, "I have adhered to certain fixed principles, and faithfully obeyed their dic-

[1] January 23, 1779.   [2] *Life of Elbridge Gerry*, i. 207.

tates without regarding the consequences of my
conduct to my friends, my family, or myself." [1]
The uprightness of his motives was indeed admitted by those who suffered most from his official
actions. Van Schaack, the friend whom Jay had
exiled to Boston for "neutrality," was allowed to
return the next year under parole. His wife, who
was dying, longed for the sea breezes and familiar sights of New York, but Jay refused her the
necessary permission to visit the city merely and
return. " I never doubted your friendship," wrote
Van Schaack in some natural depression of spirits,
" yet I own that was not the ground upon which I
expected to succeed. . . . As a man I knew you
would espouse the petition, if public considerations did not oppose it; and if they did, I knew
no friendship could prevail on you to do it." [2]
"Though as an independent American," Jay declared to Van Schaack when a refugee in England
in 1782, " I considered all who were not with us,
and you among the rest, as against us; yet be assured that John Jay did not cease to be a friend
to Peter Van Schaack." [3] To Colonel James Delancey, who had taken a royal commission and
was at the time a prisoner of war in Hartford jail,
Jay wrote recalling his early friendship: " How
far your situation may be comfortable and easy, I
know not; it is my wish and shall be my endeavor

[1] To Peter Van Schaack, 1782, *Life of Van Schaack*, p. 301.
[2] *Life of Peter Van Schaack*, p. 100.
[3] *Ibid.* p. 302.

that it be as much so as may be consistent with the interest of the great cause to which I have devoted everything I hold dear in this world ; " and he sent him a hundred pounds.

Very different was his treatment of Colonel Peter Delancey, who commanded a corps of lawless spirits known as Delancey's Boys, the cowboys of Cooper's " Spy," the murderers of Colonel Greene. " When peace was made, Mr. Jay was desirous to allay animosities, and he readily renewed his acquaintance with the royalists who had been induced by principle to join the English, but he refused to profess any regard for the perfidious and the cruel. Among the latter he considered Colonel Delancey, and therefore when he met him in London he would not know him." [1] Many of Jay's relations and friends, indeed, were either Tories or perplexed as to their duty. Many of the Philipses, a family with which Mrs. Jay was connected by descent, and her husband by adoption, were decided Tories and in due time refugees. A friend, Dr. Beverly Robinson, asked Jay to take care of his family while he consulted Colonel Philipse on his proper course of action. " The information you gave me when I was before the committee . . . that every person, without exception, must take an oath of allegiance to the States of America, or go with their families to the king's army, has given me the greatest concern. I cannot as yet think of forfeiting my allegiance to the

[1] Judge William Jay, *Jay MSS.*

king, and I am unwilling to remove myself or
family from this place, or at least out of this country." [1] Some years later, a cousin, Miss Rebecca
Bayard, wrote on behalf of her brother and his
family to expedite their passage to New York.
They had a pass from General Gates and a promise from Clinton, then governor, but were stopped
on the way.[2] The answer was kind, but firm, that
it was decided to pass no persons except on public
business. Jay even thought fit to warn Gouverneur Morris : " Your enemies talk much of your
Tory connections in Philadelphia. Take care. Do
not expose yourself to calumny." [3]

By the end of December, 1776, Westchester
County had been abandoned to the British; the
attack on Canada had failed, and Washington was
retreating through New Jersey. " In this moment
of gloom and dismay," Jay prepared an address
from the Provincial Convention to their constituents : " What are the terms on which you are promised peace? Have you heard of any except
absolute, unconditional obedience and servile sub-
mission? . . . And why should you be slaves now,
having been freemen ever since the country was
settled? . . . If success crowns your efforts, all
the blessings of freedom shall be your reward. If
you fall in the contest, you will be happy with
God in Heaven." The address was favorably re-

---

[1] From Dr. Beverly Robinson, March 4, 1777, *Jay MSS.*
[2] From Miss Rebecca Bayard, June 28, 1778, *Jay MSS.*
[3] To Gouverneur Morris, January, 1778.

ceived, and Congress at Philadelphia ordered it to be translated and printed in German at the public expense. The meagre minutes of the secret committee, when read between the lines, suggest an unsuspected extent of vacillation and disaffection throughout the State, especially in Westchester County; and a late writer, whose facts are as often exact as his comments on them are perverse, has proved that the farmers no less than the gentry were infinitely perplexed and puzzled by the conflicting claims of the king and the State.[1]   In this short period immediately following the Declaration of Independence, Jay showed the promptness and boldness and the indefatigable, unhesitating energy which the critical days demanded.

[1] Dawson, *Westchester Co. in the American Revolution, passim.*

CHAPTER IV

CONSTRUCTIVE STATESMAN

DURING the spring of 1777 Jay was engaged on the committee to frame a new form of government. "For this purpose," said his son, "he retired from the convention to some place in the country. Upon reflecting on the character and feelings of the convention, he thought it prudent to omit in the draft several provisions that appeared to him improvements, and afterwards to propose them separately as amendments. . . . It is probable that the convention was ultra-democratic, for I have heard him observe that *another turn of the winch would have cracked the cord*." [1]

The Constitution thus formed was singularly expressive of the conservative instincts of the men of the American Revolution, and of the unflinching common sense characteristic of the Dutch-Huguenot merchants of New York, of whom Jay was a natural leader. It is said, indeed, that as " there were few models to follow and improve, the work of framing a fundamental law for the State may fairly be said to have been undertaken in an almost unexplored field." [2] But such a statement needs much quali-

---

[1] Judge William Jay, *Jay MSS.*

[2] J. H. Dougherty, " Constitutions of the State of N. Y.," *Political Science Quarterly*, September, 1888, p. 490.

fication before it ceases to be misleading. John Adams had an explanation of the origin of the New York Constitution that is equally inadequate. He wrote in his old age to Jefferson [1] that, according to Duane, Jay had gone home having Adams's letter to Wythe "in his pocket for his model and foundation." But the letter to Wythe contained only the most meagre sketch of a plan of government, amounting to little more than the suggestion that legislative, executive, and judicial powers should be balanced; that there should be a representative assembly, a council chosen by the assembly, and a governor appointed by the assembly and council; the governor to appoint all officers by and with the consent of the council; and judges to hold office during good behavior.[2] The letter to Wythe did not propose, as Adams did later, as an alternative, the election of the governor by the people, and of the council by the freeholders.[3] The fact is, that the Constitution of New York was a special adaptation of the provincial government, with as few modifications as the circumstances required, and those chiefly suggested by the history of the province.[4] In the same sense, the Federal Constitution is, in the words of Sir Henry Maine, "in reality a version of the British Constitution." [5]

[1] September 17, 1823, John Adams's *Works*, x. 410.

[2] *Ibid*. iv. 193.

[3] To John Penn, *Ibid*. iv. 203.

[4] R. L. Fowler, "Constitution of the Supreme Court of N. Y.," *Albany Law Journal*, December 18, 1880, p. 486.

[5] Maine, *Popular Government*, p. 207.

"We have a government, you know, to form,"
Jay wrote; "and God knows what it will resemble.
Our politicians, like some guests at a feast, are perplexed and undetermined which dish to prefer."
This confusion of mind was, perhaps, reflected by
the choice of "State" as the title of the new government, a colorless word, though used to designate
the government of England under Cromwell.[1]

"All power whatever in the State hath reverted
to the people thereof," is the recitation in the pre-
amble; and the first section ordained that no authority should be exercised over the people of the
State but such as should be derived from and
granted by the people; a statement of a fact and
its logical corollary.   Although, nominally, the old
provincial legislature had consisted only of a single
house, the council exercised powers of a legislative
character, and this council, rather than the English
House of Lords, may have been the model of the
state Senate.[2]   As has been well said: "The bi-
cameral legislature, the power of the legislative
houses to be the sole judges of their own member-
ships, the method of choosing the presiding officer
of the more popular branch, the parliamentary
common law, the veto on legislation, the bill of
rights, the judicature, the jurisprudence, and the
franchises, were all provincial institutions, continued after the Revolution by virtue of the Constitu-

---

[1] Fowler, *Albany Law Journal*, July 21, 1879, p. 490; December
18, 1880, p. 486 n.

[2] *Albany Law Journal*, December 18, 1880, p. 487.

tion, and because they were associated with all that was wisest and best in the previous history of New York. The Revolution was not a war against these things; it was a war for these things, — the common property of the Anglican race." [1] Property qualifications were accordingly required as before; electors of the governor and senators must enjoy a freehold worth £100 ($250) a year; electors of assemblymen must have a freehold worth £20 ($50), or a tenancy worth 40s. ($5) a year, and must pay taxes. It was "a favorite maxim with Mr. Jay, that those who own the country ought to govern it." [2] But before condemning such a maxim and its application in the Constitution as "aristocratic," as modern speakers are prone to do, it is well to remember that in 1769 the Province of New York had nearly 39,000 freeholders and burgesses entitled to vote, a number in proportion to population far greater than existed in England before the Reform Bill; that there was as yet no organized demand for the franchise by the unqualified masses: and that before the French Revolution an absolute democracy was but the dream of a theorist.

As to the powers to be given to the governor, experience with the royal governors naturally suggested a policy of jealous restriction; although the success of the prerogative party in the past had been due not so much to gubernatorial power as to

[1] *Albany Law Journal*, December 18, 1880, p. 488.
[2] Jay's *Jay*, i. 70.

the occasional subserviency of the provincial Assembly, which body, through the small number of
representatives, not over twenty-seven at the time
of the Revolution, and also by reason of the protracted sessions, at first septennial and finally indefinite in duration, had naturally soon ceased to
be really representative. The governor, who was
appointed for three years, a term to which, after a
change to a two years' term, New York returned
in 1874, was held in check by two specially devised
councils, the Council of Appointment and the
Council of Revision. The former consisted of the
governor and one senator, chosen annually from
each of the five great districts into which the State
was divided for the election of senators, and had
the appointment of practically all the officers in
the State, except those of the towns. The Council
of Revision, composed of the governor, the chancellor, and the judges of the Supreme Court, had
the sole power of veto, subject to reversal by a two
thirds vote in each house. In this way the governor became little more than a mere figurehead,
without responsibility for either appointments or
vetoes; in the Council of Appointment partisanship had free opportunity to confirm its corrupt
bargains; and both councils were promptly abolished by the Constitutional Convention of 1822,
which gave the sole power of veto to the governor.
Jay himself, when governor, had reason, as will
appear, to regret his suggestion of the Council of
Appointment; which, in part, may have originated

in the old Council of the province. Had, however, Jay's construction of the language of the Constitution been followed, by which the governor had sole power of nomination, those evils would have been avoided. Against the Council of Revision, which had its analogue in the veto on provincial acts possessed by the king in Privy Council, no such objections could be raised, and its abolition, after 128 out of 6590 bills had been vetoed, was due chiefly to the growing jealousy on the part of the democracy of any supreme non-elective body.

Especially conservative were the framers of the Constitution in all that concerned the courts of law and the legal customs of the colony. Socage tenure, practically allodial, had been introduced under the Duke of York's government a century before. The continuation of the Supreme Court by mere incidental mention, and of trial by jury "in all cases in which it hath heretofore been used in the colony of New York;" and the clause moved in convention by Jay, that "the legislature . . . shall at no time hereafter institute any new court or courts, but such as shall proceed according to the course of the common law," — were reassertions of the claims of the popular party in opposition to the pro-prerogative men during the contest over the establishment of a court of equity in 1734, and during the later debate over the case of Cosby v. Van Dam, when the justices of the Supreme Court attempted to hold a court of exchequer.[1]   The

---

[1] *Albany Law Journal*, May 17, 1879, p. 492.

limitation of the tenure of the judges "during good
behavior, or until they shall have respectively at-
tained the age of sixty years," perpetuates also the
memory of the controversy with Lieutenant-Governor Colden over the retention in office of the
senile Justice Horsmanden. The only new court
created was the Court of Errors and Impeachment,
to which the justices of the Supreme Court were
nominated, sitting for the occasion with the senators. In forming this, what may now seem extraordinary tribunal, Jay and his fellow members on
the committee had doubtless before their eyes, not
the House of Lords with its special judicial powers,
but the Council of the province, which possessed
supreme appellate jurisdiction. Of this Council,
too, as of the new Court of Errors, the judges and
chancellors were members, with power to argue,
though not to vote, on appeals from their own
judgments.[1] Finally, few of the guarantees of
popular rights embodied in the Constitution had a
lineage of less than a hundred years ; for most of
them are found in the " Charter of Libertys and
Privileges," the first act of the first Assembly of
the province, in 1683, which was signed by the
governor, though disallowed by the king. Towards
the end of March, 1777, the draft of the new Constitution, in Jay's handwriting, was reported by
Duane from the committee.

After the dispiriting battles of Long Island, and
Washington's masterly retreat, came the mortify-

[1] *Albany Law Journal*, December 18, 1880, p. 489.

ing affair at Kip's Bay, the hasty retreat of Putnam's forces from New York; then followed the battle of Harlem Plains, reviving the spirit of the American troops, and that of White Plains, and Washington's retreat to the Hudson and into New Jersey. The convention, therefore, was transacting its business under the stress of unparalleled disadvantages. "In fact, such was the alarming state of affairs, that at certain periods the convention was literally driven from pillar to post, while it had alternately to discharge all the various and arduous duties of legislators, soldiers, negotiators, committees of safety, committees of ways and means, judges and jurors, fathers and guardians of their own families flying before the enemy, and then protectors of a beloved commonwealth." [1] Only a few days before, it had been necessary to allow members to smoke in the convention chambers, "to prevent bad effects from the disagreeable effluvia from the jail below." [2]

The Constitution, as drafted, was discussed section by section, and passed with but few modifications or additions; and of these Jay moved a large proportion. A section providing for voting by ballot was struck out on motion of Gouverneur Morris, but some days later Jay carried an amendment which ordered that so soon as practicable after the war all elections should be by ballot, though the legislature might at any time after a

[1] *Proceedings and Debates of Const. Conv. of* 1821, p. 692.
[2] *Journals of Prov. Cong.,* etc. i. 842.

fair trial renew the practice of *viva voce* voting.[1]
It was under this clause that the first law was
framed in New York, authorizing a secret ballot
in 1778, and so successful did it prove that nine
years later it was extended to all elections of state
officers. Such a measure was certainly never proposed in the interest of aristocracy!

The most prolonged debate of the session was
upon the question of religious toleration, over the
important clause that "the free toleration of religious profession and worship without diminution
or preference shall forever hereafter be allowed
within the State to all mankind." This charter
of freedom of conscience was one of the priceless
heirlooms bequeathed to New York by New Nether-
land, which, almost alone among the colonies, had
never listened to the denunciations of fanaticism,
had never lighted the fires of persecution. In Jay
the old Huguenot blood still ran hotly, thrilling
him with memories of Pierre Jay driven from La
Rochelle, of Bayards and Philipses seeking refuge
in Holland and Bohemia from the long arm of the
papacy. The power of the Church of Rome he
knew and feared; he urged, accordingly, amendment after amendment to except Roman Catholics
till they should abjure the authority of the pope
to absolve citizens from their allegiance and to
grant spiritual absolution. The result of his objections was the adoption of a proviso "that the
liberty of conscience hereby granted shall not be

[1] *Journals of Prov. Cong.* i. 866.

so construed as to excuse acts of licentiousness or justify practices inconsistent with the safety of the State." [1]   When the question of naturalization came up for discussion, Jay renewed the same fight, and secured the amendment, sufficient for public security though less stringent than he desired, that before naturalization all persons shall "abjure and renounce all allegiance to all and every foreign king, prince, potentate, and state, in all matters ecclesiastical as well as civil." [2]   The wording of this clause brings out, perhaps, Jay's motive in this controversy. With him it was not a religious but a political question. It was not Romanism as a religion that he feared, but Romanism as an *imperium in imperio*. That he was not a bigot was shown clearly when in July, 1775, the Provincial Congress forwarded to their delegates in the Continental Congress a "plan of reconciliation," protesting, among other things, "against the indulgence and establishment of popery [by the Quebec Act], all along their interior confines." To the answer of the delegates to the Provincial Congress Jay added this significant clause: that they thought best to make no reference to the religious article, preferring to bury "all disputes on ecclesiastical points, which have for ages had no other tendency than that of banishing peace and charity from the world." [2]

[1] *Journals of Prov. Cong.* i. 860.
[2] *Ibid.* i. 846.
[3] Theo. Roosevelt, *Life of Gouverneur Morris*, pp. 42, 43.

The Council of Appointment was constituted on Jay's motion ; but though the credit or misfortune of its creation is attributed to him, the measure was really a compromise, the extremists on one side proposing that the governor should have sole power of appointment, — a sound principle, but obnoxious to the democratic convention, — while those on the other side insisted upon confirmation by the legislature.[1]

That acts of attainder (which were limited to offenses committed before the termination of the war) should not work corruption of blood ; and that the State should assume the protection of the Indians within its boundaries, were humane provisions due to Jay. And just before the final vote, he moved a further clause that was adopted, the significance of which has been explained,[2] prohibiting the institution of any court " but such as shall proceed according to the course of the common law." [3]

On April 17, 1777, his mother died, and Jay hastened to Fishkill to attend the funeral and comfort the family. During his absence, on a Sunday, the Constitution was adopted ; it was hurriedly printed, and published April 22 by being read from a platform in front of the court-house at Kingston. Like all the early constitutions, except

[1] *Journals of Prov. Cong.* i. 377. To R. R. Livingston and Gouverneur Morris, April 29, 1777, *Jay MSS.*

[2] *Supra*, p. 73.

[3] *Journals of Prov. Cong.* i. 882.

that of Massachusetts, it was never submitted to the people; the election of delegates for the express purpose of framing a constitution being deemed a ratification in advance. Jay was at once placed on a committee for organizing the new form of government. Under the plan of organization, fifteen persons, including Jay, were created a Council of Safety " with all the powers necessary for the safety and preservation of the State, until a meeting of the legislature," and with instructions to administer the oath of office to the governor, when elected. Robert R. Livingston was appointed chancellor, John Jay chief justice, and others were appointed judges, sheriffs, and clerks, to act *pro tempore* till the institution of the new government, a period, as it happened, of some six months. An act of grace was drafted by Jay in committee, granting full pardon to any delinquent or traitor on his producing before the Council of Safety or the governor a certificate of subscription to the oath of allegiance. On further motion of Jay, the resignation by General Clinton of his command of the militia was not accepted. The thanks of the convention were then voted to the New York delegates in Congress; and the convention dissolved, May 13, ordering the Council of Safety to assemble at the same place " to-morrow morning at nine o'clock." [1] This was the close of that memorable convention, whose deliberations, said Chancellor Kent, " were conducted under the

[1] *Journals of Prov. Cong.* i. 931.

excitement of great public anxiety and constant alarm; and that venerable instrument, which was destined to be our guardian and pride for upwards of forty years, was produced amidst the hurry and tumult of arms."[1] In all this turmoil Jay and his fellow framers of the Constitution were calm and collected; inspired by the practical, precedent regarding spirit of the common law, they retained all that experience had approved, and adjusted what they added of new to harmonize with the old; therefore it was that the Constitution remained in force for over forty years, and then, "with some minor modifications, the extension of suffrage and the concentration of more power in the governor, . . . continued substantially unchanged until 1846." Subsequent changes have been in the direction of limiting the power of the legislature, and providing for the new problems presented by the sudden development of cities. One obvious defect was the failure to make provision for constitutional amendment.[2] Many things were omitted, which Jay especially regretted, — a direction that all officers should swear allegiance; a prohibition of domestic slavery; and a clause "for the support and encouragement of literature."[3] "I wish," he wrote to Morris, April 14, 1778, "you would write and publish a few civil things on our Constitution, censur-

[1] Kent, *Discourse before the N. Y. Hist. Soc.*, December 6, 1828, p. 5.

[2] Dougherty, *Pol. Science Quart.*, September, 1888, p. 494 *et passim*.

[3] Jay's *Jay*, i. 69.

ing, however, an omission in not restraining the
Council of Appointment from granting offices to
themselves."[1] In spite of defects, however, the
Constitution received general praise. " I believed
it would do very well,"[2] was John Adams's cold
expression, which meant, however, much more than
it said. " Our Constitution," Jay wrote to Ganse-
voort, " is universally approved, even in New England, where few New York productions have credit.
But unless the government be committed to proper
hands it will be weak and unstable at home and
contemptible abroad."[3] It was at that time " generally regarded as the most excellent of all the
American constitutions,"[4] of which it was the fifth
to be adopted; and by a writer whose knowledge
of the early constitutional history of the country
gives weight to any statement of his, however un-
susceptible of proof, it is asserted to have been
essentially the model of the national government
under which we live.[5]

For the next six months the government of the
State was in the hands of the Council of Safety.
They directed the release or confinement of suspected persons; regulated the prisons; conferred
with the Continental Congress on measures of defense; and provided for the coming elections. Jay
prepared a commission for holding courts of oyer

[1] *Jay MSS.*
[2] John Adams's *Works*, x. 410.
[3] June 5, 1777, *Jay MSS.*
[4] John Alex. Jameson, *Constitutional Convention*, 4th ed. § 152.
[5] John Austin Stevens, *Mag. Am. Hist.*, July, 1878, p. 387.

and terminer; reported from a committee rules for the reorganization of the Fleet prison; drafted letters to the New York delegates at Philadelphia concerning the revolt in the northeast, and was forthwith added to the Committee on Intelligence to discuss with General Schuyler at headquarters the measures requisite for its suppression.[1]

Jay was asked more than once to become a candidate for governor; but he steadily refused, for the reasons which he stated as early as May 16: "That the office of the first magistrate of this State will be more respectable as well as more lucrative, and consequently more desirable than the place I now fill, is very apparent. But . . . my object in the course of the present great contest neither has been, nor will be, either rank or money. I am persuaded that I can be more useful to the State in the office I now hold than in the one alluded to, and therefore think it my duty to continue in it." General Schuyler seems to have been the candidate of the Council of Safety, as he certainly was Jay's; but on July 9 the people elected the burly, magnetic, less aristocratic Clinton. "I hope," Schuyler magnanimously wrote to Jay, "General Clinton's having the chair of government will not cause any divisions amongst the friends of America, although his family and connections do not entitle him to so distinguished a predominance; yet he is virtuous and loves his country, has abilities and is brave, and I hope he will experience from every patriot

[1] *Journals of the Prov. Cong.* i. 948–1019.

what I am resolved he shall from me, support, countenance, and comfort." [1] All New York at this time, outside the British pale, was Whig; but, as this letter shows, there was already a divergence between the more democratic and the less democratic Whigs, though all were equally patriotic and republican. The council at once resolved that they were not "justified in holding and exercising any powers vested in them longer than is necessary," and requested General Clinton to appear and take the oath of office. But the governor elect was holding Fort Montgomery and expecting a sudden attack. "The enemy have opened the ball in every quarter," wrote Schuyler to Jay a few days earlier. "It is pretty certain that they will pay us a visit from the westward as well as from the north. I am in much pain about Ticonderoga; little or nothing has been done there this spring." [2] The evacuation of Ticonderoga followed swiftly. "I dare not speak my sentiments," wrote Schuyler again, July 14, from Fort Edward. "In the Council of Safety, to your secrecy, I can confide them. They are, that it was an ill-judged measure, not warranted by necessity, and carried into execution with a precipitation that could not fail of creating the greatest panic in our troops and inspiriting the enemy." [3] For the moment, as Burgoyne continued his southward march, the war was close indeed. Jay's family was alarmed, especially his father.

[1] July 14, 1777, *Jay MSS.*   [2] June 30, 1777, *Jay MSS.*
[3] *Jay MSS.*

"General Sullivan with 2000 Continental troops are now encamped in the town of Fishkill," is the news sent by Frederick Jay, July 18. "This affair makes the old gentleman imagine that the enemy will certainly attempt the river. I could wish he was as easy about the matter as myself."[1] Quite as easily, but less cynically, Mrs. Jay had described just such an alarm in March at Peekskill: "This very moment the doctor came into the room, his looks bespeaking the utmost discomposure. 'Bad news, Mrs. Jay.' 'Aye, doctor; what now?' 'The regulars, madam, are landed at Peekskill; my own and other wagons are pressed to go instantly down to remove the stores.' Wherever I am, I think there are alarms; however, I am determined to re-member your maxim: prepare for the worst and hope the best."[2]

The legislature was summoned by the council to convene at Kingston on the 1st of August. It is curious to notice, in the light of subsequent history, that Jay "casually hinted at holding the first session of the legislature at Albany," but found "a general disinclination to it." "Some object," he wrote to Schuyler, "to the expense of living there, as most intolerable, and others say that, should Albany succeed in having both the great officers, the next step will be to make it the capital of the State."[3] On July 31, the day before that

---

[1] To John Jay, March 23, 1777, *Jay MSS.*
[2] *Ibid.*
[3] June 20, 1777, *Jay MSS.*

set for the meeting of the legislature, General Clinton, in the presence of the Council of Safety, took the oath of office, "clothed in the uniform of the service, and sword in hand, standing on the top of a barrel in front of the court-house in Kingston." [1]

A hurried expedition was made by Jay with Gouverneur Morris, by order of the council, to the headquarters of Washington, to consult about the means of defense, and to urge the necessity of providing garrisons for the forts in the Highlands, as the term of the militia stationed there was about to expire. Soon after his return, on September 9, he opened the first session of the Supreme Court of the State at Kingston. From a letter of Jay's, it appears that this was not the first official function of the judicature since the adoption of the Constitution. "A court is directed to be held in Dutchess," he wrote to Mrs. Jay, June 6, "and I expect the like order will be given for the other counties, so that should you not hear from me so frequently ascribe it to my absence from here." [2] The Supreme Court, as has been said, was merely the old provincial Supreme Court continued. "The minutes of this term appear in the same old volume in use under the crown. Between the minutes for April term, 1776, and those for September term, 1777, are a few blank leaves, but there is no written indication of the change of government

[1] John A. Stevens, *Mag. Am. Hist.*, July, 1878, p. 387.
[2] *Jay MSS.*

that had taken place. Indeed, it would be impossible to learn from the records of the September term what had happened in the interval, were it not for the title of the first cause on the docket: the party plaintiff is ' The People of the State of New York,' and no longer ' Dominus Rex.' In all other respects the minutes disclose no immediate change in the procedure, practice, or administration of the court." [1] At Kingston, September 9, Jay, as chief justice *pro tempore*,[2] delivered an address to the grand jury of Ulster County, which for many years afterward was regarded as one of the classics of the Revolution. " It affords me, gentlemen," was the impressive opening, " very sensible pleasure to congratulate you on the dawn of that free, mild, and equal government which now begins to break and rise from amid those clouds of anarchy, confusion, and licentiousness which the arbitrary and violent conduct of Great Britain had spread, in greater or less degree, throughout this and the other American States. . . . Vice, ignorance, and want of vigilance will be the only enemies able to destroy it. Against these be forever jealous." At that moment, Burgoyne was approaching Albany and had already reached the Hudson, while New York city and the whole southern tier of counties, New York, Westchester, Richmond, and all Long Island, the richest and most

----

[1] Fowler, " Const. of the Supreme Court," *Alb. Law Journal*.

[2] His formal commission as chief justice under the Constitution was not made out till a few days later.

populous in the State, were in almost undisturbed possession of England. The extreme northeastern counties, Gloucester and Cumberland, also, were in half-declared revolt. Within the British lines Judge Ludlow still exercised the jurisdiction of the Supreme Court of the province; and these two governments continued till the evacuation, November 25, 1783. It naturally followed that the Supreme Court of the State, during Jay's term as chief justice, had little important business. During the Revolution the court never sat in banc. As, moreover, no reports are published of the decisions for the first twenty-two years of its existence, scarcely anything can be safely said of Jay as chief justice of New York.

" I am now engaged," he wrote to Morris, April 29, 1778, " in the most disagreeable part of my duty, trying criminals. They multiply exceedingly. Robberies become frequent; the woods afford them shelter, and the Tories food. Punishment must of course become certain, and mercy dormant, — a harsh system, repugnant to my feelings, but nevertheless necessary." [1] In those days the inconveniences of life were many even for a judge at Albany. " Had it not been for fish," according to Jay, " the people of this town would have suffered for want of food, occasioned by the refusal of the farmers to sell at the stipulated prices. The few goods there were in the town have disappeared. I have tried, but have not been

[1] Jay's *Jay*, ii. 23.

able, to get a pair of shoes made." [1] In the summer he seems to have been much with the governor, assisting him in official correspondence, and was constantly applied to, but in vain, to exert his influence with him in behalf of Tories or their friends who wished passports to New York. In the autumn Jay retired to the farm at Fishkill for a little much-needed rest. "I have not been without the bounds of the farm since my return to it," he wrote his wife in August; "and to tell you the truth, were you and our little boy here, I should not even wish to leave it this year, provided it would be all that time exempted from the visitation of both armies. This respite from care and business is extremely grateful. . . . Its duration, however, will probably be short, as the number of persons charged with capital offenses now in confinement requires that courts for their trial be speedily held. Delays in punishing crimes encourage the commission of crime. The more certain and speedy the punishment, the fewer will be the objects." [2] While still at Fishkill Mr. Jay received General Washington, whom his father had entertained three years before at Rye, and with whom in the service of the State he had himself conferred frequently on military matters. The object of the visit was to discuss a plan, then before Congress, for the invasion of Canada with the aid of France, and both agreed in disapproving it.

[1] To Mrs. Jay, April 9, 1778, *Jay MSS.*
[2] August 3, 1778, *Jay MSS.*

Here, too, the chief justice probably wrote the
paper, signed " A Freeholder," on the abuses of
impressment by the military, " without any law,
but that of *the necessity of the case*, which cloaks
as many sins in politics as charity is said to do in
religion." " These impresses," was the conclusion,
" may, I think, easily be so regulated by laws, as
to relieve the inhabitants from reasonable cause of
complaint, and yet not retard or embarrass the
service."

As chief justice, Jay was *ex officio* a member of
the Council of Revision, which sat from time to
time at Poughkeepsie, and which this spring, on
objections drafted by him, vetoed many anti-Tory
bills, and bills perpetuating Revolutionary methods.
The first of these bills was " an act requiring all
persons holding offices or places under the government of this State to take the oaths herein prescribed and directed ; " and a new law was subsequently passed so as to avoid Jay's objections.[1]
A number of members of the legislature had
formed themselves into a council of safety, and
declared an embargo against the exportation of
flour and grain from the State. A bill to continue
this embargo was vetoed, because it recognized the
Council of Safety, " when in fact all legislative
power is to be exercised by the immediate representatives of the people in Senate and Assembly
in the mode prescribed by the Constitution ; for

[1] February 3, 1778. Alfred B. Street, *The Council of Revision*,
p. 201.

though the people of this State have, heretofore, been under a necessity of delegating their authority to provincial congresses and conventions, and of being governed by them, and councils, and committees of safety by them from time to time appointed, yet . . . these were mere temporary expedients to supply the want of a more regular government, and to cease when that prescribed by the Constitution should take place." [1]   March 25, the council vetoed a sweeping bill to disfranchise and disqualify for office any one who since July 9, 1776, had before any committee of safety, or conspiracy, acknowledged the sovereignty of Great Britain, or denied the authority of this or any former government of this State, or given aid or comfort to the enemy, etc. The reasoning of the council was strong and concise ; the bill is unconstitutional, " because the Constitution of this State hath expressly ordained that every elector, before he is admitted to vote, shall, if required, . . . take an oath . . . of allegiance to the State, from whence . . . it clearly follows that every elector who will take such oath has a constitutional right to be admitted to such vote, and therefore that the legislature have no power to deprive him thereof, more especially for acts by him done prior to the date of the said Constitution, which was the 20th day of April, 1777, of which acts the convention, by whom that Constitution was made, had ample cog-

[1] February 20, 1778.   Street, *The Council of Revision*, pp. 203, 204. The bill passed finally with slight amendments.

nizance." . . . " Because the said disqualifications
. . . savor too much of resentment and revenge to
be consistent with the dignity or good of a free
people. Because the said disqualifications (supposing them to be constitutional and proper) are
not limited to take place only on the conviction of
the offenders in due course of law." [1] Such, however, was the intensity of party feeling, that this
bill was passed over the veto.

The same day the council vetoed a bill " for
raising moneys," by which traders and manufacturers were to be taxed £50 on every £1000 gained
in their occupations since September 12, 1776.
This was held unconstitutional, as violating " the
equal right to life, liberty, and property," because
" the public good requires that commerce and man-
ufactures be encouraged," and because it is " repugnant to every idea of justice thus, without any open
charge or accusation of offense, and without trial,
indiscriminately to subject numerous bodies of
free citizens, distinguished only by the appellation
of traders or manufacturers, to large penalties
not incurred on conviction of disobedience to any
known law, and couched under the specious name
of a tax." [2] As late as November 5, a similar bill
was vetoed, giving the assessors authority to tax at
discretion those who, " taking advantage of the
necessities of their country, have, in prosecuting
their private gain, amassed large sums of money

[1] Street, *The Council of Revision*, pp. 210, 211.
[2] *Ibid.* pp. 212, 213.

to the great prejudice of the public." Jay's objections were based on broad constitutional grounds: " An equal right to life, liberty, and property is a fundamental principle in all free societies and states, and is intended to be secured to the people of this State by the Constitution thereof; and therefore no member of this State can constitutionally or justly be constrained to contribute more to the support thereof than in like proportion to the other citizens, according to their respective estates and abilities." . . . " To tax a faculty is to tolerate it, vice not being in its nature a subject of taxation." . . . " By the principles of the Constitution, . . . except in cases of attainder, . . . no citizen is liable to be punished by the State but such as have violated the laws of the State. . . . Supposing, therefore, that the persons aimed at in this bill have acquired riches immorally, yet if they have acquired them in a manner which the legislature has not thought proper to prohibit, they are not obnoxious to human punishment, however much they may be to divine vengeance. But if, on the other hand, these persons have acquired riches in a manner prohibited by the law of the land, they ought to be tried and punished in the way directed by these laws, and not subjected to double punishment." [1]

These words, so full of reasonableness, love of legality, and hatred of injustice, may well close our account of the period that is here roughly termed

[1] Street, *The Council of Revision*, pp. 214, 215.

that of Jay's constructive statesmanship. Years are to pass before we find him again in the service of his State; but from that day to this New York has borne upon its fundamental law the deep impression of his character.

CHAPTER V

FOR many years the boundaries between New
York, New Hampshire, and Massachusetts had
been a source of controversy and confusion. The
inhabitants of the disputed territory were unusually hardy and independent, and as early as 1772
and 1773 there were riots in Gloucester and Cumberland counties against claimants of land under
title from New York. Agents were sent to England with petitions to the crown, and the case on
behalf of New York was prepared by Duane and
included in an elaborate report to the Assembly.
The breaking out of the Revolution prevented any
settlement of the question at that time. But the
Declaration of Independence was utilized by Ethan
Allen and his followers as a good opportunity to
declare the independence of the territory which
they now began to call Vermont. In January,
1777, Vermont declared itself a free and independent State, and a convention of delegates met at
Windsor, July 2, to frame a constitution. Ethan
Allen wrote a vigorous pamphlet vindicating the

right of Vermont to statehood. "There is quaintness, impudence, and art in it," wrote Jay to Morris.[1] "Strange," replied Morris, " strange that men in the very act of revolting should so little consider the temper of revolters."[2] The process of New York courts ceased to run in the northeastern counties. Troops were dispatched to quell the outbreak, but met with no success. The New York Convention at last applied through their delegates to Congress, which appointed a committee upon the letters from the convention, and a petition from the inhabitants of the New Hampshire Grants, as they were technically described. On the report of the committee, it was resolved that the Declaration of Independence in no way justified Vermont in separating from New York, and that Congress, representing the thirteen States, could not countenance anything injurious to the rights of any one of them.

Burgoyne's expedition was taken advantage of by the Vermonters to coerce the States by coquetting with the enemy; and for a time the situation was full of menace. "General Burgoyne," wrote H. B. Livingston to Jay, June 17, "has sent a summons to the people of the Grants to meet Governor Skene at Castletown, to be there acquainted with the terms on which they shall hold their property, and threatening with immediate death all who refuse their attendance. General Schuyler, in answer to this, has sent a proclamation declar-

[1] Sparks, *Morris*, i. 210.   [2] *Ibid*. i. 212.

ing that those who comply with Burgoyne's summons shall be punished as traitors. Many have
taken protection. Those who are discovered are
committed to gaol." [1] What was originally merely
an agrarian rising against claimants under legal
titles from a distant and disputed government was
thus rapidly becoming a serious political question.
Finally the New York legislature resolved that
there existed " a special case," in the sense of the
Constitution, that would justify the appointment
of Jay to Congress without vacating his seat on
the bench. He was accordingly charged with the
special mission of urging on Congress a settlement
of the territorial claims of his State, and thus
returned to the scene of his early labors.

In Congress, at the moment, the conduct of Silas
Deane, recently recalled from France, was the subject of long and vehement debate. Among other
questions involved was that of the contracts for
war material with the versatile, well-disposed, but
devious Beaumarchais. Arthur Lee, Deane's fellow commissioner, misled by the secrecy adopted
by the French government to avoid complications
with England, alleged incorrectly that the arms
were the free gift of France, and attacked Deane's
integrity. "Many persons whom you know are
very liberal of illiberality," Morris had written to
Jay in August. "Your friend Deane, who hath
rendered the most essential services, stands as one
accused. The storm increases, and I think some

[1] *Jay MSS.*

one of the tall trees must be torn up by the roots." [1]
"I think our friend D.," wrote Robert Morris,
"has much public merit, has been ill used, but
will rise superior to his enemies." [2]   Deane was a
gentleman of breeding and education, with easy
diplomatic manners, who, at the beginning of the
Revolution, was chairman of the Committee of
Safety in Connecticut, and a member of the first
Continental Congress.   When he was sent abroad
as agent of the secret committee, it was with Jay
that he regularly corresponded.   In Paris he found
himself "without intelligence, without orders, and
without remittances, yet boldly plunging into engagements and negotiations, hourly hoping that
something will arrive from America."   The truth
of his account of his dealings with Beaumarchais
is now fully proved.   It was then inconsistently
charged that the articles sent were of poor quality,
and that they were gifts of France not intended to
be paid for.   But Deane had written at the beginning: " Mons. Beaumarchais has been my minister
in effect, as this court is extremely cautious, and I
now advise you to attend carefully to the articles
sent you, as I could not examine them here.   I was
promised they should be good, and at the lowest
prices." [3]   Only a year before, Captain Nicholas
Rogers, in transmitting to Jay some of Deane's
letters, incidentally gave testimony to Deane's wor-

[1] G. Morris to Jay, August 16, 1778, *Jay MSS.*
[2] September 8, 1778, *Jay MSS.*
[3] To Jay, December 3, 1776.

thiness at that time. "You will use a certain
liquid (that Mr. Deane told me you had) upon the
margin of the printed sheets so as to make legible
what Mr. Deane has wrote; should it not have its
proper effect, which I am afraid of, as the letters
were put into a tin box in a barrel of rum which
was eat through, and I am afraid has damaged
them, the enclosed letter is of the same contents.
. . . I liv'd at Paris in the same house with Mr.
Deane and had the Pleasure of being particularly
intimate with him. . . . I should be happy to inform you and answer you any questions concerning
the most of Mr. Deane's transactions the last summer, which he perform'd with the warmth 'of the
most zealous of Patriots." [1] That Deane subsequently, embittered, perhaps, by persecution, became, in Jay's opinion, a traitor to his country,
ought not to be allowed to affect one's judgment
of his antecedent conduct. Certainly, with the
knowledge that he possessed at the time, Jay was
in honesty bound to defend and sustain his friend,
and he did so; thus winning unawares the approbation of the French envoy, who was personally
and officially interested in the same cause.

To the outspoken attacks of Lee, Deane at last
responded by a bitter article in a newspaper com-
menting on the character of Lee and the delay of
Congress. In Congress and out of it the article
created intense excitement. "Mr. President Laurens brought the newspaper with him to the House,

[1] June 4, 1777, *Jay MSS.*

and from the chair proposed that it should be read, in order that it might become the subject of certain resolutions. The House not thinking it proper to come into that measure, he resigned the chair, saying that he could no longer hold it consistent with his honor. They were disgusted and adjourned. The next day his friends attempted to replace him, but did not succeed. A new president was elected." [1] Such is the colorless description of the stormy scene given by Jay, who was chosen the new president.

Among the many congratulations Jay received, that from his wife, though touched with womanly regret, must have pleased him most: "I had the pleasure of finding by the newspapers that you are honor'd with the first office on the Continent, and am still more pleased to hear this appointment affords general satisfaction. . . . I am very solicitous to know how long I am still to remain in a state of widowhood: upon my word I sincerely wish three months may conclude it; however, I mean not to influence your conduct, for I am convinced that, had you consulted me as some men have their wives about public measures, I should not have been *Roman matron* enough to have given you so entirely to the public." [2] "Sally!" was the old-fashioned reply, with sedate words still pulsating with love and longing for home; "Sally! the charms of this gay city would please me more if you partook of them. I am afraid to think of

[1] *Jay MSS.*   [2] December 28, 1778, *Jay MSS.*

domestic happiness; it is a subject which presents
to my imagination so many shades of departed joys,
as to excite emotions very improper to be indulged
in by a person in my station, determined at every
hazard to persevere in the pursuit of that great
object to which we have sacrificed so much." [1]

The history of Jay's presidency of Congress is
too much that of the country to be written here.
It is necessary to refer only to affairs especially
intrusted to him.   The condition of the currency
was such as to cause the gravest anxiety.   "Our
money," wrote R. R. Livingston to Jay in October, 1778, "is so much depreciated as hardly to be
current, and, as a necessary consequence of this,
our expenses have increased beyond all conception.
According to a calculation which I have made, it
costs as much to maintain the army two months
now, as it did to maintain them for the whole of
the year 1776.   It is absolutely necessary that we
should get out of this war soon." [2]   Accordingly,
as one of his first duties, Jay was directed to write
a letter to the States explaining the action of Congress in limiting the issue of paper money, and
calling on the States for funds to meet current
expenses.   If the letter hardly showed a thorough
knowledge of the principles of finance, it must be
remembered that few statesmen of that day had
such knowledge, and it at least answered the purposes of the moment.   It stated simply the causes

[1] January 31, 1779, *Jay MSS.*
[2] October 8, 1778, *Jay MSS.*

of depreciation, which was held, in this case, to be *artificial*, or due to lack of confidence in the government, and not *natural*, due to excessive issue. The rest of the letter aimed to restore public confidence by affirming the honest intentions of Congress to fulfill their engagements, and proving their ability to do so by reference to the enormous undeveloped wealth of the country, and the indefinite increase of population to be expected from immigration. It is easy to notice now that the amount of paper then issued was far in excess of what could possibly be maintained at par in the natural course of business. But a bankrupt in need of money cannot afford to be logical, and an appeal to an optimistic patriotism was then the only resource. In later life, to Jay, as to many other Federalists, the future of the country seemed dark and unpromising; but now the optimistic close of his letter to the States only expressed his own serious confidence that the evils of the present were temporary, and that dawn was soon to break. "Calm repose and the sweets of undisturbed retirement," he wrote to Washington, "appear more distant than a peace with Britain. It gives me pleasure, however, to reflect that the period is approaching when we shall be citizens of a better ordered state, and the spending of a few troublesome years of our eternity in doing good to this and future generations is not to be avoided or regretted. *Things will come right, and these States will be great and flourishing.* The dissolution of our government threw us into a

political chaos. Time, wisdom, and perseverance
will reduce it into form. . . . In this work you are,
in the style of one of your professions, a master-
builder, and God grant that you may ever continue
a free and accepted mason." [1]

The matter of Vermont was, of course, Jay's
especial charge, and this proved extremely difficult
of adjustment. Congress was reluctant to intervene in any local territorial dispute, however important. There were many different interests to
reconcile, and all the members of Congress were
not disinterested. "There is as much intrigue in
this State House," wrote Jay to Washington, "as
in the Vatican, but as little secrecy as in a boarding-
school." [2] For the greater part of a year there was
no progress to report. At length, in August, 1779,
he advised the legislatures of New York and New
Hampshire to authorize Congress to settle the line
between them, and the legislature of New York,
in addition, to empower Congress to adjust their
private controversy with the people of Vermont.[3]
This done, Jay moved and carried resolutions submitting the disputed boundaries to arbitration by
commissioners representing New York, New Hampshire, and Vermont. This explicit recognition of
the new claimant to statehood was a surrender of
the technical claims of New York, which he justified
with characteristic common sense in a letter to Gov-

[1] April 21, 1779, *Jay MSS.*
[2] April 26, 1779, *Jay MSS.*
[3] To Governor Clinton, August 27, 1779.

ernor Clinton: "In my opinion it is much better
for New York to gain a permanent peace with her
neighbors by submitting to these inconveniences,
than, by an impolitic adherence to strict rights, and
a rigid observance of the dictates of dignity and
pride, remain exposed to perpetual dissensions and
encroachment."[1] Almost the last official act of
Jay as delegate was the drafting of bills embodying
resolutions of Congress that met the assent of all
three States; and his task was apparently accomplished. But the Congress had no power of coer-
cion, and the dispute remained open till after the
ratification of the Constitution, when it was settled
forever, somewhat ignominiously, by the transfer
of $30,000 from the treasury of Vermont to the
treasury of New York.

Jay was continued in Congress by special vote
of the New York legislature till October 15; but
he was already contemplating retirement from public life, so neglected had been his private affairs,
so necessitous had become the condition of his
family. On August 10 he gave in his resignation of
the chief justiceship of New York and insisted on
its acceptance, simply remarking: "I shall return
to private life, with a determination not to shrink
from the duties of a citizen. During the continuance of the present contest I considered the public
as entitled to my time and services." Now that
our victory is assured, was perhaps the innuendo,
I may be honorably discharged. "Popularity,"

[1] Jay's *Jay*, i. 92.

he repeated a few days later to Clinton, " is not among the number of my objects. A seat in Congress I do not desire, and as ambition has in no instance drawn me into public life I am sure it will never induce me to continue in it. Were I to consult my interest I should settle here and make a fortune; were I guided by inclination I should now be attending to a family who, independent of other misfortunes, have suffered severely in the present contest." [1] So dangerous was the country about Fishkill that Peter Jay, at a hint of a visit from his son, urged him not to come : for " gangs of villains make frequent excursions from our neighboring mountains for prey," and might find his " person too tempting an acquisition to be neglected." [2] The old merchant was indeed much broken and in no little distress : " I am," he lamented, " unfortunately too much reduced to attend effectually to business. . . . I 've not yet got an inch of ground ploughed for wheat. . . . I have no prospect yet of getting any salt for salting my beef and pork this fall, nor have I anybody to look out for me. Hard times ! " [3] His sister Eve had married a clergyman, who died soon afterwards, leaving her in extreme poverty; and she and her son, Peter Jay Munro, were taken entire care of by Jay, at a time when he was complaining to Governor Clinton that the New York delegates were " not allowed sufficient to maintain, or rather sub-

[1] August 27, 1779, *Jay MSS.*   [2] *Jay MSS.*
[3] September 1, 1779, *Jay MSS.*

sist, themselves." [1] Her gratitude was adequate, and must have been overwhelming to Jay: " Give me leave, sir, to tell you that you are not only a kind brother, but a very affectionate father and husband to me, and a most tender father to my poor son." [2] Public duty, however, obliged him to leave to his brothers, Frederick and Sir James, the care of the family.

Politicians have occasionally been known, perhaps, to avow a preference for a quiet home life in the country, with no over-keen desire to be taken at their word. But the sentiment was often on Jay's reticent but truthful lips at every period of his life ; and he proved his sincerity by his thirty years of voluntary retirement. The same story of simple tastes and strong affections is told by his letters written while president of Congress to his wife. She was at Persipiney, New Jersey, with her father, when Jay sat one night thinking of her in his room. " It is now nine o'clock, my fellow lodgers out, and, what seldom happens, I am perfectly alone, and pleasing myself with the prospect of spending the remainder of the evening in writing a letter to you. As it rains and snows there is less probability of my being interrupted, and for that reason I prefer it to moonshine or starlight." What a charming introduction, one might think, to a little volume of priceless gossip and confidences ! But no, the letter is only to say that he

[1] August 27, 1779, *Jay MSS.*
[2] From Mrs. Munro, October 18, 1779.

loves her, and is lonely without her ; prudence forbids any anecdotes, any news, for have not two of
his letters just fallen " into the enemy's hands at
Elizabeth Town "?[1]   "I esteem it a blessing," he
writes again, "that (when absent from you) soli-
tude is so far from being irksome, that I often
court and enjoy it. Hence it is that, altho' few
are more fond of society, I oftener walk and ride
without than with company. There is a kind of
satisfaction in being able, without any breach of
politeness, to pursue one's own inclination, to ride
as fast or as slow, to stop as short or as long, to
take this or that road, as may be most agreeable.
. . . In this unfriendly month [of March], Nature,
you know, appears in a rude and dirty garb; so
that as yet I must be silent about 'lonely devious
walks' thro' 'verdant fields' or 'shady groves ;'
nor would it be in season to say a word of 'gentle
breezes,' 'melodious birds,' or 'the hum of bees
inviting sleep sincere.' "[2]

It was, however, more than twenty years before
his modest wishes were gratified, and then she
whom he loved so could not share his pleasure.
Now a new and unsought appointment was be-
stowed on him, full of new trials and not unexpected disappointments; and on October 1 Jay resigned the chair of Congress, receiving a vote of
thanks "in testimony of their approbation of his
conduct," as he was passed on to labors in a new
field.

[1] To Mrs. Jay, March 5, 1779.   [2] To same, March 17, 1779.

CHAPTER VI

THE treaties with France, concluded February 6, 1778, recognized American independence, and provided that, in case England should declare war against France, the two powers should make common cause, and that neither of them should conclude a truce or peace until the independence of the United States had been secured. Though Vergennes had declared three months before that no such treaty could be made without the consent of Spain, on account of the obligations of the Bourbon Family Compact, and the necessity of a Spanish alliance in the event of the war likely to be precipitated, the treaty was not, in fact, communicated to Spain till after its signing; but a secret clause was inserted providing for her accession to its terms. England, as was expected, regarded the treaty, long denied with a brazen face by the French minister at London, as an act of war, and for the next two years France was fighting England single-handed so far as European allies were concerned. The aid of Spain was essential, and to

gain this Vergennes, through his minister, Montmorin, at Madrid, bent all his powers of artifice
and persuasion.

Charles III. of Spain hated the idea of another
war, and wished only to end his days in peace.[1]
He was a conscientious man and devoted to his
family, and Louis XV. was his nephew; but he
was haughty, suspicious, and stubborn; he was
piqued at being thought a tool of France, and the
abrupt ending of the last war made him fear that,
without a special guarantee, France, after drag-
ging him into this new struggle, might again conclude a separate peace, regardless of the interests
of Spain.[2] His minister, Florida Blanca, indignant at the American treaty, hindered in every
way the early French naval expeditions, cleverly
avoided explanations, and finally suggested that
the only way to induce Spain to declare herself
was by agreeing not to make peace without securing
the restitution of Gibraltar, Florida, and Jamaica.
In the mean while, with the notion of deceiving
England till the time should be ripe for a sudden
blow, he was playing the part of a mediator, and
Lord Weymouth was coquetting with him with
dissimulation as deep as his own.

This negotiation revealed the actual wishes of
the two courts. France submitted, as her lowest
terms, the political and territorial independence of
the United States, the withdrawal of the English

[1] Vergennes to Montmorin, October 24, 1778, Doniol, iii. 24.
[2] Montmorin to Vergennes, Doniol, iii. 495, 497.

commissionership from Dunkirk, a fair partition
of the Newfoundland fisheries, according to the
treaty of Utrecht, and, if possible, a modification
of the navigation laws.[1] Spain proposed in addition that England should keep Canada and Nova
Scotia, but that Spain should take so much of
Florida as was necessary for the monopoly of the
navigation of the Gulf of Mexico.[2] The Spanish
court, as Montmorin thought, exaggerating the
prosperity and progress of the United States,
deemed it essential to leave " seeds of division and
jealousy between" them and England.[3] That court
was not only perfectly indifferent to the claims of
the United States,[4] but was convinced that in no
long time they would become her enemies, and was,
therefore, bent on keeping them from the Mississippi, and as far from her own colonies as possible.
As neighbors, the Americans would be as objectionable as the English. When read in the light
of these intentions, the word Florida becomes indefinitely comprehensive. Even the independence
of America was objected to, and France was blamed
for having guaranteed it. Would not a truce serve
the purpose? It was obvious that Spain was holding off till France, no longer able to do without

[1] Vergennes to Montmorin, October 13, 1778, Doniol, iii. 551.

[2] Montmorin to Vergennes, October 15, 1778, Doniol, iii. 556,
557.

[3] Montmorin to Vergennes, October 19, 1778, Doniol, iii. 558,
559.

[4] Doniol, iii. 575.

her, would, at the dictation of Spain, submit to
any terms of alliance, even the sacrifice of the sovereignty of the United States. France had now to
modify her views, or to risk losing Spanish coöperation altogether.[1] The terms of Spain, by changing the objects of the war, might prolong it indefinitely; but Vergennes had to accept even so hard
a bargain, and, while complaining bitterly of the
"gigantic pretensions" of Spain,[2] he signed the
treaty of Aranjuez, April 12, 1779.

In this treaty is to be found the key to the political situation in 1779 and during the three years
following. By it Spain agreed to make no treaty
with or concerning the United States without the
participation of France; if France should conquer
Nova Scotia the fisheries were to be shared between
them; and neither party was to lay down arms till
Gibraltar was secured to Spain, and to France the
abolition of the English commissionership at Dunkirk, or whatever other benefit she might chose
instead.[3]

While the attitude of Spain remained still undetermined, the state of public opinion in America
was of course to France a matter of the first importance. If Congress should insist on the Mississippi, Florida, and the western territories, all
which were included in the Spanish conception of
Florida, they ruined the possibility of either a sat-

[1] Doniol, iii. 576.
[2] Vergennes to the king, Doniol, iii. 588.
[3] De Circourt, p. 335.

isfactory peace or a successful war, for Spain would
then refuse to act either as mediator or ally. As
president of Congress, Jay was present at the numerous meetings of the Committee on Foreign Affairs, when Gérard urged the necessity of moderat-
ing their claims to meet the views of Spain. Soon
after Jay's installation Gérard gave him a dinner,
and for two hours with Mirales, the Spanish envoy,
and several members of Congress, he smoked and
listened to Gérard's argument that policy required
" a permanent line of separation " between Spanish
and American possessions, and that only by so limiting themselves could the States remove the European belief that they were naturally turbulent and
ambitious, like their English fathers. Jay diplomatically suggested that France was as much interested in this arrangement as Spain, and Gérard,
seeing that no definite propositions were following,
dropped the subject with the reply that that was
all the more reason for adopting it.[1] Then and at
other times Gérard urged the danger to the colonies of too extensive boundaries, and fancied that
Jay assented to the idea of bounding the colonies
as they were at the beginning of the Revolution.[2]
That would exclude the Mississippi; and Gérard
argued, according to his instructions, that a claim
to the navigation of the Mississippi or to the western territory beyond it was absurd, and was op-

[1] De Circourt, pp. 260, 261, Gérard to Vergennes, December 22,
1778.

[2] De Circourt, p. 266, Gérard to Vergennes, January 28, 1779.

posed to the policy of France and Spain, since the
United States could not be held to succeed to the
claims or rights of Great Britain, which were still
open to be conquered by Spain. For any such purpose France, he said, would certainly not continue
the war.[1] Similar opinions Gérard expressed to
Jay often in his own rooms as the evening deep-
ened towards midnight, and Jay has left a record
of his views at the time which concurred closely
with Gérard's: that we had no right to the Floridas, and that the Mississippi "we should not want
this age."[2] Of Jay, accordingly, Gérard had the
highest opinion: "he is a man of enlightened understanding," he wrote to Vergennes, "free from
prejudice, capable of broad views; he is sincerely
attached to the alliance and an enemy of the English. He takes infinite pleasure in the idea that
this triumvirate, as he calls it, of France, Spain,
and America, will defy the forces of the whole
world. He talks with frankness and good faith,
and yields willingly to the good arguments one
presents to him. I am much mistaken if we shall
not have reason to regret if his presidency is as
short as it seems likely to be."[3] Jay was at all
times an excellent listener, and to this useful and
amiable trait may be due not a little of Gérard's
enthusiasm. It was, however, not a wholly one-
sided bargain at this stage in the war to secure

[1] De Circourt, p. 264.
[2] Jay's *Jay*, i. 95, 100.
[3] De Circourt, p. 263, Gérard to Vergennes, December 22, 1778.

a triple alliance between France, Spain, and the United States, with a recognition of independence, in exchange for the western wilderness and waters. But when Jay found that Spain had declared war for her own purposes without regard to America, the whole situation appeared changed, and thereafter in his opinion there remained nothing worth the sacrifice even of part of the Mississippi.

Gérard had long urged Congress to come to some understanding with Spain; suggesting that on these lines they might obtain from that country an acknowledgment of their independence and a treaty of commerce. At length, in September, 1779, Congress voted on the appointment of a minister to treat with Great Britain. On the first two ballots, six States voted for John Adams, five for Jay, and the vote of one State was divided. New England was stanch for Adams, to champion the claim to the fisheries, though Adams was obnoxious to France; while Jay was the candidate of New York. The next day the nomination for a minister to Spain was opened, and the friends of Adams, the pro-English party, so called among them, declared for Arthur Lee, the enemy of Deane and Gérard; finally, Adams was appointed peace commissioner to Great Britain, and Jay minister to Spain. The choice of Jay, Gérard informed Vergennes, "leaves nothing to be desired. To great intelligence and the best intentions, he unites an engaging and conciliatory mind and character."[1]

[1] Gérard to Vergennes, September 27, 1779, *Stevens MSS.*

Jay was well aware of the satisfaction of Gérard, and also of the Spanish envoy, Mirales. " I have reason to think," was his dry comment, " that both of them entertained higher opinions of my docility than were well founded." [1]

It was not an attractive position, — that of an unrecognized envoy of a country little known and less liked, begging money at a haughty and penurious court. Franklin, who had been appointed to Spain January 1, 1777, had postponed his journey, merely inclosing to Aranda the resolution of Congress which offered Spain help in reducing Pensacola, — an offer that was never properly acknowledged; and Arthur Lee, who succeeded Franklin, had left Spain in disgust, having succeeded in wringing from repeated promises of millions only a meagre hundred and seventy thousand livres; unable to negotiate a loan, much less a treaty.[2] Nevertheless, Jay accepted at once, though with modest expectations. On October 16 he received his instructions, — to induce Spain to form a commercial treaty similar to that with France, to acquire a port on the Mississippi in Spanish territory, and to obtain a loan of five millions, or at least a subsidy, in exchange for the Floridas. The navigation of the Mississippi was to be preserved at all hazards. Four days later Jay set sail in the Confederacy, the government frigate that had been ordered to take Gérard back

---

[1] Jay's *Jay*, i. 100.
[2] Bolles, *Financial Hist. of the U. S.* p. 246 n.

to France, on the arrival of his successor, Luzerne.
With Jay went his wife, to the distraction of old
Governor Livingston and his wife, who had no
time to bid their daughter good-by; his nephew,
Peter Jay Munro; his brother-in-law, Colonel Livingston, afterwards judge of the United States
Supreme Court, as his private secretary; and Mr.
Carmichael, a member of Congress, as his public
secretary. A violent storm disabled the ship and
forced the captain to make for Martinique, where,
on December 18, they cast anchor in the harbor
of St. Pierre, narrowly escaping an English fleet,
which captured on the same day nine French
merchantmen off Port Royal. Some indiscreet
attempts on the part of Gérard to discover Jay's
instructions had created a coolness between the
two diplomats, which was increased by a difference of opinion on the proper course to be taken
after the storm. But Adams certainly exaggerated
greatly when he thought this petty dissension led
Jay to a general distrust and dislike of Frenchmen. At Martinique, the officers of the Confederacy naturally fraternized with French officers
who chanced to be on shore, and Jay, finding the
Americans distressed for lack of money, character-
istically advanced them a hundred guineas. The
idea of their being " obliged to sneak . . . from
the company of French officers," he wrote, "for
fear of running in debt with them for a bowl of
punch, was too humiliating to be tolerable, and too
destructive to that pride and opinion of independ-

ent equality which I wish to see influence all our officers." [1]

Ten days were lost at Martinique; then, on a frigate lent by the governor, the party reëmbarked for Toulon, and January 22, 1780, disembarked unexpectedly at Cadiz, whither they were driven by English men-of-war. Jay was now, as he expressed it, " very disagreeably circumstanced," without letters of credit or recommendation to any one there, with no money even, except what he borrowed through the courtesy of a fellow-passenger.[2] He at once sent Mr. Carmichael to Madrid, with instructions to sound the sentiments of the court, and discover how far their relations to the United States were independent of France, — a significant direction. Meanwhile, Mr. and Mrs. Jay were cordially entertained by the governor of Andalusia, Count O'Reilly, who gave Jay a confidential account of the politics of the court, and of the personal character of those who composed it, not excepting the king, — accounts which Jay afterwards found to be perfectly accurate. When the spring came they moved to Madrid, to be near the first secretary of state, Count Florida Blanca, a man of whom Montmorin said: "At times cold and phlegmatic, at times violent, he is in these opposite moods equally self-opinionative. . . . By the bent of his mind, too, he is inclined to dissimulation." [3]

---

[1] Jay's *Jay*, i. 105.

[2] Sparks, *Diplomatic Corresp. of Amer. Rev.* vii. 220.

[3] Montmorin to Vergennes, December 7, 1778, Doniol, iii. 610 n.

At Madrid, Jay received no official recognition; that, Count Florida Blanca declared, was to depend "on a public acknowledgment and future treaty." Consequently he could not attend the court, and was neglected by the nobles and officials. Some time was spent at first in answering elaborate inquiries about the social and military condition of the States; and then came a long and, as it seemed at the time, an important interview with the minister at Aranjuez: some money was promised, and the one obstacle to a treaty was said to be " the pretensions of America to the navigation of the Mississippi ; " but Count Florida Blanca hoped that " some middle way might be hit on." [1] Jay's sense of diplomatic honor was now severely tested : he had promised the French minister, Montmorin, to inform him of the course of the negotiations, but this conversation was confidential. " I was reduced," Jay confessed, " to the necessity of acting with exquisite duplicity, — a conduct which I detest as immoral, and disapprove as impolitic, — or of mentioning my difficulties to the count, and receiving his answers." He told the count, it need not be said, and was allowed to keep his promise.[2] Such frankness must have seemed naïve, perhaps amusing, to the clever young diplomat, who, at that very moment, held locked in his own breast the all-important secret of the treaty of Aranjuez.

[1] Sparks, *Dipl. Corr. of Amer. Rev.* vii. 256.
[2] *Ibid.*

The question of the navigation of the Mississippi was a novelty in international diplomacy. The United States was the first power to insist on the right of a people who live along a river to sail through the dominion of other powers to its mouth;[1] they also claimed the same right under the reservation to Great Britain in the treaty of Paris of the right of navigation. But it was the mediæval policy of Spain to keep the Gulf of Mexico a closed sea from Florida to Yucatan. Florida Blanca, indeed, in September, went so far as to say that the exclusive navigation of the Mississippi was the principal object of the war, and more important than the capture of Gibraltar.[2] Spanish obstinacy is proverbial, and on this point was as invincible as Cumberland (the English agent sent to draw Spain into a separate peace) found it to be on the question of the cession of Gibraltar. The credit of the United States was, moreover, seriously hurt by Congress suddenly drawing bills on Jay and their other ministers abroad, to be met by loans to be begged from the various courts. Any chance of compromise was at once lost with the suspicious, selfish court of Spain.

The first bills to appear were drawn on Laurens, who was supposed at home to be at The Hague, but who, in fact, had been caught by an English cruiser, and was lying in the Tower. Then bills

[1] Schuyler, *American Diplomacy*, pp. 265, 266.
[2] Sparks, *Dipl. Corr. of Amer. Rev.* vii. 456.

were presented to Jay for acceptance, drawn on himself; and not until months had elapsed did the explanation come from the Committee for Foreign Affairs, that, even before news came of his arrival, bills for $100,000 had been so drawn at six months' sight, and negotiated to raise money for the purchase of military stores; and that, so soon as his arrival was reported, still further bills for $25,000 more were also drawn. "I would throw stones with all my heart," wrote Jay, "if I thought they would reach the committee without injuring the members of it."[1] But he tried to get this draft "on the bank of hope," as he called it, cashed by Florida Blanca, suggesting that the action of Congress showed their reliance on the friendship of Spain. All these bills, which for the next year and a half made Franklin and Jay sleepless and sick with mortification and anxiety, were accepted by them personally, and were paid in the end by France, with only trivial help from Spain. Florida Blanca insisted on some equivalent from the United States; he suggested frigates to be built in America, and manned to attack East Indian convoys; but, as Jay said, Congress had only the money it got from these bills to buy the frigates with. He argued rather shrewdly that the colonies ought to be assisted because they were in arms against the enemies of Spain and France for the sole purpose of winning an honorable peace for all three nations. But money was difficult to procure,

[1] Sparks, *Dipl. Corr. of Amer. Rev.* vii. 304, 305.

even in Holland, the richest country in Europe; for the long wars had exhausted every treasury, and " if America was a beggar, England was a far greater." [1] As Jay expressed it, " the fact is, there is little corn in Egypt." [2] The net result of his long efforts was the loan of $150,000; and at length he was forced by promises, that were not kept, to suffer one batch of bills, not amounting to over $25,000, to be protested; but in a month they were redeemed, and American credit was restored by the successful importunity of Franklin and the wise generosity of France.

When affairs were once more in good train, everything was ruined by the news of the loss of Charleston, the effect of which on the timid court was, in Jay's words, " as visible the next day as that of a bad night's frost on young leaves." So matters were again for months at a standstill. Meantime, no news had come from friends in America, the letters being intercepted or suppressed; and his own dispatches Jay had to send down by his secretary to the seaboard to be given personally to the captain of any casual American vessel. His only child had been left in America, and a baby born in Spain lived scarcely a month. Jay had to follow the wandering court from town to town, to Madrid, to Aranjuez, to San Ildefonso, and traveling was so expensive that Mrs. Jay had

[1] Bolles, *Financial Hist. of the U. S.* 2d ed. pp. 256, 257.
[2] Jay to Franklin, September 8, 1780, E. E. Hale, *Franklin in France*, i. 412.

generally to be left behind at the capital. When his letters do come they contain little to cheer. Secretary Thomson writes that by March, 1780, the paper dollar had fallen to a penny in value,[1] a depreciation by which the Jay family suffered severely; and his brother Frederick tells how a party of "De Delancey Boys" broke into his father's house, stole money and plate, and slightly wounded Mrs. Frederick Jay with a bayonet.[2] Though greatly straitened, Jay sent home gifts of the most useful things he could think of, and found time to discuss and provide for the old family servants.

In his official family also there was unhappiness: his secretary proved untrustworthy, and a young man in his charge, from a perverse spirit of malignant mischief, increased the discord. A letter from Jay to Franklin, introducing Prince Masserana, gives a glimpse of the lonely life he led at Madrid: "I am much indebted to the politeness of this nobleman, and except at his table have eaten no Spanish bread that I have not paid for since my arrival in this country."[3] As discomforts multiplied, Jay became more and more proud and reserved. "I never find myself," he confessed to Franklin, "less disposed to humility or improper compliances than when fortune frowns."

---

[1] From Charles Thomson, October 12, 1780, *Jay MSS.*

[2] From Frederick Jay, November 8, 1781, *Jay MSS.*

[3] To Franklin, October 25, 1780, Hale, *Franklin in France*, i. 416.

The Marquis d'Aranda complained of Jay, indeed, in a private letter that was quoted, "*qu'il parait toujours fort boutonné,*" — a curious complaint to come from a Spanish nobleman. In fact, Jay had a great admiration for the man and the statesman, calling him the ablest Spaniard he had met: "I think it probable," was his characteristic acknowledgment of the marquis's criticism, "we shall be yet on more familiar terms, for though I will never court, yet I shall with pleasure cultivate his acquaintance."[1] Delay in the payment of his salary helped to make the unfortunate envoy's situation seem at times intolerable: "to be obliged to contract debts and live on credit is terrible,"[2] is a painful cry, wrung from the heart of a man like Jay. Some distractions there were of course, though we do not know whether Jay continued his sight-seeing so vigorously as during the first summer in Spain. Then, in July, he went with Brockholst Livingston to a bull-fight, when "one of the knights who fought on horseback was killed and two wounded;" and every evening that summer there was a comedy,[3] which they doubtless occasionally attended.

In the spring of 1781 the French ambassador surprised Jay by suggesting that the negotiations

[1] To Franklin, February 21, 1781, Hale, *Franklin in France*, i. 422.

[2] To Franklin, April 1, 1781, Hale, *Franklin in France*, i. 426.

[3] J. B. Livingston to Gov. Livingston, July 12, 1780, *Mag. Am. Hist.* iii. 512.

failed because Florida Blanca expected further overtures about the Mississippi, and believed Jay's discretion to be greater than he admitted.[1] What was meant did not become clear till some weeks later, when directions came from Congress to insist no longer on the free navigation of the Mississippi below the thirty-first degree of latitude. A month more and Jay's instructions were still further modified, permitting him to negotiate without reference to the treaties with France. The Southern States chiefly interested in the fate of the Mississippi, Virginia, Georgia, and South Carolina, had indeed changed their policy radically, — partly persuaded by the infinitely various arguments of Luzerne, partly because English successes in the South made them fear a permanent loss of territory if Spain did not help them, or if a peace were suddenly negotiated on the basis of *uti possidetis*, before the British troops had withdrawn. Jay disapproved of these new instructions, and said so. Spain, he argued, was now at war for her own purposes, and would be induced by no cession to be more liberal or to fight harder. He tried, however, to renew negotiations. Better wait for a general peace, was the reply he got. Pressure of business was also a standing excuse. At last he was asked to draft propositions with a view to a treaty of alliance between Spain and the States, and he did so instantly. But the abandonment of the right to navigate the Mississippi he carefully

[1] Sparks, *Dipl. Corr. of Amer. Rev.* vii. 456, 457.

made void if the alliance were postponed to a general peace. To these propositions no answer was ever given. "This court," Jay wrote to Franklin in November, 1781, "continues to observe the most profound silence. . . . Heretofore the minister was too sick and too busy; at present his secretary is much indisposed." [1] In the autumn of 1781 a person was appointed to treat with Jay, but when applied to he never had instructions. In the spring of 1782 Jay proposed to demand a categorical answer, but was dissuaded by the French ambassador.[2] He determined to go to the Escurial and urge his business, but again the French ambassador bade him "wait with patience." [3] Thus month after month was wasted, as Jay gloomily expressed it, in "expectation, suspense, and disappointment." Political disturbances in the Spanish colonies might account for some coolness towards the American envoy at the close of 1781, but the real explanation of Jay's ill-treatment was the positive unfriendliness felt by Spain for the Americans, — detestation of them as republicans, and jealousy of them as territorial rivals. In such circumstances a treaty such as Jay was intrusted to make was out of the question.

The mediation proffered about this time by the Empress of Russia and the Emperor of Germany was, in Jay's opinion, unlikely to be effectual; in-

[1] November 21, 1781, *Jay MSS.*
[2] Sparks, *Dipl. Corr. of Amer. Rev.* viii. 11.
[3] *Ibid.* p. 33.

deed, he thought, as did Vergennes, that those
powers were more friendly to England than to
France.[1] What he wished was a close defensive
alliance between France, Spain, and America, an
alliance that Holland might probably be induced
to join. Then a vigorous campaign "would give
us a peace worth our acceptance." At the moment, he saw that Spain wanted Gibraltar and
Jamaica, and was far from being tired of the war;
and he anxiously sounded Montmorin as to the
steps France was taking to influence Spain towards
an American alliance. On this point Montmorin,
though "well attached to the American cause,"
showed a "mysterious reserve." Yet Jay still
had "full confidence in the friendship of France;"
though he was gradually learning to take an independent stand. "In politics," he explained to
Franklin, "I depend upon nothing but facts, and
therefore never risque deceiving myself or others
by a reliance on professions which may or may not
be sincere."[2] In reality, France was indignant at
the neglect of America by Spain, at her indifference to American credit, at her unwillingness to
compromise. Spain ought to try more to gain the
friendship of the Americans, said Montmorin in
June, 1782, for fear of their considering a separate
peace, especially if their independence is assured
and a peace comes to be hindered only by the demands of Spain. But, he added, this court of

[1] To B. Franklin, August 20, 1781, *Jay MSS.*
[2] *Ibid.* loc. cit.

Spain thinks of nothing but the chance of winning Gibraltar.[1]

The hands of France, however, were tied by the treaty of Aranjuez. France was committed to a continuation of the war till Spain should get Gibraltar, and meantime American independence became a subsidiary object. "Spain knew her own business and interest, and France had no right to press her on such points;" such was Vergennes's final answer to Jay through Montmorin. At last Jay told the latter openly that he thought England would be the first nation to acknowledge American independence, for France did not wish "to see us treated as independent by other nations until after a peace, lest we should become less manageable in proportion as our dependence upon her shall diminish;" and the count waived the subject.

In May, 1782, Jay was invited to dinner by Count Florida Blanca, but the invitation was soon explained to have been a mistake, and when renewed to Jay "as a private gentleman" was very properly declined. This was the last mortification Jay was destined to suffer from the Spanish court.

Franklin and Jay had long been intimate friends in spite of the difference of forty years in their ages. In the spring of 1781, when Franklin, in a moment of discouragement, sent to Congress his resignation, he urged Jay to take his place at Paris, and suggested his writing to his friends

[1] Montmorin to Vergennes, June 8, 1782, De Circourt, iii. 45.

" accordingly." [1] But Jay thought the change impolitic, wrote home to that effect, and Franklin's
resignation was not accepted.[2] In the following
summer Jay, whom the influence of Luzerne had
retained in Spain when Congress thought of recalling him, Franklin, Laurens, and Jefferson had
been joined with Adams as commissioners for a
general peace; and now in April, 1782, while
Laurens was a prisoner on parole, Adams at The
Hague, and Jefferson still in America, Franklin
summoned Jay to his assistance: "Here," he wrote
in Paris, "you are greatly wanted, for messengers
begin to come and go, and there is much talk of a
treaty proposed; but I can neither make nor agree
to propositions of peace without the assistance of
my colleagues. . . . You would be of infinite service." [3] Jay at once asked the advice of Montmorin, who, on consulting Florida Blanca, made
no objection; Jay could treat with Aranda, then
the Spanish ambassador at Paris, and, in any case,
Mr. Carmichael might stay behind and act in
Jay's stead. "Jay has doubtless made up his
mind," Montmorin concluded, "to leave Spain,
which he dislikes extremely, and which, as a matter
of fact, must have been very disagreeable to him
for more than two years past." [4] Without delay
Jay shook from his feet the unfriendly dust of

[1] From B. Franklin, April 12, 1781, *Jay MSS.*
[2] To B. Franklin, August 20, 1781, *Jay MSS.*
[3] From B. Franklin, April 22, 1782, Jay's *Jay*, ii. 94.
[4] Montmorin to Vergennes, May 5, 1782, De Circourt, iii. 343.

Madrid and started for Paris.　Mrs. Jay fell sick
on the journey with fever and ague, and as " the
posthorses at the different stages had been engaged
for the Comte du Nord," who had left Paris with
a great retinue, " they did not reach their destina-
tion till June 23." [1]

[1] Sparks *Dipl. Corr. of Amer. Rev.* viii. 113.

CHAPTER VII

NEGOTIATOR OF PEACE: THE ATTITUDE OF
FRANCE IN 1782

THE instructions to the American commissioners, appointed to treat with Great Britain, were
based on the theory that, without the active coöperation of the French court, the States would be
at the mercy of England, that France was engaged
to procure them the best terms obtainable, and
that gratitude and policy alike necessitated absolute confidence in the Count de Vergennes, French
minister for foreign affairs. For the successful
conduct of the negotiations, it was essential for the
commissioners to determine whether this theory of
Congress was correct. The facts now known show
us that it was incorrect.

France, by her treaty with Spain, had formed
obligations inconsistent with the interests of the
States. By it the object of the war had been
changed from securing independence for America
to winning Gibraltar for Spain, from that which
was already within the grasp of the allies to that
which was in any case a remote contingency, and
was, as it happened, an impossibility; and all this
had been brought about without the knowledge of

the country most vitally interested in the war, the
one country whose existence as a nation was at
stake.   The treaty was very possibly unavoidable,
as is urged by the latest, best informed, and most
voluminous apologist of France, M. Doniol.[1]   But
whether such was the case or not is immaterial
from the American point of view ; so long as the
facts were withheld from Congress the conduct of
Vergennes was disingenuous, and the American
ministers, so far as they suspected or knew the
facts, were no longer justified in intrusting to him
the fortunes of their country.

It was, however, not merely regard for the prejudices, or even the " gigantic pretensions," of
Spain that made France an inefficient friend to
America in reaping the fruits of the Revolution ;
her attitude in 1782 was perfectly consistent with
what had been the secret policy of her government since before the Declaration of Independence.
These matters may be discussed now without the
bitterness and partisan feeling which the discussion
excited in 1783 and in 1798.   We no longer con-
found the morality of a people with the policy of
its government, — even in a democracy ; and such
confusion would be still more unjust in the case of
a non-representative government of the eighteenth
century, above all in the France of Louis XVI.
Jay himself made no such error, but carefully
discriminated between the French people and the

[1] *La Participation de la France dans l'établissement de l'inde-
pendance des Etats-Unis*, Paris, 1883.

French government: " It is true," he said, " that I returned from that country to this, with opinions unfavorable to their court ; but not only without a wish unfriendly to them, but, on the contrary, with sentiments of good-will and regard."[1] "It is not," he added, " from the characters of this or that administration or prevailing party in the government that the character of a nation is to be inferred."[2] Even though the official conduct of a nation, in international negotiations, is crudely selfish, and the language of its ministers is an effectual concealment of the truth, neither people nor ministers are necessarily blamable ; for the first duty of a nation is self-preservation, and the first duty of a negotiator is to his own country, as is a lawyer's to his client. It certainly can hardly be said that now, after the lapse of a hundred years, controversies between nations are ever adjusted on altruistic principles, from motives purely of gratitude and affection ; and if such is the fact, it is no longer possible honestly to take a sentimental view of the peace negotiations of 1783.

As early as 1775 M. Malouet, the French minister of the navy, was told that the people wished France to interfere in behalf of the colonies ; and he at once replied, in the true spirit of the old régime, that it was as illogical as it was dangerous for an absolute monarchy to place itself at the head of a democratic revolution.[3] Such, too, was

---

[1] To R. G. Harper, December 21, 1795, Jay's *Jay*, ii. 263.
[2] Jay's *Jay*, ii. 262. [3] *Mémoires*, iii. 335.

the opinion of the king, who was afraid of the effect upon his own subjects of a bad example;[1]
and in his policy of neutrality he was supported
by Maurepas and Necker. If Vergennes thought
otherwise, it was certainly from no love of republican institutions, of the sentiment of liberty, or of
the Americans personally. " With respect to principles," wrote Tom Paine, before he became a hire-
ling of Luzerne, " Vergennes was a despot."[2]   He
was the steady opponent of the more liberal ministers of the king, Choiseul, Turgot, and Necker; he
hated such revolutionary ideas as liberty of the
press, liberty of speech, and parliamentary government, and accordingly he detested the Americans
as " rebels."[3]   But the deepest feeling in the minister's heart was hostility to England, and a patriotic longing to wipe out the disgrace of the treaty
of 1763. " The inveterate enmity of that power
to us," he wrote in a memoir to the king in 1775,
" makes it our duty to lose no opportunity for
weakening it. The independence of the insurgent
colonies must therefore be encouraged." " I hope
to live long enough," he said again a little later in
private, " to see England humiliated and American
independence acknowledged."[4]   The profession of
faith he made to Montmorin was doubtless perfectly
honest : " My country's good is dear to me.   I am

[1] Soulavie, *Louis XV*. iii. 409.

[2] *Rights of Man*, 1791, i. 92.

[3] Tratchevsky, *La France et l'Allemagne sous Louis XVI.* p.
18.

[4] *Moniteur Universel*, 1789, i. 45 n.

no less devoted to that of Spain ; to contribute to
the one and the other, that is all my ambition ; "
and his regard for the interests of Spain may well
have come from a belief in the importance of the
closest union between the two branches of the
House of Bourbon, without that personal motive,
which has been suggested, that, not being of noble
lineage, he was ambitious to die a grandee of
Spain.

The policy of France was much discussed in secret memoirs and letters to the king, but always,
very naturally, with a single eye to French interests. Turgot, early in the Revolution, in an elaborate paper, urged that the best thing for France
would be a long English-American war ending in
victory for England, because nothing could be
more enfeebling to a military power than to try to
govern by force so distant a country. The worst
event for France would be a speedy ending of the
war, no matter who won, for that would leave the
troops of England free to be turned against her
European foes. Such was the state of affairs when,
after having received vague encouragement from
the French emissary, Bonvouloir, the Secret Committee for Foreign Affairs in Congress sent Deane,
a gentleman of means and education, disguised as
a merchant, to sound the intentions of the court,
and to procure money and arms. Deane engaged
the romantic imagination and ingenious pen of
Beaumarchais, who, by a series of adroitly worded
memoirs, and seconded by the good-will of de Ver-

gennes, persuaded the king that peace could be preserved only by preventing the complete triumph of either England or the colonies, and that, to effect this, sufficient aid must be given the Americans to "put their forces on an equality with those of England, but nothing beyond." [1] From that time the king was convinced, but against his will, or rather against his instincts and his conscience; and whenever documents relating to the war that followed were given him to sign, he is said to have complained pathetically, "Must I sign, for reasons of state, what I don't think right?" [2] By secret grants from the treasuries of France and Spain, on the suggestion of de Vergennes, Beaumarchais was enabled, through the fictitious firm of Rodrigue, Hortalez et Cie., to supply the colonies with much-needed war material in exchange for promised cargoes of tobacco, which, however, never came; and within a year he even succeeded in sending them ships of war and officers.

After the Declaration of Independence, Deane, Franklin, and Arthur Lee were commissioned to attend to the affairs of the United States in Europe. In December Franklin landed at Nantes, to the great excitement of the populace, and his entry into Paris was like a royal triumph. Then he retired to Passy, and there lived a life so happy in winning and keeping public affection, that it was

[1] February 29, 1776. De Loménie, *Life of Beaumarchais*, iii. 122.

[2] *Moniteur Universel*, 1789, i. 45 n.

well described by Cabanis as "a masterpiece of art."

In February, 1777, the commissioners agreed to separate, and Franklin remained attached to the court of France, whose vacillation was suddenly ended by the unexpected events of the war in America. It had been doubted whether the colonies could withstand a serious campaign. But the capitulation of Burgoyne was a complete answer to all doubters, and with the prospect of success France saw her chance for intervention. When it was known that England was proposing terms of reconciliation, though it was pardon only that Lord Howe had to offer, and not redress of grievances, de Vergennes could wait no longer. The terms proposed were, as he thought, so clearly hostile to France, — though it is not obvious how, — that no time was to be lost in preventing their acceptance. American independence, moreover, he was convinced, would be useful to France. For these various reasons, as he explained to M. Gérard,[1] the minister opened negotiations at Paris for a treaty of amity and commerce, and for a treaty of eventual alliance. The treaty of commerce recognized the United States as independent in fact, but, except for its friendly reciprocity, was not historically important; the treaty of alliance, however, provided for the war with England that was sure to be forced or precipitated by the acknowledgment of independence. The end of the alliance, said the

[1] Instructions to Gérard, De Circourt, iii. 255, 256.

treaty, is to maintain the independence of the United States.

These treaties were for years afterwards referred to by France as a singular instance of generosity to the helpless, friendless colonists. And for years it seems to have been a general opinion that the treaty of alliance bound the United States to France by ties unusually confidential, close, and permanent. It did, indeed, result in America receiving, to promote the common cause of France, Spain, and the colonies, active help from France in men and money, at a time when threatening bankruptcy and despair made such help priceless. By such timely aid France may be said to have in fact enabled the States to win what they did win at the peace; and all this aid, comfort, and goodwill may well have been an expression, far truer than the official French chicanery during the negotiations, of the feelings, the vague sentiments and longings, of the French people, dumb as yet and not self-conscious, but who cheered when they saw the white head of Franklin, and in a few years' time made Europe ring with watchwords in part caught from him. The final benefit, however, guaranteed to the colonies by the treaty was curiously meagre: "the treaty," said de Vergennes, " only guarantees [the] independence [of the Americans] and their eventual conquests; " [1] and in return for this the Americans promised not to make peace with England without securing their inde-

[1] Vergennes to Luzerne, September 25, 1779.

pendence. This was the *quid pro quo;* [1] and these
were all the mutual covenants of the two nations,
so far as they had actual reference to the making
of a peace. Such certainly was the French interpretation of the spirit and words of the treaty.
Independence was insisted on, because de Vergennes thought with Lord Chatham and George
III. that its acknowledgment would be the beginning of the end of the British empire. Yet even
independence need not be expressly acknowledged;
a tacit recognition of it would satisfy both the
terms of the treaty and the interests of France. [2]

If the French government had allied itself to
the struggling colonies from sympathy with their
motives and pity for their wrongs, it would naturally take a friendly interest in their ambition and
effort to establish themselves so as to secure a
great and peaceful future. But even in the instructions to Gérard, the first French minister to
the States, de Vergennes explains and emphasizes
the indifference, or rather the opposition, of France
to every claim which our people really believed
just, and which events have proved to have been
essential to their welfare. The principle of French
policy was that, the independence of the States
once established, they should be so hemmed in by
foreign powers, and so limited in size, that fear of

[1] Montmorin to Florida Blanca, October 15, 1778, Doniol, iii.
522.

[2] Gérard to Congress, July 14, 1779, *S. J.* ii. 198; Vergennes
to Luzerne, September 25, 1779.

English aggression would keep them permanent
dependents on France. For this reason England
was to retain Canada.[1] The Floridas were to go
as Spain should choose; and as to the navigation
of the Mississippi, if Spain should insist, the Americans were to be discreetly prepared to give it up,[2]
and to trust to the "magnanimity" of the king of
Spain.[3] Luzerne was, indeed, directed to "encourage Congress to confide in Spain," and this long
after the treaty of Aranjuez, when de Vergennes
knew that Spain cared for nothing in the war but
her own selfish interests, which she regarded as
opposed to American claims, even to American
welfare. There was also no necessity, Gérard was
instructed, for the Americans to reach as far north
as the fisheries of Newfoundland. "The fishery
along the coast," wrote de Vergennes to Luzerne,
"belongs . . . exclusively to England, France par-
ticipating by special treaties. The Americans have
forfeited their share in British fisheries by declaring their independence of England. . . . The
United States should . . . not grudge France
the slight advantage of extending her fisheries."[4]
France and England, Luzerne very naturally suggested some years later, should guarantee the fishery to each other.[5] The selfish motive here disclosed leads one to wonder whether the readiness

[1] De Circourt, iii. 255, 310.
[2] Vergennes to Gérard, August 26, 1778, Doniol, iii. 569, 578.
[3] Vergennes to Luzerne, September 25, 1779.
[4] *Ibid.*
[5] Luzerne to Vergennes, January 11, 1782.

with which France yielded all the western territory to Spain was not half justified by a secret consciousness that, if desirable, a cession of it might later be induced by proper pressure, as was in due time the cession by Spain to France of Louisiana.

France, then, had many purposes concerning America to effect at the eventual peace, — purposes the precise opposite of the claims dearest to the Americans themselves, her allies. This policy was tortuous and difficult, and imposed upon France, so far as possible, the task of controlling the selection of the American commissioners, and of dictating their instructions. In a word, it was necessary for France to control completely the negotiations for peace. To this end, Gérard, Marbois, and Luzerne employed all the arts of the European diplomacy of the period, dissimulation, flattery, what Flassan calls the "*mensonge politique*," and what de Vergennes refers to as "*donatifs*," and M. de Circourt as "*sécours temporaires en argent*." "His majesty," wrote de Vergennes to Luzerne, "further empowers you to continue the donations which M. Gérard has given or promised to various American authors, and of which he will surely have handed you a list." This list has not yet been disclosed, and the topic is one which even M. de Circourt shows a desire to avoid. "This delicate subject," he says, "has been even in my time the subject of criticisms and controversies into which we need not enter."[1]

[1] De Circourt, iii. 283.

These methods met with a success that can be explained only by the surprisingly facile character of some members of Congress, and the almost incredible simple-mindedness and credulity of others. Congress, in those early days, as pictured in the private correspondence of the French agents and ministers, does not altogether represent that Amphictyonic Council of honorable, unselfish patriots into which it has now become transfigured by the magic consecration of time. Some thirty years afterwards, Gouverneur Morris was sitting over the polished mahogany at Bedford with John Jay, when he suddenly ejaculated through clouds of smoke, "Jay, what a set of d——d scoundrels we had in that second Congress!" "Yes," said Jay, "that we had," and he knocked the ashes from his pipe.[1] "The tone of Congress," says Mr. C. F. Adams, in his review of the situation, "had gradually become lowered. The people were suffering from exhaustion by the war, especially in the Southern States."[2]

It thus became possible for the accomplished envoys of the French court gradually to create a party devoted wholly to French interests. "I can do what I please with them," wrote Bonvouloir of the members of Congress in 1775.[3] Gérard, also, so soon as he was appointed in 1778, set himself to persuade the public of the disinterestedness of France by suggesting suitable arguments to writers

[1] Family tradition.   [2] John Adams's *Works*, i. 341.
[3] Durand, p. 10.

for the newspapers who signed themselves often by
such names as Gallo-Americanus and Americanus.[1]
Tom Paine was engaged for a thousand dollars a
year to inspire " the people with sentiments favorable to France and the alliance," [2] and Paine was
then secretary to the Committee on Foreign Affairs. In no long time Luzerne was a power in
the House. In the autumn of 1781 R. R. Livingston was elected to the new secretaryship for foreign affairs. " He is not ignorant," wrote Luzerne
to de Vergennes on November 1, " of the part I
took in his election." [3]

Before Adams was chosen to treat for peace
with England, his instructions were carefully
adapted to suit the views of Luzerne. The first
definite statement of the boundaries claimed by
the States, as reported by a committee of Congress, February 23, 1779, was: *Northerly*, the ancient limits of Canada to Lake Nepissing, thence
W. to the Mississippi; *Westerly*, the Mississippi.
The boundaries specified in the *ultimata* adopted
March 19 were substantially the same, that on the
south, and for the most part that on the north,
being identical with those actually acquired at the
peace. The instructions to Adams, resolved upon
August 14, 1774, were to the same effect. But
Luzerne was alert and energetic, and did not let

[1] Gérard to Vergennes, April 11, September 1, 1778; May 29,
1779, *Stevens MSS.*

[1] Durand, p. 137.

[3] Luzerne to Vergennes, May 14, August 27, 1778, *Stevens MSS.*

them long remain unchanged. In January, 1780, he presented to Congress the views of Spain: that the United States should extend no farther to the westward than settlements were allowed by the proclamation of 1763; that they should have no territory on the Mississippi, and therefore no right to navigate it; while even lands east of the river, in which settlements were prohibited, are held to be still British possessions. In February and March he urged the same and similar arguments.[1] The chief position now pressed was the importance of conciliating the court of Madrid. But the Southern States resented extremely any sacrifice of their claims; for Virginia was reaching out towards the Mississippi and the foundations of Kentucky were laying. So between these two fires Congress long delayed precise instructions. June 6 and 7, 1781, there was a long debate on the boundaries. So many were in favor of taking the Ohio for a boundary, wrote Luzerne to de Vergennes, that it would only have depended on him to get such a motion passed, but " it seemed to me that circumstances might arise in which it would be necessary to withdraw the boundaries still farther." [2] The matter of boundaries is dependent on the events of the war, was de Vergennes's comment, and Congress is wise in not defining them.[3] The final instructions to the commissioners referred

---

[1] Luzerne to Vergennes, February 11, March 13.
[2] Luzerne to Vergennes, June 13, 1781.
[3] Vergennes to Luzerne, September 7, 1781.

them to these former instructions, but omitted to tie them by absolute directions. By a secret article, however, they were ordered to try to get the boundaries as stated. It is not surprising, perhaps, that on November 23 Luzerne communicated to Congress the satisfaction felt by France with the discretion left to the ministers.

Luzerne was equally successful in the matter of the fisheries; after long debates, and in spite of the ceaseless efforts of Elbridge Gerry and the delegates from Massachusetts, — at times the New England party succeeding, at times the French, — a share in the fisheries, so far from being an ultimatum, appeared in the final instructions only as a condition precedent to a treaty of commerce with Great Britain in case any such should be negotiated. The wishes of Congress are subordinated to French convenience, was Luzerne's cry of delight to de Vergennes.[1] It is true that Marbois assured Congress that in regard to the fisheries the king would do his best to procure every advantage for the United States.[2] But M. Marbois was in this matter, to say the least, curiously misinformed. The question is simply this, said Luzerne, discussing the fisheries with Mr. Thompson, a member of Congress: Has Congress a right to insist on France procuring for them this advantage? One has only to read the treaty to see that France is only bound to secure independence for America.[3]

[1] June 3, 1780.   [2] Marbois to Vergennes, July 11, 1781.
[3] Luzerne to Vergennes, January 5, 1782.

The subject may be closed with this curt remark of de Vergennes: "The Americans doubtless do not flatter themselves that in the last analysis we will let the peace depend on the greater or less extension that may be granted to them as to the fisheries." [1]

When in the autumn of 1779 the election came on of a minister to negotiate for peace, the New England party chanced to be strong enough at the moment to elect the champion of the American fishermen, John Adams. Already suspected and disliked by France, Adams soon made her detest him by his independent manners; and Franklin conveyed to Congress the disapprobation felt for his fellow countryman by de Vergennes, an act, perhaps, hardly justified by diplomatic propriety. In the spring of 1781 de Vergennes urged on Luzerne the policy of having Adams instructed to take no step without the king's consent, — as the next best thing to having him removed for good. [2] Luzerne, accordingly, spoke confidentially to the president and various members of Congress about the danger of Adams losing for America an opportunity of making peace on reasonable terms. As a result, he hoped two associates would be sent him, or directions to govern himself by de Vergennes's advice. [3] He labored earnestly with the committee on instructions as to the folly of leaving

---

[1] Vergennes to Luzerne, March 23, 1872.

[2] Vergennes to Luzerne, March 9, 1781, April 19, 1781.

[3] Luzerne to Vergennes, June 1, 1781.

the negotiation to Adams's sole discretion. It was, he said, the affection of France for the United States that made her so anxious in the matter.[1] Now the committee was charged to draw up a resolution, of which article 4 provided that the American minister should be guided by the advice of France. The article, as drafted, required the utmost confidence in the French ministers, and forbade concluding peace without consulting them. That was not enough, exclaimed Luzerne to the chairman; it was necessary that Adams should have to follow the advice of France, if she thought it essential.[2] Accordingly, June 8, the instructions were amended so as to read: "You are to make the most candid and confidential communications upon all subjects to the ministers of our generous ally, the King of France; to undertake nothing in the negotiations for peace or truce without their knowledge or concurrence; and ultimately to govern yourself by their advice and opinion." At last Luzerne was satisfied. "I regard in effect," he said, "the negotiation as being actually in the hands of the king, with the exception of the question of independence and the treaties." [3] The resolution had passed with but three States against it, a happy result which he attributed chiefly to the absence of Samuel Adams, and to the rupture of the New England League for which he was indebted to his old pensionary, General Sullivan.

[1] Luzerne to Vergennes, June 8, 1781. Cf. *S. J.* ii. 438.
[2] Luzerne to Vergennes, June 11, 1781.   [3] *Ibid.*

The success of his schemes almost turned Luzerne's head with joy, for elsewhere he speaks of the "unlimited confidence" placed in France.[1] Yet it is to be noticed that these most unwise instructions were passed, not for the benefit of France, but purely for the sake of America, because it was believed that in such way the best terms could be procured at the peace. Luzerne had previously disclaimed that France had any selfish object in the matter; now, when complaints arose, Luzerne urged Congress to reconsider their decision, and hinted that "France would be glad to be relieved of the responsibility if she consulted her own interest."[2]

When doubts of the honesty of France were expressed, Luzerne was directed to discredit them by assurances that were but repetitions of these earlier statements, which must have had no small share in effecting the purposes of France. You may assure them, said de Vergennes, that, "far from wishing to abuse the influence he might have on the negotiations of the American ministers, the king will employ it only for the best advantage of the United States; and that, if he does not succeed in procuring them all the terms that each of them individually might wish, the fault will certainly not be his, but due to circumstances."[3] A more definite

---

[1] Luzerne to Vergennes, June 13, 1781.

[2] Luzerne to Vergennes, June 23, 1781.

[3] Vergennes to Luzerne, September 7, 1781; November 23, 1781, S. J. iii. 83.

pledge of faith it would be hard to draft, — and yet Rayneval seems to have forgotten it when he discussed the American claims with Shelburne in London.

These instructions — of which there was so much unnecessary talk when the preliminary articles of peace reached America, and which assume such sanctity even in the imagination of M. Doniol — were not founded on any treaty obligation, but were enacted under a mistake of fact for the purpose of gaining from England, by the good offices of France, terms which, as appears by the official correspondence of de Vergennes and his diplomatic agents, France had secretly determined to oppose. The attitude of France in 1782, as sketched in that correspondence, was not that presented by Luzerne and credited by Congress ; and no treaty satisfactory to the United States could possibly have been negotiated except by one who saw the facts as they were, and was bold enough to act accordingly. Adams may have been such a man, but his temperament was that of a fighter rather than of a diplomatist, and, suspected as he was by France of unfriendly prejudice from the beginning, he could have had but slight opportunity of success. Now to tie his hands still more, following up Luzerne's suggestion to give Adams "two adjoints," Jay,[1] Franklin, Jefferson, and Laurens were added to the commission. As for the peace negotiations, wrote Luzerne, they will depend

[1] Jay being named first.

henceforth on his colleagues as much as on him. "Mr. Jay is the one whose reports in the course of the negotiation will make most impression on Congress, because he passes as being the least violent either for or against us, and I am very sure that his accounts will have much influence on the opinion Congress will form of our conduct at the peace." [1]

[1] Luzerne to Vergennes, September 25, 1781.

Shelburne

CHAPTER VIII

THE NEGOTIATIONS

1782–1783

WHEN Jay reached Paris on June 23, 1782, the negotiations, strictly speaking, had not yet begun. All the belligerent powers, except Spain, were eager for peace; the ministry of Lord North had been driven from power in March by a series of votes of "want of confidence," and the Rockingham ministry had taken office only on condition that the king would not veto the concession of independence to America; while France was convinced of the necessity of entering into direct negotiations at Paris in order to forestall the intervention of the imperial courts of Austria and Russia, whose offers of mediation were half accepted by England, in whose favor they seemed unfairly prejudiced.[1] Franklin had opened unofficial intercourse with the ministry, through Oswald, "a pacifical man,"[2] and Grenville, "a sensible, judicious, intelligent, good-

[1] "Observations relative to Pacification (French), June 20, 1782," *Stevens MSS.;* Vergennes to Montmorin, June 22, 1782, *Stevens MSS.;* Montmorin to Vergennes, August 22, 1782, *Stevens MSS.*

[2] Franklin's *Works,* ix. 267.

tempered, and well-instructed young man," [1] the
former being the personal envoy of Shelburne, secretary of state for home and the colonies, and the
latter the personal envoy of Fox, secretary of state
for foreign affairs.   Each of these ministers was
endeavoring to secure the American negotiations
for his own department.   Grenville had received
successively several commissions, but only to treat
with France and not technically including America; while as yet Oswald had no commission at all.
In these preliminary overtures, however, some suggestions had been made by Franklin which proved
useful: that the only engagements America had
with France were comprised in the treaty of commerce and the treaty of alliance, and that so soon
as England conceded the independence of America,
" the treaty she had made with France for gaining
it ended." [2]   De Vergennes had proposed that the
negotiations of France and America should be separate, though they were to move *pari passu* and
the two treaties were to be signed simultaneously; [3]
and this idea Franklin communicated to Grenville,
who acceded to it gladly. [4]   The proposition that
France should accept the grant of independence as
her full compensation de Vergennes rather scorn-
fully rejected. [5]   For, " even admitting America to
be the sole object of France in the war, there still

[1] Franklin's *Works*, viii. 35.
[2] Grenville to Fox, May 14, 1782, *Stevens MSS.*
[3] Bancroft, x. 540; Franklin's *Works*, ix. 290.
[4] Grenville to Fox, May 30, 1782, *Stevens MSS.*
[5] Grenville to Fox, May 10, 1782, *Stevens MSS.*

remained Spain to satisfy, and that power had never had anything in common with America, whose independence she had not yet recognized;"[1] a frank admission that France might prolong the war for objects in which, in the words of Fox, "it is not even pretended that America has any interest either near or remote."[2] It seems then to have been agreed that America should negotiate with England directly, not through de Vergennes or the mediating courts, and separately by herself, without further communication with France than was required by comity, "bienséance," to use Franklin's term, and by the interpretation the American ministers should, in their discretion, put upon their instructions. These instructions, so far as they imposed confidence in France, were not at that time construed by Franklin literally, for he did not communicate to de Vergennes the one important suggestion which he made with regard to the terms of peace; namely, the cession of Canada, a suggestion that he would hardly have included even in his informal "notes for conversation" had he been aware that it was opposed equally by England, France, and his own government. So early as 1778 it was the settled design of France and Spain "to keep the English in the possession of Nova Scotia and of Canada,"[1] and Gérard was instructed to dissuade Congress from their plan of conquering

---

[1] Grenville to Fox, May 30, 1782, *Stevens MSS.*

[2] Fox to Grenville, May 26, 1782, *Stevens MSS.*

[3] Vergennes to Gérard, December, 1778, De Circourt, iii. 264.

Canada, as the king thought the possession of it by England would be a useful means of keeping America dependent upon France.[1] The English ministry declared the cession of Canada to be " out of the question," [2] and Washington considered its possession to be undesirable. Such was the state of affairs when Jay arrived on the scene.

The first letter he wrote to America testified to his regard for Franklin: " I have endeavored to get lodgings as near to Dr. Franklin as I can. He is in perfect good health, and his mind appears more vigorous than that of any man of his age I have known. He certainly is a valuable minister and an agreeable companion." [3] The next day, writing to Montmorin, he showed how far he was from any prejudice against the French: " What I have seen of France pleases me exceedingly. Doctor Franklin has received some late noble proofs of the king's liberality in the liquidation of his accounts, and the terms and manner of paying the balance due on them. No people understand doing civil things so well as the French. The aids they have afforded us received additional value from the generous and gracious manner in which they were supplied, and that circumstance will have a proportionable degree of influence in cementing the connection formed between the two countries." [4]

[1] Vergennes to Gérard, December, 1778, De Circourt, iii. 255.
[2] Fitzmaurice, Life of Shelburne, iii. 183–186.
[3] Jay to Livingston, June 25, 1782, Dipl. Corr. viii. 114, 115.
[4] Jay to Montmorin, June 26, 1782, Jay's Jay, ii. 100.

Jay lost not a moment before setting about the business of his mission. The entries in his diary run: "1782, 23d June. Arrived in Paris about noon. Spent the afternoon at Passy with Dr. Franklin. He informed me of the state of the negotiation, and that he kept an exact journal of it. 24th. Waited upon M. Vergennes with the Dr.[1] The count read us his answer to the British minister. 25th. Wrote to Count Aranda. Wrote to the secretary for foreign affairs. 26th. After breakfast with the Dr. met with Mr. Grenville."[2] The paper that de Vergennes read to Jay and Franklin was presumably a copy of the verbal answer he had made to Grenville on the 21st, which, to quote his own words to Montmorin, "was drawn up solely with the view of prolonging the negotiation to gratify our desires and the convenience of our allies. In fact the four points on which I ask for arrangements would take up quite six months."[3] June 29 Jay and Franklin called upon Aranda, the Spanish ambassador, who had been authorized to continue the negotiations attempted at Madrid. A suggestion of the necessity of mutual concessions was made by the ambassador, but nothing of importance was transacted immediately, as the next day Jay fell ill, and was unable to take any part in affairs for several weeks.

During Jay's illness another change of ministers

[1] Dr. Franklin.
[2] Jay's *Jay*, i. 136.
[3] Vergennes to Montmorin, July 20, *Stevens MSS.*

occurred in England. Rockingham died on July 1, and the next day the king offered the vacant office to Shelburne "with the fullest political confidence." The Whig party at cnce objected to what was unquestionably a constitutional exercise of the prerogative, and Shelburne's acceptance was followed by the resignation of Fox, Burke, Sheridan, and others of Fox's intimate friends. Pitt became chancellor of the exchequer, Townshend home and colonial secretary, and Lord Grantham secretary for foreign affairs. This was, indeed, a ministry, to use the king's phrase, "on a broad bottom," but decidedly liberal. In the House of Lords Shelburne stated that his views on the subject of American independence were still the same as heretofore, that it would be a fatal misfortune to England, but that now he was obliged to yield to necessity. He would, however, make every exertion to prevent the court of France from dictating the terms of peace ; the sun of England would set with the loss of America, but he was resolved to improve the twilight and prepare for the rising of that luminary again.[1] On the 11th Parliament rose, and Shelburne was prepared to give his whole attention to concluding the negotiations before it should reassemble in November. He at once sent Benjamin Vaughan, the political economist, to Paris to assure Franklin, who was an intimate friend, that there was to be no change of policy; and to Oswald he wrote : " I beg him to believe

[1] Fitzmaurice, *Life of Shelburne*, iii. 239, 241.

that I can have no idea or design in acting towards him and his associates but in the most liberal and honorable manner." [1]

On July 9, in an interview with Oswald, Franklin drew up a series of articles to be communicated to Shelburne, as a basis for negotiation. The articles marked *necessary* were: (1) Independence, full and complete, in every sense, and the withdrawal of all troops; (2) A settlement of boundaries; (3) A confinement of the boundaries of Canada to at least what they were before the Quebec Act; (4) A freedom of fishing on the Banks of Newfoundland and elsewhere for fish and whales. The articles marked *advisable* were: (1) An indemnity to many people who had been ruined by the destruction of towns; such an indemnity, Franklin said, "might not exceed five or six thousand pounds;" (2) Some acknowledgment of the error of England in distressing the country; (3) American ships and trade to have the same privileges in the United Kingdom as British ships and trade; (4) The cession of Canada and Nova Scotia. [2] At the close of this interview Franklin withdrew his suggestion, made in his "notes for conversation" in April, that the royalists might be compensated by the sale of waste lands in Canada; and declared that, owing to the inability of Congress to control the parti lar States, the claims of

[1] Shelburne to Oswald, June 30, Fitzmaurice, *Life of Shelburne*, iii. 243.

[2] Fitzmaurice, *Life of Shelburne*, iii. 243, 244.

the royalists could not be considered. Oswald concluded his report with the remark, "I could not
perceive that he meant that the progress and conclusion of their treaty was to have any connection
or would be influenced by what was doing in the
treaties with other powers." [1]

When Fox resigned, Grenville thought fit to
resign also, and was succeeded by Fitzherbert, the
English minister at Brussels. But before leaving
Paris, Fitzherbert alarmed Franklin by spreading a
report that Shelburne had no intention of granting
independence. The report was instantly denied by
Shelburne: "There never have been two opinions,"
he assured Oswald, "since you were sent to Paris,
upon the most unequivocal acknowledgment of
American independency;" and he promised him a
commission, with instructions from Townshend "to
make the independency of the colonies the basis
and preliminary of the treaty." [2] This language
seems at first sight unequivocal; but it has misled
some historians into supposing that what was intended was an acknowledgment of independence,
without reference to a treaty, — an acknowledgment as absolute as was subsequently extorted by
Jay through the representations of Vaughan. The
language of Shelburne, however, on this occasion
differs little from the vote of the cabinet, May 23,
on the motion of Fox, " to propose the independ-

[1] Oswald to Shelburne, July 11.
[2] Shelburne to Oswald, July 27, 1782, Hale, *Franklin in France*
ii. 90.

ency of America in the first instance, instead of
making it a condition of a general treaty;"[1] a
motion which Shelburne and a majority of the cabinet construed to mean that independence was proposed merely as "the price of peace," as a basis to
treat upon.[2] As to the articles drawn up by Franklin, Shelburne hoped that those "called *advisable*
will be dropped, and those called *necessary* alone
retained as the ground of discussion."[3]

On August 6 a copy of the promised commission
arrived, empowering Oswald to treat and conclude
with the commissioners of "the said colonies or
plantations," etc. The next day Oswald called
upon Franklin at Passy, who read the commission
and said "he was glad it was come," and "that he
hoped we shou'd do well enough and not be long
about it." Thus Oswald remarks in his journal,
having in mind Franklin's earlier suggestion that
on the granting of independence the treaty with
France came to an end. "That could not but be
very agreeable to me," he continued, "if my expectations had not been so soon after dampt by the
. . . unpleasant reception from Mr. Jay." This
conversation with Jay, which occurred the following day, is perhaps of sufficient interest to justify
free quotation from Oswald's journal. Jay, he
wrote, "is a man of good sense, of frank, easy, and

[1] June 30. Hale, *Franklin in France*, ii. 61 n.

[2] Fitzmaurice, *Life of Shelburne*, iii. 219.

[3] Shelburne to Oswald, June 27, 1782, Hale, *Franklin in France*,
ii. 90.

polite manners. He read over the copy of the commission . . . and then said: By the quotation from the Act of Parliament in the commission he supposed it was meant that Independence was to be treated upon, and was to be granted, perhaps, as the price of peace; that it ought to be no part of a treaty; it ought to have been expressly granted by Act of Parliament, and an order for all troops to be withdrawn, previous to any proposal for treaty; as that was not done, the king, he said, ought to do it by Proclamation, and order all garrisons to be evacuated, and then close the American war by a treaty." Then, after mentioning "many things of a retrospective kind," Jay added that "the great point was to make such a peace as should be lasting." Oswald noticed the expression which he had often heard from de Vergennes and Franklin, and was curious to know what meaning Jay attached to the words. "What security," he asked, "could be given for a continuance of peace, save a treaty, which, like the Treaty of Paris, was apt to prove very inadequate security?" Jay replied, "He would not give a farthing for any parchment security whatever. They had never signified anything since the world began, when any prince or state, of either side, found it convenient to break through them. But the peace he meant was such, or so to be settled, that it should not be the interest of either party to violate it." As to France, he said that by their treaty the Americans could not make peace but in concurrence with the Eng-

lish settlement with France; that the independence of America was not a sufficient indemnity to
France, and, if granted as such, would put them
under a greater obligation to France than they
inclined to, as if to her alone they were indebted
for their independence. The treaty of alliance
with France must be fulfilled; for "they were a
young republic just come into the world, and if
they were to forfeit their character at the first out-
set, they would never be trusted again, and should
become a proverb among mankind." Jay spoke
"with such a freedom of expression and disapprobation of our conduct at home and abroad respecting America," concluded Oswald, "as shews we
have little to expect from him in the way of indulgence. And I may venture to say that, although
he has lived till now as an English subject, though
he never has been in England, he may be supposed
(by anything I cou'd perceive) as much alienated
from any particular regard for England as if he
had never heard of it in his life. . . . I sincerely
wish I may be mistaken, but think it proper to remark, as Mr. Jay is Dr. Franklin's only colleague,
and being a much younger man and bred to the
law, will of course have a great share of the business assigned to his care."

On the 10th Jay and Franklin consulted, by
appointment, with de Vergennes, to whom Franklin had sent a copy of the commission. De Vergennes advised them to proceed under it, as soon as
the original should arrive. Jay observed that "it

would be descending from the ground of independence to treat under the description of colonies," — by which phrase the States were described in the commission. De Vergennes replied that an acknowledgment of independence, instead of preceding, must in the natural course of things be the effect of the treaty, and that it would not be reasonable to expect the effect before the cause. On the whole, the French court considered that the American ministers should accept the commission on condition that England would accept their own commissions as made out by Congress.[1] To Montmorin and Luzerne, de Vergennes subsequently expressed similar opinions.[2] Jay's theory of de Vergennes's motives he explained fully to Franklin: He thought that the French minister wished to postpone the acknowledgment until the objects of Spain had been secured, " because, if we once found ourselves standing on our own legs, our independence acknowledged, and all our other terms ready to be granted, we might not think it our duty to continue in the war for the attainment of Spanish objects. I could not otherwise account for the minister's advising us to act in a manner inconsistent with our dignity, and for reasons which he himself had too much understanding not to see the fallacy of. The Doctor imputed this

---

[1] " Reflections (French) on the bill of July 25, 1782," *Stevens MSS.*

[2] To Montmorin, August 22; to Luzerne, September 27, *Stevens MSS.*

conduct to the moderation of the minister, and to his desire of removing every obstacle to speedy negotiations for peace. He observed that this court had hitherto treated us very fairly, and that suspicions to their disadvantage should not be readily entertained. He also mentioned our instructions as further reasons for our acquiescence in the advice and opinions of the minister." [1] Jay, indeed, had divined, with an accuracy hard to surpass, the fears of the court of Spain, which by the treaty of Aranjuez Vergennes was compelled to regard. " When once independence has been definitely offered to the United States," Montmorin wrote from Madrid, August 12, expressing his own opinion and that of Florida Blanca, " if it is not followed immediately by peace it will not be difficult to persuade them that the continuation of the war has an entirely different object from their interests." [2] That de Vergennes had an ulterior motive was, indeed, obvious enough, from the inconsistency of his present argument that independence should be the effect of the treaty, with his previous assertion to Grenville, in Franklin's presence, that it was no favor to France, since independence existed in fact before France interfered, and with his still earlier refusal, inspired possibly by Adams, to accede to the Russo-Austrian plan of mediation, because it contemplated an English

[1] To R. R. Livingston, September 18, 1782, *Dipl. Corr.* viii. 135.

[2] Montmorin to Vergennes, August 12, 1782, *Stevens MSS.*

negotiation with the States as colonies, and not as
an independent power of equal rank with the others.
Franklin, however, was unconvinced by Jay's reasoning; for on the morning of August 11, Sunday,
he told Oswald that "Mr. Jay was a lawyer, and
might possibly think of things that did not occur
to those who were not lawyers. And he at last
spoke as though he did not see much difference;
but still used such a mode of expression" that
Oswald could not positively say that he would not
insist "on Mr. Jay's proposition, or some previous
or separate acknowledgment." [1]

There was, however, no room to mistake Jay's
meaning. "I urged upon Oswald," he wrote, "in
the strongest terms the great impropriety, and consequently the utter impossibility, of our ever treating with Great Britain on any other than an equal
footing, and told him plainly that I would have no
concern in any negotiation in which we were not
considered as an independent people;" and with
Oswald's approval he drew up a declaration, recog-
nizing the colonies as independent States, which,
after being submitted to Franklin, was delivered
to Oswald on the 15th. They consented, however,
to waive the declaration, when the Englishman
showed that he was instructed to grant independence if the commissioners refused to treat otherwise, and they agreed to accept a stipulation of independence in a separate preliminary article. On
August 17 Oswald communicated these demands

[1] Hale, *Franklin in France*, ii. 112.

to the ministry, though his commission under the great seal had arrived the day before, and Franklin and Jay were discussing it with de Vergennes, who repeated his previous arguments. "Upon the whole," wrote Oswald, "they would not treat at all until their independence was so acknowledged as that they should have an equal footing with us and might take rank *as parties to an agreement*." [1] "The American commissioners," he wrote again, "will not move a step until independence is acknowledged; until the Americans are contented, Mr. Fitzherbert cannot proceed." [2]

Jay also prepared a letter explaining the attitude of the commissioners. "If Parliament meant to enable the king to conclude a peace with us on terms of independence, they necessarily meant to enable him to do it in a manner compatible with his dignity, and consequently that he should previously regard us in a point of view that would render it proper for him to negotiate with us. As to referring an acknowledgment of our independence to the first article of a treaty, permit us to remark that this implies that we are not to be considered in that light until after the conclusion of the treaty, and our acquiescing would be to admit the propriety of our being considered in another light during that interval. It is to be wished that his majesty will not permit an obstacle so very un-

[1] To Shelburne, August 17, 1782, *Stevens MSS*.
[2] To Shelburne, August 18, 1782; Oswald to Townshend, August 18, *Stevens MSS*.

important to Great Britain, but so essential and indispensable with respect to us, to delay the reestablishment of peace." This letter was considered too positive by Franklin, who, moreover, as Jay wrote to Livingston, "seemed to be much perplexed and fettered by our instructions to be guided by the advice of this court. Neither of these considerations had weight with me; for as to the first, I could not conceive of any event which would render it proper, and therefore possible, for America to treat in any other character than as an independent nation; and as to the second, I could not believe that Congress intended we should follow any advice which might be repugnant to their dignity and interest." Fitzherbert, writing on August 17, informed Grantham of de Vergennes's attempt to excite new jealousies and misunderstandings between England and America, which convinced him that the grant of American independence at the moment would not be agreeable to France, " as the band between them would thereby be loosened before the conclusion of a peace." But so averse was the ministry to acceding to the terms of Jay, that they offered to waive the claims of British creditors for debts prior to 1775, and of the refugees for compensation, "for the salutary purposes of precluding all further delay," as Townshend expressed it.

At last, however, Oswald was instructed, that, if this concession would not suffice, " in the very last resort " he might inform the commissioners that the king would recommend Parliament to enable him to acknowledge independence "absolutely and irrevocably, and not depending upon the event of any other part of a treaty. But upon the whole, it is his majesty's express command that you do exert your greatest address to the purpose of prevailing upon the American commissioners to proceed in the treaty, and to admit the article of independence as a part, or as one only of the other articles."[1] In other words, the cabinet had determined to reject Oswald's proposal.[2] On September 5 Oswald sent Franklin an extract from this letter of Grantham's, and a day or two later made another vain attempt to persuade Jay to rest satisfied with his commission in its present form. On the 8th Franklin fell ill with a serious attack of the gout.[3]

In the mean while important events had occurred which convinced Jay that the French court was opposed to American claims in other matters than that of independence. When, in July, Jay renewed his negotiations with Aranda, the latter stated the Spanish claims with great definiteness, and subsequently sent him a map of the boundaries proposed.[4] Aranda argued that the western territory, so far as it was not still in the possession of the Indians, belonged to Spain by virtue of her

[1] Townshend to Oswald, September 1, 1782, Fitzmaurice, *Life of Shelburne*, iii. 255, 256.

[2] Fitzmaurice, *Life of Shelburne*, iii. p. 254.

[3] Franklin's *Works*, ix. 403–405.

[4] *Dipl. Corr.* viii. 150.

conquest of West Florida and her posts on the
Mississippi and the Illinois. Jay proposed for
discussion a boundary east of the Mississippi, running from a lake near the confines of Georgia to
the confluence of the Kanawha with the Ohio and
thence to Lake Erie; and on August 10 he left
with de Vergennes a map marked according to
these views. De Vergennes withheld his opinion,
but Rayneval, the minister's confidential secretary,
said that he thought the Americans claimed too
much, and Franklin seemed to agree with Rayneval.[1] On August 26 Jay and Aranda held another
conference on the boundaries, and Aranda asked
Jay to state his views in writing.[2] On September
5, upon an invitation from Rayneval, Jay talked
over the matter with him at Versailles; and on the
6th Rayneval sent Jay a paper stating his personal ideas.[3]

The argument of Rayneval was simple in its
logic but startling in its conclusions. America's
only claim to the western territory was under the
rights of Great Britain, but in 1775 England had
admitted that Ohio belonged to France, and in
1761, 1763, and 1775 that the lands west of the
Alleghanies were Indian territory. He therefore
proposed that lands to the north of the Ohio should
belong to England, lands to the south of latitude
31° north to Spain; also that a line should be
drawn along the Cherokee and the Cumberland to

[1] *Dipl. Corr.* viii. 152.   [2] *Ibid.* viii. 154.
[3] *Ibid.* viii. 155.

the Ohio, and that the Indians to the west of this line should be under the protection of Spain, and those to the east under the protection of the United States.[1] "It was not to be believed," Jay wrote, "that the first and confidential secretary of the Count de Vergennes would, without his knowledge and consent, declare such sentiments and offer such propositions, and that, too, in writing;" and John Adams,[2] and, in a similar case, Fitzherbert, reached the same conclusion.[3] De Vergennes disowned all responsibility for the paper in 1783 :[4] "it might be considered as non-existent in relation to the king's ministers." But a year earlier, when the matter was still fresh, his tone to Luzerne was different : "A confidential note has been sent to Mr. Jay, in which it is almost proved that the boundaries of the United States south of the Ohio are confined to the mountains, following the watershed."[5] Jay could not have forgotten that arguments similar to Rayneval's had been made to him repeatedly in the summer and autumn of 1779 by Luzerne. Then sacrifices were to be made to Spain to induce her to join in the war ; now similar sacrifices were proposed to induce her to end it. "The policy of Spain at this moment amounts to this," wrote Montmorin on July 8, "to negotiate, if it is absolutely impossible to avoid it, . . . but to delay

[1] *Dipl. Corr.* viii. 154, 156.
[2] *Ibid.* vii. 68.
[3] To Grantham, August 29, 1782, *Stevens MSS.*
[4] To Luzerne, July 21, 1783, *Stevens MSS.*
[5] To Luzerne, October 14, 1782, De Circourt, iii. 290.

as long as possible the moment for explaining herself, in the hope that the siege of Gibraltar will be
favorable. . . . One cannot disguise from one's
self the fact that, in view of this state of things, it
is almost wholly for Spain that we continue the
war. I hope that this truth may not be too obvious
to the Americans, who have no reason to be interested in satisfying that power, and who would soon
be wearied of the war if it had only this object." [1]

That summer in the month of June two papers
were prepared in the French department for foreign affairs.[2] The first of these urged the importance of limiting the United States, so as to restrain them so long as possible from ambitious
projects; England must renounce Georgia, and
Florida must be ceded to Spain. "We regard it
as necessary for the solidity of the future peace," is
the conclusion, " to separate the English absolutely
from this part of the continent. The ambitious
views they have shown in wishing to have the Mississippi for a boundary, the extension they have
hastened to give to their commerce in this part of
the world, the communications that they have established with New Mexico, are sources of discord
that must be eliminated." [3]

On September 10 an intercepted letter to de
Vergennes from Marbois, Luzerne's secretary at

[1] *Stevens MSS.*

[2] So stated by Mr. Bancroft, who selected these papers for publication. To Hon. John Jay, December 11, 1882.

[3] De Circourt, iii. 33.

Philadelphia, was transmitted to Jay through English hands. He speaks of the opposition which
Samuel Adams is raising in Massachusetts to any
terms of peace that do not preserve American rights
to the fisheries; and Marbois suggests that the
king should intimate to Congress or the ministers
"his surprise that the Newfoundland fisheries have
been included in the additional instructions; that
the United States set forth therein pretensions
without paying regard to the king's rights," etc.
"It is remarked by some," the letter concludes,
"that as England has other fisheries besides Newfoundland, she may perhaps endeavor that the
Americans should partake in that of the Great
Bank, in order to conciliate their affection, or procure them some compensation, or create a subject
of jealousy between them and us; but it does not
seem likely that she will act so contrary to her
true interest; and were she to do so, it will be
better to have declared at an early period to the
Americans, that their pretension is not well
founded, and that his majesty does not mean to
support it." [1] Franklin doubted whether this letter reflected the opinions of the French ministry.[2]
"The channel ought to be suspected," he wrote to
Livingston. "It may have received additions and
alterations; but supposing it all genuine, the forward, mistaken zeal of a secretary of legation
should not be imputed to the king." De Vergennes vindicated himself in similar terms: "The

[1] Jay's *Jay*, i. 490, 491, 494.   [2] Franklin's *Works*, ix. 463.

letter, by a forced interpretation, was designed to
render us suspected in regard to the fisheries. In
the first place, the opinion of M. de Marbois is not
necessarily that of the king; and in the next place,
the views indicated in that dispatch have not been
followed." [1] As a matter of fact this opinion of
M. de Marbois was identical with that of the king,
and it was not followed because circumstances
made it impracticable. The authenticity of the
letter was confessed by Marbois himself to Edward
Bancroft, when they were returning on the same
ship together after the peace,[2] and subsequently to
Mr. W. B. Lawrence.

That America had no right to the fisheries after
becoming independent of the crown of Great Britain had been the familiar theme of Gérard and
Luzerne, and was stated and restated with almost
wearisome iteration in their correspondence. Luzerne's understanding about the matter is shown
by a letter of August 15 to de Vergennes. He
reports that returning prisoners bring news that
England fears that the ambition of France and
Spain may put a stop to the negotiation, and is
prepared to offer America independence on condition that she remains neutral during the rest of
the war; that several members of Congress assured him that, though " Spain and Holland might
have special interests to discuss, it was not for
the Americans to examine their nature and basis,

---

[1] Vergennes to Luzerne, September 7, 1783.
[2] John Adams's *Works*, i. App. p. 674,

but . . . though the pretensions of the belligerent powers should be as exorbitant as England asserted, that the United States ought not to lay down their arms till we had procured to all our allies the satisfaction they might wish." "I took this," continued the discreet Luzerne, "as being meant to show that Holland and Spain were bound in their turn to continue the war to procure the fisheries for America. I replied that they could reckon on the moderation of the powers at war with England."[1] The opinions of Rayneval certainly coincided singularly with those of Marbois. Fitzherbert, about this time, just before Marbois's letter reached Jay, happened to "drop something" to M. de Rayneval about the American claim to the fisheries. "He [Rayneval] signified to me," Fitzherbert wrote to Grantham, "in pretty plain terms that nothing could be further from the wishes of this court than that the said claim should be admitted, and moreover that we, on our part, were not only bound in interest to reject it, but that we might do so consistently with the strictest principles of justice."[2]

On September 9 Jay heard that Rayneval had left Versailles for England, traveling under an assumed name. Only a few days before Rayneval had explained to Jay his intended absence by saying that he was going into the country for a few days. Knowing the confidence de Vergennes had

[1] Luzerne to Vergennes, August 15, 1782, *Stevens MSS.*
[2] Fitzherbert to Grantham, August 29, 1782, *Stevens MSS.*

in his secretary, and having conclusive reasons now for distrusting the policy of France, Jay assumed that the object of Rayneval's mission was to suggest such a division of the western territories as would be satisfactory to Spain, and a partition of the fisheries between France and England. The next day Jay decided to urge Vaughan to go to England to express the American view to Shelburne in opposition to Rayneval; for Vaughan was still in Paris as Shelburne's unofficial personal agent, and had full knowledge of all that had been passing. Vaughan at once consented, and wrote to Shelburne asking him to conclude nothing with Rayneval till his own message had been heard, and on the 11th he too left Paris. "It would have relieved me," Jay wrote to Livingston, "from much anxiety and uneasiness to have concerted all these steps with Dr. Franklin; but on conversing with him about M. Rayneval's journey, he did not concur with me in sentiment respecting the object of it, but appeared to me to have great confidence in the count [Vergennes], and to be much embarrassed and constrained by our instructions."

The mission of Rayneval was primarily suggested by certain informal proposals which Admiral de Grasse, then a prisoner on parole, had communicated to de Vergennes as from Lord Shelburne. Montmorin, to whom de Vergennes had inclosed them with remarks indicating some doubts of their authenticity, wrote that he and Florida Blanca were astounded at the English propositions, and that the king and ministry " approve of your determination, and think it suitable that some one should be sent to England to assure himself of the intentions of Lord Shelburne and his colleagues." [1]

"My instructions were as simple as they were laconic," wrote Rayneval many years afterwards. "They asked that I should demand the admission or disavowal of the note communicated to M. de Grasse. The first article of the note concerned the independence of America. . . . Nothing was prescribed in relation to the other conditions to be made with the American commissioners." [2]   And he further said that when the English minister introduced other American questions, he referred to his ignorance and lack of instructions, and in what he did say strengthened rather than weakened the demands of the Americans.   One conference, with the arguments he used, Rayneval describes in the notes of his mission: "At last came the turn of America.   My Lord Shelburne had warned me that they would have much difficulty with America about the boundaries as well as about the fishery of Newfoundland; but he hoped the king would not support them in their demands.   I answered that I had no doubt of the eagerness of the king to do what depended on him to restrain the Americans within the limits of justice and reason.   And my lord wishing to know what I thought of their

[1] Montmorin to Vergennes, August 25, *Stevens MSS*.
[2] Rayneval to Monroe, November 14, 1795, Rives, *Madison*, i. 655, App. O.

pretensions, I answered that I was ignorant of
those concerning the fishery, but that, whatever
they might be, it seemed to me that there was a
safe principle to follow in this matter, namely:
that the fishery in the high sea is *res nullius*, and
that the fishery along shore belongs of right to the
owners of the shores, so far, at least, as there are
no limitations by treaty. As to the extent of the
boundaries, I supposed the Americans would take
that in their charters, that is to say, they would
wish to reach from the Ocean to the Pacific. My
Lord Shelburne treated the charters as absurd,
and the discussion did not last longer because I
did not wish either to sustain or deny the American pretension; I only said that the English
minister would find in the negotiations of 1754,
relating to the Ohio, the boundaries that England,
then the sovereign of the United States, thought
right to assign them." [1] This, perhaps, was the
conversation mentioned briefly but significantly by
Lord Edmond Fitzmaurice in his "Life of Shelburne." "They then proceeded to speak about
America. Here Rayneval played into the hands
of the English ministers by expressing a strong
opinion against the American claims to the Newfoundland fishery, and to the valley of the Mississippi and the Ohio. These opinions were carefully
noted by Shelburne and Grantham." [2]

Almost simultaneously with Rayneval, Vaughan
arrived in London, instructed by Jay to impress

[1] De Circourt, iii. 46.   [2] *Ibid.* iii. 203.

upon the ministry that, as every idea of conquest had become absurd, nothing remained for England but to make friends with those whom she could not subdue; and that the way to do this was by liberally yielding every point in the negotiation essential to the interest and happiness of America; of which the first was that of treating on an equal footing. With independence granted, too, America would be at liberty to conclude peace so soon as France was satisfied, without regard to Spain. As to the terms of peace, admission to the fisheries was essential; the charters proved the right of the Americans to extend to the Mississippi; and the peace should be so free from seeds of distrust or jealousy that America would find no need to form alliances with other nations. Finally it was necessary for ministers to take a decided and manly part.[1]

So effective was this reasoning, that the real meaning of the situation was perceived at once. Vaughan, as he said nearly fifty years afterwards, was asked but a single question: " L. [Lansdowne, for such at that time was Lord Shelburne's title] only asked me, ' Is the new commission necessary?' and when I answered Yes, it was instantly ordered, and I was desired to go back with it, which I did, carrying the messenger who had charge of it in my chaise. The grant of the commission showed how things stood, and I departed joyfully." [2] The feel-

[1] Jay to Livingston, *Dipl. Corr.* viii. 165.
[2] Benjamin Vaughan to Peter A. Jay, January 14, 1830, Jay, *Address before N. Y. Hist. Soc.* p. 50.

ings of the ministers are explained by Fitzmaurice,
in the "Life of Shelburne." "It became clear to
the cabinet," he says, "that a profound feud had
sprung up between the Americans and their European allies, and that all they had to do was to avail
themselves of it. They at once decided to accept
the American proposition as to the terms of the
commission to Oswald. Lord Ashburton gave it
as his opinion that it came within the terms of
the Enabling Act. The new commission was then
made out at once and dispatched to Paris by
Vaughan." [1] That Vaughan's mission had effected
a complete change of policy, that the signing the
new commission was part of the new plan, not a
continuation of the old, as is supposed by some
writers, are facts shown conclusively by Shelburne's
letter to Oswald announcing it: "Having said and
done everything which has been desired, there is
nothing for me to trouble you with except to add
that we have put the greatest confidence, I believe,
ever placed in man, in the American commissioners. It is now to be seen how far they or America
are to be depended upon. I will not detain you
by enumerating the difficulties which have occurred. There never was a greater risk known; I
hope the public will be the gainer by it, else our
heads must answer for it, and deservedly." [2]

To persons not versed in public affairs the

[1] Fitzmaurice, *Life of Shelburne*, iii. 267.

[2] Shelburne to Oswald, September 23, 1782, Fitzmaurice, *Life of Shelburne*, iii. 267, 268.

wording of a commission may seem a matter of
minor importance. What difference could it make
whether Oswald was empowered to treat with the
colonies as such, or with the United States, so long
as independence was to be granted absolutely by
the first clause of the treaty? The difference was,
that in the first case independence still remained
something to be bargained for; also, most important of all, that the States were technically colonies
of Great Britain till the treaty was signed, and
could claim the fisheries, or the western territory
as such, only by virtue of their charters, or by
established custom. But, as de Vergennes repeatedly stated, these claims could not be logically sustained by the colonies as against England, since
their rights were derived through their connection
with the crown. The "United States," however,
treating for peace with Great Britain, were in an
entirely different position. The two powers were
on an equal footing; the only question was how
to make a permanent peace between them. The
colonial claims, well founded or not, became unimportant; instead of a treaty of more or less grudg-
ing concession from a superior power to its revolted
colonies, the treaty became one of territorial partition between equals seeking a permanent basis
of conciliation. Indeed, the preliminary grant of
independence may be said to have carried with it
a grant of the western territory.

The mission of Vaughan marked also a complete change of policy on the part of the Amer-

icans. Heretofore their attitude was that of suspicion towards England and reliance on France;
now mutual confidence was established between
the English ministry and the American commissioners, and both parties were anxious to arrange
satisfactory terms of peace as speedily as possible,
without further reference to France or her ally,
Spain. The bold, prompt decision of Jay, reached
without consulting even his single colleague in
Paris, growing out of his clear perception of the
facts as they really were, by his rejecting all com-
promises, though thereby the negotiations with
France and Spain should be brought to a stop, had
at last resulted in placing the American negotiations in a condition in which a satisfactory conclusion on all points was now little more than a
matter of detail to be settled by a few frank conversations.

"On the 27th of September," wrote Jay to
Livingston, "Mr. Vaughan returned here from
England with the courier that brought Mr. Oswald's new commission, and very happy were we
to see it. . . . Mr. Vaughan greatly merits our
acknowledgments." [1] The day before, in the ante-
room of de Vergennes at Versailles, Aranda had
made a final attempt to induce Jay to discuss a
treaty with Spain without a communication of his
powers, as Spain had not acknowledged the independence of the United States; and Jay had declared that both the terms of his commission and

[1] *Dipl. Corr.* viii. 201.

the dignity of America forbade his treating on any other than *an equal footing*.[1] De Vergennes, happening to interrupt them, again opposed Jay's argument, but to no purpose. On the same day Jay met Rayneval, who spoke in favor of his *conciliatory line*, and by his conversation gave rise to the suspicion that Spain had been recently confirmed in her claims by French advice.[2] This was the last attempt at negotiation with Spain in Europe. From first to last she had refused to acknowledge the independence of the United States, and had pursued a policy which, even in the eyes of de Vergennes, was ungenerous and unwisely selfish.

Under the new commission progress was rapid, though some delay was caused by the illness of Franklin. "Upon my saying," wrote Oswald on October 2, "how hard it was that France should pretend to saddle us with all their private engagements with Spain, he [Jay] replied: 'We will allow no such thing. For we shall say to France: The agreement we made with you we shall faithfully perform; but if you have entered into any separate measures with other people not included in that agreement, and will load the negotiation with their demands, we shall give ourselves no concern about them.'"[3] Accordingly on October 5, without consulting de Vergennes, Jay handed to Oswald a plan of a treaty, to the terms of which

[1] *Dipl. Corr.* viii. 202.
[2] Jay, *The Peace Negotiations*, p. 127 n. 2.
[3] Oswald to Townshend, October 2, *Stevens MSS.*

three days later Oswald assented, and which he transmitted at once to England. This plan proposed for the northeastern boundary the rivers St. John and the Madawaska; the "northwest angle" of Nova Scotia, so called, to be determined, and the line drawn thence according to the treaty of 1763. This and the other boundaries were settled in the first article, Oswald not "asserting the claims of the English crown over the ungranted domains, deeming that no real distinction would be drawn between them and the other sovereign rights, which were necessarily to be ceded."[1] These other articles provided for a perpetual peace, secured the right to the fisheries, including a liberty to dry fish on the shores of Newfoundland, and established the navigation of the Mississippi, to which Jay added a clause for reciprocal freedom of commerce.[2] No provision was made for debts contracted prior to 1775, nor for compensation to the royalists, both Franklin and Jay refusing to yield in either respect, while Oswald was authorized not to insist on them.[3] "Mr. Jay said to me last night," wrote Oswald on the 8th, "once we have signed this treaty we shall have no more to do but to look on and see what people are about here. They will not like to find we are so far advanced."[4] And to a desire to keep the negotia-

[1] Fitzmaurice, *Life of Shelburne*, iii. 269.
[2] *Ibid.*; *Dipl. Corr.* x. 88, 92.
[3] Fitzmaurice, *Life of Shelburne*, iii. 269, 281.
[4] Oswald to Shelburne, October 8, 1782, *Stevens MSS.*

tion separate, and conclude it before France was ready, Oswald attributed his own seeming haste in agreeing to Jay's terms. " I knew," he wrote in explanation, " it hath always been the wish of the ministry of this court that the Americans should go no faster in their treaty than they do themselves, and, indeed, that the main question regarding America should not be too quickly determined. On this account I thought it best to assent to the propositions as offered, in this general way."[1] " I look upon the treaty," he said, " as now closed."

But meantime news was received in England of the great victory at Gibraltar, when Lord Howe succeeded in relieving the fortress in spite of the combined fleets of France and Spain, after a siege of three years. The ministry at once determined to resist the demands which de Vergennes had formulated on October 6, and to try to modify the American demands as well, considering that the feud between the allies was already established, and that in no case would the Americans continue the war for purely Spanish purposes. To strengthen Oswald and relieve him of the responsibility of making new demands, Henry Strachey, at one time secretary to Clive and to Lord Howe's commission, and now under-secretary for foreign affairs, was sent to his assistance. He was instructed to urge the French boundary of Canada, and the claims of England to the lands between the Missis-

[1] Oswald to Townshend, October 11, 1782, *Stevens MSS.*

sippi and the western boundaries of the States,
with a view to securing compensation for the refugees;[1] to confine the Americans to a drift fishery,
without the right of drying fish, and to omit the
clause respecting freedom of commerce.   Above
all, the claims of the refugees were to be secured,
and the payment of the debts prior to 1775;
" honest debts must be honestly paid and in honest
money."

While Strachey was on his way, armed with
books and papers relating to the northern boundaries, Jay met Rayneval at dinner at Dr. Franklin's, and the secretary again contested the American claims to the backlands and to the fisheries.
But fortunately the man who had the most accurate
knowledge of the fishery claims and of the boundary of Massachusetts, John Adams, was also hurry-
ing to Paris at Jay's summons, and arrived there
on October 26.

Adams at once called on an old friend and countryman, Ridley, who, as Adams noted in his diary,
was "full of Jay's firmness and independence;
Jay has taken upon himself to act without asking
advice, or even communicating with the Count
de Vergennes, and this even in opposition to an
instruction," which, interjected Adams, " has never
yet been communicated to me. . . . Jay declares
roundly, that he will never set his hand to a bad
peace.   Congress may appoint another, but he will

[1] Fitzmaurice, *Life of Shelburne*, iii. 280, 281, 282; Shelburne
to Oswald, October 21, 1782.

make a good peace or none."[1] Adams expected to call on Franklin on Sunday, but heard that he had "broke up the practice of inviting everybody to dine with him" that day "at Passy; that he is getting better; the gout left him weak; but he begins to sit at table."[2] On Monday, October 28, Jay wrote: "Mr. Adams was with me three hours this morning. I mentioned to him the progress and present state of our negotiation with Britain, my conjectures of the views of France and Spain, and the part which it appeared to me advisable for us to act. He concurred with me in sentiment on all these points."[3] But Jay does not mention here or elsewhere the discomfort and distress which did not escape the keen eyes of his kind-hearted visitor. "I found Jay," Adams wrote, "in very delicate health, in the midst of great affairs, and without a clerk. He told me he had scarcely strength to draw up a statement of the negotiation hitherto, but that he must do it for Congress. I offered him the assistance that Mr. Thaxter could afford him in copying, which he accepted."[4] In their opinions on the state of European affairs at the moment, they were in perfect harmony: "Nothing that has happened since the beginning of the controversy in 1761," were Adams's strong words, "has ever struck me more forcibly or affected me more in-

[1] John Adams's *Works*, iii. 299, 300.

[2] *Ibid.* 299.

[3] Jay's *Jay*, i. 152.

[4] Adams to Jonathan Jackson, November 17, 1782, John Adams's *Works*, ix. 514.

timately than that entire coincidence of principle and opinion between him and me."

Franklin's private views were still widely divergent from those of his colleagues. In July of the following year he made the definite statement to Livingston: "With respect to myself, neither the letter from M. Marbois, handed in through the British negotiators (a suspicious channel), nor the conversation concerning the fishery, the boundaries, the royalists, etc., recommending moderation in our demands, are of weight sufficient in my mind to fix an opinion that this court wished to restrain us in obtaining any degree of advantage we could fairly prevail on our enemies to accord;"[1] and long after the preliminary articles were signed, he was fond of saying that M. de Vergennes had never deceived him. Yet he apparently did not resent Jay's independent action in sending Vaughan to Shelburne, though he was now a man of seventy-six, while Jay was only thirty-seven years of age. The friendship between the two was never strained, far less broken; throughout the following spring and summer they lived together at Passy in the most affectionate intimacy, and within a year Franklin appointed Jay one of his executors.[2] Never a word was said by either reflecting on the character or the wisdom of the other. It is, then, strange that the biographers and admirers of Franklin should have thought fit, without regard to facts, to dispar-

[1] July 23, 1783, *Dipl. Corr.* iv. 138, 139.
[2] September 11, 1783.

age the services of the man whom Franklin himself
ever loved and esteemed.   Mr. Sparks took this
tone, remarking : " In vain did Dr. Franklin essay
to remove these groundless impressions from the
mind of Mr. Jay ; " [1] the groundless impressions
being that France and Spain were opposed to the
American claims.   Elsewhere referring to Jay's
refusal to accept de Vergennes's advice to treat under the designation of "colonies," the same writer
speaks of Franklin groaning "during the month
wasted *upon this nonsense*."   More recently Mr.
Henry Cabot Lodge has asserted that "the negotiations seemed almost concluded, when Jay appeared
on the scene at Paris." [2]   While Jay, "disliking
and mistrusting Spain, and believing Franklin too
ready to yield to France, checked the negotiation,
which was prospering so well with Shelburne." [3]
And finally one of the last of Franklin's biographers, the Rev. Edward E. Hale, refers to the wording of Oswald's commission as "a point which he
[Franklin] *rightly* thought of minor importance,"
and then, speaking of Vaughan's mission, says : " It
seems also impossible to decide just what credit
should be assigned to Mr. Jay.   It must be acknowledged that he acted in a manner contrary to his
instructions.   It must also be acknowledged that
matters turned out very much according to his
mind.   But that settles nothing.   The question

[1] Sparks, *Franklin*, p. 482.
[2] Lodge, *Hist. of the English Colonies in America*, 518.
[3] *Ibid.*

must be, 'Did Vaughan's mission decide Shelburne
to accede to the desires of America?' And this
can never be certainly known."[1]

The conduct of Franklin during the negotiations
can surely be explained without any disparagement
of his colleagues. The Adams family, in three successive generations, have offered three such explanations, each of them adequate. If that of John
Adams is rejected, as the perhaps hasty and exaggerated expression of that blunt, eccentric man,
and that of John Quincy Adams as also colored
possibly by unconscious prejudice though stated
with classic elegance, one may accept without
offense the explanation so fairly offered by Charles
Francis Adams: that Franklin was, in the first
place, minister to the court of France, and that he
was only subsequently and secondarily a negotiator
of the peace, and that in his primary capacity,
with the grave responsibilities it imposed, he could
neither with propriety, nor with advantage to this
country, exhibit the boldness of Jay, who acted
simply as a negotiator with England unhampered
by the obligation to the court of France, which
affected Franklin.

But whatever his private opinions may have
been, they were not allowed by Franklin to influence his public conduct, and from this time to the
conclusion of the treaty he acted in perfect harmony with his colleagues. On the 29th Oswald
introduced Strachey, who had arrived the day

[1] Hale, *Franklin in France*, ii. 146.

before, to Jay, and then, after being joined by
Adams, all went out to Dr. Franklin's, at Passy,
and at both these places Adams made his memorable suggestion that the questions of payment of
the debts and of compensating the Tories were
distinct. That evening, apparently, Adams spent
with Franklin. "I told him, without reserve,"
wrote Adams, "my opinion of the policy of this
court, and of the principle, wisdom, and firmness
with which Mr. Jay had conducted the negotiation
in his sickness and my absence, and that I was
determined to support Mr. Jay to the utmost of
my power in the pursuit of the same system. The
Doctor heard me patiently, but said nothing. At
the first conference we had afterwards with Mr.
Oswald, in considering one point and another,
Dr. Franklin turned to Mr. Jay and said, 'I am of
your opinion, and will go on with these gentlemen
in the business without consulting this court.' "[1]
This may have been at the first regular meeting
of the commissioners, on October 30, to examine books and papers. It was doubtless on some
earlier and more private occasion that the characteristic incident occurred, related by Trescott,[2] and
quoted by Parton:[3] "'Would you break your instructions?' Franklin asked him one day. 'Yes,'
replied Jay, taking his pipe from his mouth, 'as
I break this pipe;' and so saying Jay threw the

[1] John Adams's *Works*, iii. 336.
[2] *Diplomacy of the U. S.* i. 121.
[3] Parton, *Life of Franklin*, ii. 488.

fragments into the fire." The significance of this
public acknowledgment by Franklin must not be
overlooked, for thereby he became fully entitled to
the credit, or discredit, of breaking the instruction
to act constantly by the advice of France, which
credit, or discredit, is usually reserved only for Jay
and Adams.

Adams's happy suggestion to separate the claims
of the Tories from those of the British creditors
struck "Mr. Strachey with peculiar pleasure. I
saw it instantly smiling in every line of his
face," wrote Adams in his diary. Franklin and
Jay agreed to the payment of all just debts; and
Strachey at once wrote home that he thought something might be gained.[1] On the 30th and 31st the
northeastern boundary was discussed. The English at first wanted the whole of Maine, or at least
the Penobscot and Kennebec, but Adams convinced
even that "most eager, earnest, pointed spirit," as
he called Strachey, by exhibiting official documents
of former royal governors of Massachusetts. The
boundary of Maine was by a compromise settled at
the St. Croix, by which, as was afterward decided
by the commissioners appointed under Jay's treaty
of 1794, was meant the Schoodic; and thence a
choice was given for the northern boundary of the
States between two lines, one along the forty-fifth
parallel, the other through the centre of the lakes
to the source of the Mississippi. The next day,
November 2, the fisheries were discussed, and the

[1] October 29, 1782.

Americans surrendered the right of drying fish, on condition that Nova Scotia should be substituted for Newfoundland; but Jay and Adams both objected strongly to the English notion of separating the English and American fisheries. On November 3 compensation to the royalists was urged by Strachey, but to no purpose. The greater part of November 4 was spent by Adams and Jay at Oswald's with Strachey; "from 11 to 3, in drawing up the articles respecting debts, and Tories, and fishery;" the last article Adams drafted himself; and a suggestion was accepted by Oswald that the claims of the royalists should be recommended by Congress to the States.[1] In the evening, till near eleven o'clock, Jay and Adams were at Oswald's again with Strachey, "as artful and insinuating a man as they could send," said Adams;[2] and they agreed to clauses concerning the debts and the confiscation of lands belonging to Tories. The same day Strachey made a final appeal by letter for " stipulations for the restitution, compensation, and amnesty," to which the commissioners replied: " We should be sorry if the absolute impossibility of our complying further with your proposition should induce Great Britain to continue the war for the sake of those who caused and prolonged it." On November 5 Strachey returned to England, taking with him a copy of the articles with a marked map; a copy which Jay compared scrupulously with the original draft,

[1] John Adams's *Works*, iii. 302.   [2] *Ibid.* iii. 303.

allowing no alteration. " I did not expect to find
him so uncommonly stiff about the matter," [1] complained Oswald ; while Strachey wrote : " You will
see by the treaty all that could be obtained." Jay
was particularly anxious that this treaty should be
accepted. " He hoped," wrote Oswald to Townshend, on November 6, " we would not let this
opportunity slip, but resolve speedily to wind up
the long dispute, so that we might become again as
one people ; " and he suggested that the American
negotiators were now in a better situation than
when their instructions were given, and that if the
business were reopened they might claim compensation for British depredations.

During Strachey's absence the commissioners received further light on the policy of de Vergennes,
when Adams visited him for the first time on the
10th, and informed him that they and the English
differed on two points, the Tories, and the Penobscot. De Vergennes and Rayneval both advocated
the cause of the Tories, with the object, as Adams
suggested to Oswald's secretary, Whitefoord, of
keeping up in America " a French party and an
English party." [2] On the 15th he discussed the
question of the Tories again with Oswald, with the
result that the next day Oswald urged through
Vaughan that Jay should go to England, as he
thought Jay could convince the ministry. But
Jay replied that if he should go it must be either

---

[1] Oswald to Strachey, November 8, 1782.
[2] John Adams's *Works*, iii. 307.

" with or without the knowledge and advice of
this court, and, in either case, it would give rise to
jealousies: he would not go." [1]   Adams, however,
felt confident, " because," as he wrote to Livingston, " I find Mr. Jay precisely in the same sentiments, after all the observations and reflections he
has made in Europe, and Dr. Franklin, at last, at
least appears to coincide with us. We are all
three perfectly united in the affair of the Tories
and of Sagadahoc, the only points in which the
British minister pretends to differ from us." [2]   A
few days later he discussed with Franklin the
French policy of trying to deprive the United
States of the fisheries and the Mississippi, and
Franklin agreed that the French were blind to
their true interests. " We must be firm and
steady and should do very well," said Adams: and
Franklin replied, he " believed we should do very
well and carry the points." [3]   The day before, de
Vergennes had made another argument in behalf
of the Tories, and three days later Lafayette gave
Jay a message from Aranda that, " as the lands
upon the Mississippi were not yet determined
whether they were to belong to England or Spain,
he could not yet settle that matter." [4]

In the mean time Vaughan had followed Strachey and Rayneval to England, to explain the

[1] John Adams's *Works*, iii. 312.
[2] November 11, *Ibid*. viii. 9.
[3] *Ibid*. iii. 321.
[4] November 23, *Ibid*. iii. 327.

American position, and Oswald had written to
Townshend reporting a conversation with Jay and
Adams in which they said " that if peace with
Great Britain was not to be had on any other
terms than their agreeing to these provisions,"
relating to the Tories, "the war must go on,
although it should be for seven years to come, and
that neither they nor the Congress had any power
in the matter." [1]   But Shelburne was determined
to make a final attempt to save the royalists, and
drew up fresh instructions securing them indemnity; he also sought payment of debts accrued
subsequently to 1775, and limitation of the right
of fishing to a farther distance from shore.[2]   To
coerce the commissioners he suggested that their
cause would not gain by being deferred till Parliament should meet, on December 5, the date to
which the prorogation had been extended.   Fitzherbert also, who was added to the commission,
was directed " to avail himself of France so far
as he may judge it prudent from circumstances."
But the instructions really meant much less than
they seemed to; Shelburne could not hope to remain in power if the negotiation failed.   "It is
our determination," he had written to Fitzherbert
in October, "that it shall be either war or peace
before we meet the Parliament;" [3] and accordingly
Oswald was authorized to sign whenever Fitzherbert, Strachey, and himself thought it expedient.

[1] November 15, 1782.
[2] Fitzmaurice, *Life of Shelburne*, iii. 298.   [3] *Ibid*. iii. 287.

"The Tories stick; Strachey is coming again, and may be expected to-day," said Oswald to Jay, as he read his dispatches on the 22d.[1] On the 24th Strachey arrived in Paris, and the day following, all the commissioners met at Oswald's lodgings. Strachey announced that the cabinet unanimously condemned the article respecting the Tories. "The affair of the fisheries, too, was somewhat altered," wrote Adams in his diary. "They could not admit us to dry on the coasts of Nova Scotia, nor to fish within three leagues of the coast, nor within fifteen leagues of the coast of Cape Breton. The boundary they did not approve: they thought it too extended, too vast a country, but they would not make a difficulty. . . . I could not help observing that the ideas respecting the fisheries appeared to me to come piping hot from Versailles."[2] "The restitution of the property of the loyalists," was however, "the grand point on which a final settlement depended. Jay asked if this was the ultimatum of the ministry, and Strachey answered reluctantly 'No,' and admitted that Oswald had absolute authority to conclude and sign." Adams then, by documents, disproved the exclusive rights of the French to any part of the fishery; he argued the dependence of New England on the fishery, and remarked that "if a germ of war was left anywhere" it would most probably be in that article.

[1] John Adams's *Works*, iii. 324.
[2] *Ibid.* iii. 327, 328.

The proposition concerning the royalists was unanimously rejected, Franklin being especially emphatic. For the next four days the discussion continued. On the 28th Adams drew up an article on the fishery, and the same day Laurens arrived for the first time, and inserted, on the day of signing, the clause, which afterwards caused so much controversy, prohibiting the British troops from " carrying away any negroes or other property of the inhabitants." On the 29th Strachey endeavored to have the word "liberty" substituted for "right" in the fishery clause, but was boldly answered by Adams. Fitzherbert proposed sending a courier to London for advice before signing, but was met by the suggestion that, if so, the courier should take also a memorial for damages done by British troops. After consulting together, the English commissioners agreed to accept the American terms about the fisheries, and their ultimatum: that there should be no further persecution of the royalists, and that Congress should recommend the various state legislatures to restore confiscated estates of English citizens and of Americans who had not taken up arms.[1] Notice of their agreement was then communicated to de Vergennes.[2] "Are we to be hanged or applauded," wrote Strachey that evening, "for thus rescuing you from the American war? If this is not as good a peace as was expected, I am confident it is

[1] Bancroft, x. 589.
[2] Franklin's *Works*, ix. 488.

the best that could have been made." On November 30 the treaties were signed, sealed, and delivered, and all went out to Passy to dine with Dr. Franklin.[1] It was merely provisional articles that were signed as yet, but they were to constitute the treaty of peace between Great Britain and the United States so soon as a definite treaty should be concluded between Great Britain and France. The government was to be bound only by what Oswald should sign; and the commissioners were prompt to seize the happy moment. "We must have signed," said Adams, "or lost the peace. The peace depended on a day. If we had not signed, the ministry would have changed."[2]

Relying perhaps on the instructions of Congress, and underestimating the ability of the American commissioners, de Vergennes had taken little pains to inform himself of the progress of the negotiations. "It behooves us to leave them to their illusions," he wrote to Luzerne, in October, "to do everything we can to make them fancy that we share them, and unostentatiously to defeat any attempts to which these illusions may carry them if our coöperation is required." . . . They "have all the presumption of ignorance, but there is reason to expect that experience will erelong enlighten and improve them."[3] On November 23 he wrote again that the king was not obliged "to prolong

[1] Strachey to Nepean, November 29, 1782, *Stevens MSS.*
[2] John Adams's *Works*, viii. 88.
[3] October 14, 1782, *Stevens MSS.*

the war in order to sustain the ambitious pretensions which the United States may form in reference to the fishery or the extent of boundaries." [1]
When the provisional articles were shown to him,
de Vergennes wrote to Rayneval that the English
had rather bought a peace than made one, and
that their concessions exceeded anything he had
believed possible ; [2] and Rayneval replied that the
treaty seemed to him like a dream. At the time
no offense was expressed by the French court, not
a word of reproach but only of congratulation by
de Vergennes. It was not till more than a fort-
night afterwards that a rumor prevalent in England, that the preliminary articles were a final
settlement, and a consequent fear that in such
case the United States might join England against
France, moved de Vergennes to write his sharp
letter of December 15 to Franklin,[3] and urge Luzerne to inform Congress of the irregular action of
the commissioners. But Franklin's astute, diplomatic reply, pleading guilty of "neglecting a point
of bienséance," and hoping that, to avoid gratify-
ing the English, "this little misunderstanding
. . . will be kept a secret," together with the passing of the temporary alarm, induced Vergennes to
countermand his letter to Luzerne ; and in token
of his good-will he promised Franklin a new loan
of six million livres. It is certainly unnecessary

[1] Vergennes to Luzerne, De Circourt, iii. 294.
[2] December 4, 1782, *Stevens MSS.*
[3] Sparks, *Franklin,* ix. 449.

to search for a cause of offense where de Vergennes so obviously found none.

January 20, 1783, the commissioners published a formal declaration that so long as peace was not concluded between France and England the preliminary articles did not change the relations between England and the United States. The same day preliminary articles of peace were signed at Paris between Great Britain and France, and Great Britain and Spain, and a cessation of arms was proclaimed between Great Britain and the United States. From that day the provisional articles took effect.

The opposition to the terms of peace in Parliament drove Shelburne from office, and in the interim of a month, which took place between his resignation and the accession to power of the coalition ministry on April 2, under the Duke of Portland, Oswald was recalled and replaced by David Hartley, with instructions to secure amendments to the Provisional Articles and to negotiate a commercial treaty. Hartley proposed articles in favor of the royalist landowners, and the Americans suggested stipulations for the payment of prisoners' expenses; while Franklin drafted an article protecting non-combatants in the event of a future war. But none of these were adopted. In commerce the Americans demanded perfect reciprocity; while Hartley was instructed by Fox[1] to insist on the admission of British goods into America

[1] April 10, 1783, Jay, *Peace Negotiations*, p. 163.

while excluding American goods from British ports, especially from the West Indies. De Vergennes, wrote Fitzherbert April 18, desired to attract American trade to France, and Franklin concurred with him, while Adams and Jay would give the preference to England. " I hope," wrote Jay in March, " we shall soon be in the full possession of our country and of peace ; and as we expect to have no further cause of quarrel with Great Britain, we can have no inducement to wish or to do her injury; on the contrary, we may become as sensible to her future good offices as we have been to her former evil ones. A little good-natured wisdom often does more in politics than much slippery craft." [1] If Shelburne had continued in office, a commercial treaty might have been arranged, but with his fall a reaction of feeling set in against America, and the ministries that followed one another, with shifting personalities and indefinite policies, thwarted the efforts of the commissioners. Fox doubted the authority of Congress, and by a royal proclamation of July 2 the West India carrying trade was confined to British ships. Finally, on July 27, the commissioners decided to drop all commercial articles in the definitive treaty, and leave everything of that kind to a future special treaty. On September 3, with the exception of the so-called separate article concerning the boundaries of Florida, which the events of war had made unnecessary, the Provisional Articles were adopted as

[1] To Benjamin Vaughan, March 28, 1783, Jay's *Jay*, ii. 116.

the final treaty between England and America, and were signed at Paris in the morning. A special courier conveyed the news to de Vergennes at Versailles, whereupon the definitive treaties between France and Spain and Great Britain were signed in the presence of the ambassadors of the mediating imperial courts, an empty compliment in which England refused to participate.

By the treaty the United States gained more than Congress had ventured to propose or even hope for. "The boundaries must have caused astonishment in America," de Vergennes had written in July to Luzerne. "No one can have flattered himself that the English ministers would go beyond the head-waters of the rivers falling into the Atlantic."[1] Territory was acquired to the extent of more than twice what was proposed by France and Spain to England in the summer of 1782. In spite of the opposition of the powerful ally, on whose good offices Congress relied to obtain any satisfactory terms at all, the right to the fisheries, the navigation of the Mississippi, and an unimpeded opening to the Pacific were secured. To Jay, more than to any other of the commissioners, his contemporaries awarded the credit for this diplomatic triumph. "The New England people," wrote Hamilton, "talk of making you an annual fish offering as an acknowledgment of your exertions for the participation of the fisheries." "The principal merit of the negotiation was Mr. Jay's,"

[1] July 21, 1783, *Stevens MSS.*

said John Adams, whose praise was seldom excessive:[1] and at the time he wrote: "A man and his
office were never better united than Mr. Jay and
the commission for peace. Had he been detained
in Madrid, as I was in Holland, and all left to
Franklin as was wished, all would have been lost."[2]
Fitzherbert, when Lord St. Helens, in 1838, added
his testimony from the English point of view, that
"it was not only chiefly but solely through his
[Jay's] means that the negotiations of that period,
between England and the United States, were
brought to a successful conclusion."[3] Nor is it
without significance that de Vergennes should have
complained of "characters so little manageable as
those of Jay and Adams."[4] Further, it is worth
noting that, though Jay had successfully opposed
the policy of France, a Frenchman could appre-
ciate his motives: "I do not credit him with gratitude to us," wrote Luzerne to de Vergennes, "but
he is incapable of preferring England to us; he
glories in being independent, and his desire to
prove his attachment to his country sometimes
makes him unjust. But we need not fear from
him any premeditated act prejudicial to the alliance."[5]

[1] John Adams to John Jay, November 24, 1800, Jay's *Jay*,
i. 418.
[2] John Adams to Jonathan Jackson, November 17, 1782, John
Adams's *Works*, ix. 516.
[3] Lord St. Helens to Judge William Jay, July 29, 1838.
[4] Vergennes to Luzerne, December 24, 1783, *Stevens MSS.*
[5] Luzerne to Vergennes, September 26, 1783, *Stevens MSS.*

In the autumn Mr. Jay's family took a house at Chaillot, near Passy, on the road to Paris, and there Mrs. Jay and the children spent several months, while Jay himself went to England to try the waters of Bath for his health, having first obtained from Congress special leave of absence. His wife wrote: "Everybody that sees the house is surprised it has remained so long unoccupied. It is so gay, so lively, that I am sure you'll be pleased. Yesterday the windows were open in my cabinet while I was dressing, and it was even then too warm. Dr. Franklin and his grandsons, and Mr. and Mrs. Coxe and the Miss Walpoles, drank tea with me, likewise, this evening, and they all approve of your choice. As the sky is very clear and the moon shines very bright, we were tempted to walk from the saloon upon the terrace, and while the company were admiring the situation, my imagination was retracing the pleasing evenings that you and I have passed together in contemplating the mild and gentle rays of the moon."[1] Dr. Franklin was a near neighbor, and sometimes enjoyed an old friend's privilege of making fun of pretty Mrs. Jay's devotion to her husband. "Dr. Franklin charges me to present you his compliments," she says, "whenever I write to you, but forbids my telling you how much pains he takes to excite my jealousy at your stay. The other evening, at Passy, he produced several pieces of steel; the one he supposed you, at Chaillot, which being placed near another piece,

[1] From Mrs. Jay, November 6, 1783.

which was to represent me, it was attracted by
that and presently united; but when drawn off
from me, and near another piece, which the Doctor
called an English lady, behold, the same effect!
The company enjoyed it much, and urged me to
revenge; but all could not shake my faith in my
beloved friend." [1] "It gives me pleasure," was
Jay's reply from Bath, "to hear that the Doctor
is in such good spirits. Though his magnets love
society, they are nevertheless true to the pole, and
in that I hope to resemble them." [2]

While Mrs. Jay was reading "Evelina," which
Miss Walpole lent to her, watching the ascent of
a "globe of Montgolfier's," exchanging repartees
with Dr. Franklin and having the children inocu-
lated, Jay was at Bath, having stayed only a few
days in London, and making but one short trip
to Bristol to attend to a bequest in the will of
his cousin Peloquin. In London he found many
Americans, and was most scrupulous in adjusting
his behavior to them according to their patriotism.
"Having been very well assured that the conduct
of Judge Ludlow, Mr. Watts, H. White, and P.
v. Schaack had been perfectly unexceptionable,"
he wrote to Egbert Benson, "and that they had
not associated with the abominable Tory Club in
London (which filled the public papers with the
most infamous lies against us), I received and re-

[1] From Mrs. Jay, November 18, 1783, *Queens of American Society*, p. 67.
[2] *Ibid.*

turned their visits. Vadill also made me a visit, but I never returned it. Reports of the cruelties practiced by my old friend Jas. De Lancey of W. Chester News also kept us asunder. I wish these reports may prove as groundless as he says they are. He was an honest friend to me, and I sincerely lament the circumstances which prevent my taking him by the hand as cordially as ever. I have not seen any of Gen. De Lancey's family. I once met Billy Bayard on the street, but we passed each other as perfect strangers." [1] At Bath he saw much of the well-known Countess of Huntington. " She inquired about you in a very friendly manner, and is an enthusiast for America," he tells his wife. " Her heart is much set on the conversion of our Indians; she will find it a difficult task, but her wishes are laudable, though perhaps too sanguine." [2] The waters, aided by rhubarb and much walking, cured his dysentery and sore throat, and he returned to Paris in January.

He refused repeated offers of an appointment to London or Paris, urging the propriety of making Adams the first minister from America to England, and declaring his intention to become and remain a private citizen and a lawyer. After a long and unnecessary delay caused by dilatoriness of his secretary, Carmichael, in settling his accounts with Barclay, the agent of Congress, he at length left Paris with his family on May 16 for Dover,

[1] To E. Benson, December 15, 1783, *Jay MSS.*
[2] December 5, 1783, *Jay MSS.*

where he took ship for New York. "Your public and private character," wrote David Hartley in a farewell letter, "has impressed me with unalterable esteem for you as a public and private friend; . . . if I should not have the good fortune to see you again, I hope you will always think of me as eternally and unalterably attached to the principles of renewing and establishing the most intimate connection of amity and alliance between our two countries." John Adams wrote to Barclay: "Our worthy friend, Mr. Jay, returns to his country like a bee to his hive, with both legs loaded with merit and honor." [1]

[1] To Thomas Barclay, May 24, 1784, *Hist. Mag.* 1869, p. 358.

CHAPTER IX

SECRETARY FOR FOREIGN AFFAIRS

1784–1789

ON July 24, 1784, Jay was once again in New York, after an absence from the country of some five years. He was welcomed by the city fathers with an address and the freedom of the city in a gold box, "as a pledge of our affection and of our sincere wishes for your happiness." He had intended to "become a simple citizen," as he wrote from France to Van Schaack, and to take up again the practice of his profession; but on landing he found that Congress had two months before appointed him secretary for foreign affairs. This office had been established in 1781, and had been occupied by Chancellor Livingston till June, 1783, when he resigned, according to Luzerne,[1] on account of the insufficient salary. It then remained vacant till the following May, when Congress, hearing from Franklin of Jay's expected return, elected him the same day on the motion of Elbridge Gerry. For some months Jay withheld his acceptance, as he was unwilling, for reasons of private business, to be detained at Trenton, where

[1] Luzerne to Vergennes, May 19, 1782, *Stevens MSS.*

Congress had been in session and was to reassemble in September, and also because he was reluctant to assume such responsibility without the privilege of selecting his own clerks, a power which Congress had heretofore reserved to itself. Meantime he was elected a delegate to Congress by the state legislature; but on December 21, Congress having decided to adjourn to New York, and yielding in the matter of the appointments of his subordinates, Jay accepted the secretaryship, and resigned his seat on the floor.

Almost immediately afterwards he was tempted to become a candidate for governor; but he refused to desert the federal service, saying: "A servant should not leave a good old master for the sake of a little more pay or a prettier livery." To the more conservative Whigs, who were soon to be known as Federalists, the official conduct of Governor Clinton had become intensely objectionable, partly on account of his appointments to office of personal adherents, partly because he was the most vehement partisan of those harsh laws against the royalists, which Jay and Hamilton regarded as both unjust and impolitic. General Schuyler, who with Livingston was also named as an anti-Clinton candidate, urged Jay again and again, with singular self-effacement, to reconsider his refusal, since he was "the only man capable of stemming the torrent of evil, which with accelerating rapidity was rolling to the goal of debasement." But to Jay the occasion did not seem sufficiently critical, and even this fervent and florid appeal was in vain.

While Livingston had held the place, the secretary for foreign affairs had been little more than a mere clerk of Congress, and Jay now applied himself to the reorganization of the department, having the papers filed for the first time in a methodical manner, and asserting and maintaining on every occasion the dignity of the office. He protested earnestly and successfully against the impropriety of permitting foreign correspondence pertaining to his department to be communicated to Congress before being submitted to his scrutiny.[1] He made frequent use of his privilege to appear on the floor of Congress, and to speak on questions of foreign policy; and Congress constantly asked for and deferred to his advice. In a short time the secretaryship thus became the first office in consequence under the Confederation; for through it was transacted the correspondence between the federal government and the several States as well as that with foreign nations. "The political importance of Mr. Jay increases daily," wrote Otto to de Vergennes in January, 1786. "Congress seems to me to be guided only by his directions, and it is as difficult to obtain anything without the coöperation of that minister as to bring about the rejection of a measure proposed by him."[2] Yet all this time the accommodations provided for

[1] Madison's *Works*, i. 142.
[2] Bancroft, *Const. Hist.* pp. 479, 480.

the foreign office were miserably insufficient. " As late as 1788 there were, . . . besides the secretary and his assistants, only two clerks, or just enough, as may be inferred from a report of this date, for one of them to be in the office while the other went to luncheon. The quarters of the office, the report tells us, consisted of only two rooms, one of them being used as a parlor, and the other for the workshop." [1]

In the summer of 1785, the court of Spain appointed practically a resident minister to the United States, though under the modest title only of *encargado de negocios*, Don Diego de Gardoqui, with a view to settle the controversy about the navigation of the Mississippi, which had been guaranteed to the United States by the treaty of peace; also to arrange a commercial treaty. The negotiations were at once intrusted to Jay (whom it had been previously decided to send to Spain for that purpose), with full power; which, however, was limited later by the instruction "to stipulate the right of the United States to their territorial bounds and the free navigation of the Mississippi . . . as established in their treaties with Great Britain." [2] In 1783 Count Florida Blanca, in conversation with Lafayette, had seemed to yield the Spanish claims to the western territory, to which, indeed, Spain had no valid title; but Gardoqui now asserted that this understanding

[1] J. F. Jameson, *Essays on the Const. Hist. of the U. S.* p. 165.
[2] *Secret Journals*, iii. 586.

was a mistake. "In a word," wrote Jay to Lafayette, "they do not mean to be restricted to the limits established between Britain and us." [1] Gardoqui was equally inflexible against yielding the free navigation of the Mississippi. But he was willing to conclude a commercial treaty on liberal terms, a matter of first importance to the Northern States, where, especially in New England, grave commercial distress existed, for which such a treaty was thought to be the only remedy.

Jay was finally convinced that the crisis would justify a surrender of the navigation for a period of twenty-five or thirty years. August 3, 1786, in a speech before Congress, he stated his reasons concisely: first, because no treaty can be made unless that question is settled; secondly, because the navigation of the Mississippi is not now important, or likely to be so for many years; thirdly, because, as we are not prepared for war, Spain can exclude us from that navigation indefinitely. "Why, therefore," he concluded, "should we not (for a valuable consideration, too) consent to forbear to use what we know is not in our power to use?" [2] These reasons were logical but inconclusive, since they disregarded the one decisive fact that the Southwest was becoming rapidly populated by colonists who strongly insisted on the free navigation of their great river. "The act which abandons it," wrote Jefferson, "is an act of sepa-

[1] June 16, 1786, Jay's *Jay*, ii. 187.
[2] *Secret Journals*, iv. 45, 53.

ration between the eastern and the western country." [1] Jay, doubtless, was not unmindful of the
instructions, which Congress had sent to him in
Spain only four years before, on the motion of the
Southern delegates: to resign absolutely all claim
to the Mississippi south of the thirty-first parallel. It was, indeed, due wholly to the sagacity
which had been then shown by him that the United
States still possessed any claims to the river to
arbitrate. Now, however, the political situation
had changed completely with the march of events;
" while Congress was discussing the points of the
treaty a nation was created," [2] and a nation which
could not be disregarded. Accordingly, on August 28, every Southern delegate save one voted
to revoke the secretary's commission to negotiate.
The motion was defeated, and the next day, by
vote of seven States to five, Jay was again given
unlimited power. " It rests wholly with Jay,"
wrote Madison to Randolph, " how far he will proceed with Gardoqui, and how far he will communicate with Congress." [3]

The next month Jay reported that he had arranged an article saving the right of navigation,
while suspending its use for the period of the
treaty, but that the negotiation was " dilatory, unpleasant, and unpromising." [4] Finally Congress

1 To Madison, January 30, 1787, Jefferson's *Works*, ii. 87.
2 Lyman, *Diplomacy of the U. S.* i. 285.
8 March 11, 1787, *Madison Papers*, ii. 622.
4 Jay to Gardoqui, October 17, 1788, *Jay MSS.*

revoked Jay's powers, in view of the change of
government about to take place by reason of the
adoption of the new Constitution.   Jay's suggestion, discussed as it was only in secret session, and
thought by the Southern statesmen to sacrifice the
rights of the South to the convenience of the North,
was the chief cause of the opposition of North Carolina and Virginia to the ratification of the Constitution ; and that it was an error of judgment was
frankly admitted by Jay himself in 1788.[1]   But he
was actuated by national, not sectional motives, in
advising what he knew to be a choice of evils; and
in the words of one of his severest critics: "In
the game of applied politics, often a calculus of
probabilities among contingent events and impon-
derable forces, a statesman may sometimes show
more wisdom in being fortuitously wrong as the
event turns out, than in being fortuitously right
according to a drift and posture of events which
could not be foreseen." [2]

For some years the claims of Beaumarchais to
compensation, now urged by the agents of France,
were debated in Congress, a discussion which was
unfortunately destined to continue a long while yet
before the end could be achieved.   Jay had little
to do with the matter, but his views were positive.
"There can be," he wrote to Jefferson in Paris,
"but little clashing of interests between us and
France. . . . These engagements, however, give

[1] *Secret Journals*, iv. 452.
[2] James C. Welling, *The Land Politics of the U. S.* p. 19.

me much concern. Every principle of honor, justice, and interest calls upon us for good faith and punctuality, and yet we are unhappily so circumstanced, that the moneys necessary for the purpose are not provided." Indeed, though his political opponents found it convenient to denounce Jay as unfriendly to France, his official conduct regarding her was that of a friend. In reporting on the complaints by French merchants of laws of Massachusetts and New Hamphire discriminating against French vessels, he urged that Congress should recommend the repeal of such acts. "The French," he said, "have extended liberty of commerce to the United States beyond what they were bound to do by the treaty, and it certainly would not be kind to repay their friendly relaxation" by unnecessary restrictions.[1] "But the commerce of the country," he added, "must suffer from partial and discordant regulations . . . until it is under one direction." Since 1782, a convention defining the rights and duties of consuls had also been in negotiation with France, but it came to nothing, though Jay clearly saw its necessity. "The foreign consuls here," he said, "have no other authority than what they may derive from the laws of nations, and the Acts of particular States. The propriety of these Acts appears to be questionable, especially as national objects should be regulated by national laws."

Jay was also anxious to effect a commercial

[1] *Dipl. Corr.* 1783–89, i. 176.

treaty with France on the basis of perfect reciprocity. Besides urging his views on Jefferson, the
minister to France, he wrote to Lafayette very
freely: " Without any attempt to dress my ideas
à la mode de Paris — have we any reason to flatter ourselves that you will encourage us to drink
your wines by permitting your islands to eat our
bread? . . . Commercial privileges granted to us
by France at this season of British ill humor
would be particularly grateful, and afford conclusive evidence against its being the plan of the two
kingdoms to restrict our trade to the islands." [1]
" Toleration in commerce," he wrote a few years
later to the same friend of America, " like toleration in religion, gains ground, it is true; but I am
not sanguine that either will soon take place to
their due extent." [2] To Jay, indeed, the benefit
of free trade seemed axiomatic. " How freely
would it redound to the happiness of all civilized
people," he exclaimed in a letter to Lord Lans-
downe, " were they to treat each other like fellow
citizens! Each nation governing itself as it
pleases, but each admitting others to a perfect
freedom of commerce. The blessings resulting
from the climate and local advantages of one country would then become common to all, and the
bounties of nature and conveniences of art pass
from nation to nation without being impeded by
the selfish monopolies and restrictions with which

[1] To Marquis de la Fayette, January 19, 1785, *Jay MSS.*
[2] To Marquis de la Fayette, April 26, 1788, *Jay MSS.*

narrow policy opposes the extension of divine benevolence." [1]

In the autumn of 1785 the Algerines declared war, or, rather, resumed their piracies, on the cessation of tribute. The war Jay did not deem a great evil, but rather hoped that it might become "a nursery for seamen, and lay the foundation of a respectable navy." [2] He recommended at once, but in vain, the organization of a board of admiralty, the building of five forty-ton ships, and the arming of American traders in the Mediterranean at public expense. In 1787 he wrote to Lafayette: "The great question, I think, is whether we shall wage war or pay tribute? I for my part prefer war." [3] But he only succeeded in persuading Congress to allow Jefferson, in 1788, to provide for the subsistence of American captives at Algiers out of the fund set apart for their redemption. [4]

Much complaint and public clamor arose from the retention by Great Britain of the northwestern posts, in violation of the seventh article of the treaty of peace. But when John Adams, the American minister at London, formally protested, the English government retorted that the fourth article, securing every facility for the collection of debts due to Englishmen, was violated with equal openness by the United States. The correspond-

[1] April 20, 1786, *Jay MSS.*

[2] To the President of Congress, October 13, 1785.

[3] November 16, 1787, *Jay MSS.*

[4] To the President of Congress, September 12, 1788, *Jay MSS.*

ence was referred to Jay. "The result of my inquiries into the conduct of the States relative to the treaty," he wrote to Adams, "is, that there has not been a single day since it took effect on which it has not been violated in America by one or other of the States; " [1] and these conclusions were, with a candor rare in a public officer, embodied with appropriate recommendations in his report to Congress on October 13. " The amount of the report, which is an able one," said Madison in a letter to Jefferson, " is, that the treaty should be put in force as a law, and the exposition of it left, like that of other laws, to the ordinary tribunals." [2] Congress passed resolutions accordingly, and ordered them transmitted to the several States, together with a circular letter written by Jay, urging the repeal of all laws in contravention of the treaty; but the States as usual paid little heed.

Besides these more important transactions, there was much to occupy the time of the secretary for foreign affairs. There were reports to make on individual claims against the government urged by M. Otto, the representative of France, or by Mr. Temple, who had been received as British consul, on Jay's advice, as a matter of comity. On the recommendation of Jay a consul was appointed at Canton,[1] with which port a promising trade was already begun. For reasons that do not appear,

[1] To John Adams, November 1, 1786, Jay's *Jay*, ii. 191.
[2] *Madison Papers*, ii. 294.
[3] January, 1786.

but apparently on Jay's suggestion that there should be some official supervision of the mails, Congress by a secret act, September 7, 1785, authorized him in his discretion to open letters in the post-office;[1] a singular grant of arbitrary power which he is said never to have exercised.

Then, as now, heads of departments were beset by applicants for office or favor; but in granting these Jay was unusually punctilious. He refused curtly his brother Frederick's request to ask Gardoqui to recommend him as a reputable merchant to sell a damaged cargo. He even declined to serve John Adams, by recommending Adams's son-in-law, Colonel Smith, to succeed him at London. "In other countries," was Jay's answer, "it is not unusual to consult . . . the opinion of the secretary for foreign affairs respecting the officers to be appointed in that department. . . . But the case is different here. Although Congress commonly refer the propriety of measures to my consideration, yet they uniformly forbear to consult me about the persons to be appointed to any place or office however important. . . . These considerations have led me to make a rule to keep within the limits of my department, and not to interfere or to endeavor to influence any elections or appointments in Congress."[2]

Jay had other business, not connected with the secretaryship. In 1785 he was appointed by the

[1] From Secretary Thomson, September 8, 1785, *Jay MSS.*
[2] To Colonel W. S. Smith, July 20, 1787, *Jay MSS.*

State of New York one of its agents to determine its controversy with Massachusetts concerning boundaries; but he resigned early the next year. When a committee was appointed by Congress on a plan for the government of future territories, he was requested to attend and advise. " Shall the government," he wrote to James Monroe, " be upon colonial principles, under a governor, council, and judges of the United States, . . . and then admitted to a vote in Congress with the common right of the other States; or shall they be left to themselves until that event?" [1]

Under an act of New York for the gradual manumission of slaves, a society was formed for promoting it and protecting such as were freed. In 1786 Jay was appointed by the society one of the trustees for receiving donations, and two years later was elected to its presidency, which he retained till, being chief justice, he thought proper to resign.

Always a devout Episcopalian, he was a delegate from New York to the General Convention of the church, which met at Philadelphia in June, 1786. There he drafted the letter sent to the English bishops, requesting ordination for the American candidates, while defending the alterations made in the liturgy. On its dissolution the convention honored him with a special vote of thanks.[2]

The secretary for foreign affairs was expected to perform certain social duties. On returning from

[1] April 20, 1786, *Jay MSS.*   [2] *Jay MSS.*

Europe he took a house in New York for a year, and began building one for himself at No. 8 Broadway, which was finished the following spring. Here was naturally the centre of official entertainment so long as New York remained the capital. In Mrs. Jay's "Dinner and Supper List for 1787 and 1788" appear the names of most of the well-known colonial families, and of the most noted statesmen who were brought to New York by the Congress under the Confederation and the first Congress under the Constitution. "Mrs. Jay gives a dinner almost every week," wrote Mrs. Smith to her mother, Mrs. John Adams, "besides one to the *corps diplomatique* on Tuesday evening."[1] On May 20, 1788, she wrote again: "Yesterday we dined at Mrs. Jay's, in company with the whole *corps diplomatique*. Mr. Jay is a most pleasing man, plain in his manners, but kind, affectionate, and attentive; benevolence is stamped on every feature. Mrs. Jay dresses showily, but is very pleasing on a first acquaintance. The dinner was *à la Française,* and exhibited more European taste than I expected to find."[2] It was doubtless in a simpler style that Mr. and Mrs. Adams were entertained there in the spring of 1789, for Mrs. Adams, to judge from her letter thanking Mrs. Jay for her hospitality, was treated quite as one of the family. "Our mush and lemon brandy were of great service to us, and we never failed to toast the donor, whilst our hearts were warmed by the recol-

[1] *Queens of American Society*, p. 75.   [2] *Ibid.*

lection. I hope, my dear madam, that your health is better than when I left you, and this not for your sake only, but for that of your worthy partner, who I am sure sympathized so much with you, that he never really breakfasted the whole time I was with you." [1]

By the year 1788 the wheels of government had fairly stopped, the Confederation was little more than a name, and the duties of the secretary for foreign affairs consisted mainly in proving to Congress the futility or absurdity of any action. For this reason the negotiations with Spain were summarily closed; the treaty with England was incapable of enforcement; and when a loan was proposed, necessary as money was, he felt obliged to say: " Congress can make no certain dependence on the States for any specific sums, to be required and paid at any given periods, and consequently is not in a capacity safely to pledge its honor and faith as a borrower." [2] It was his own experience which he embodied in his analysis of the weakness of the government in his " Address to the People of the State." " They [the Congress] may make war, but are not empowered to raise men or money to carry it on. They may make peace, but without power to see the terms of it observed. They may form alliances, but without ability to comply with the stipulations on their part. They may enter into treaties of commerce, but without power to

[1] February, 1779, *Jay MSS.*
[2] Lamb, *Hist. of New York*, ii. 292.

enforce them at home or abroad. They may borrow money, but without having the means of repayment. They may partly regulate commerce, but without authority to enforce their ordinances. They may appoint ministers and other officers of trust, but without power to try or punish them for misdemeanors. They may resolve, but cannot execute, either with dispatch or with secrecy. In short, they may consult, and deliberate, and recommend, and make requisitions, and they who please may regard them." [1]

The national life was not secured by the treaty of peace, which only gave an opportunity for it; and the time between 1783 and the adoption of the Constitution of 1788 was, perhaps, " the most critical period of the country's history." [2] The people were restless under the depression of trade and the depreciated currency; rioting threatened in many States, and in Massachusetts became rebellion. " I am uneasy and apprehensive," wrote Jay to Washington, " more so than during the war. Then we had a fixed object, and though the means and time of obtaining it were often problematical, yet I did firmly believe that we should ultimately succeed, because I did firmly believe that justice was with us." The liberty so dearly won seemed about to be lost forever in the imminent anarchy. " If

---

[1] *Address*, p. 6; Ford, *Pamphlets on the Constitution*, Brooklyn, 1888, p. 67.

[2] Trescot, *Diplomatic History*, p. 9.

[3] June 27, 1786, Marshall, *Life of Washington*, ii. 107.

faction should long bear down law and government," were his gloomy words to Adams, "tyranny may raise its head, and the more sober part of the people may even think of a king." [1]

The reasons for the failure of the Confederation were obvious, and Jay laid his finger on those that were fundamental. "To vest legislative, judicial, and executive powers in one and the same body of men, and that, too, in a body daily changing its members, can never be wise. In my opinion those three great departments of sovereignty should be forever separated, and so distributed as to serve as checks on each other." [2] This principle became the corner-stone of the federal Constitution. Government by committees was another chief cause of executive procrastination and inconsistency. "In my opinion," Jay wrote to M. Grand in Paris, "one superintendent or commissioner of the treasury is preferable to any greater number of them; indeed, I would rather have each department under the direction of one able man than of twenty able ones;" [3] and modern publicists have reached the same conclusion. Finally, coerceive power in the federal government was essential; "a mere government of reason and persuasion," was Jay's unwilling testimony, "is little adapted to the actual state of human nature." [4]

[1] To John Adams, May, 1786.
[2] To Thomas Jefferson, August 18, 1786, Jay's *Jay*, i. 256.
[3] April 28, 1785.
[4] To Thomas Jefferson, April 24, 1787.

The remedy lay in securing a more centralized form of government, acting on the people directly and not merely through the States. Jay was in this sense a Federalist from the ' ginning; a strong federal union he considered the real aim and spirit of the Revolution; what was new was rather the doctrine of extreme state rights of the so called anti-Federalists. " It has, until lately, been a received and uncontradicted opinion," he stated in the " Federalist," " that the prosperity of the people of America depended on their continuing firmly united; and the wishes, prayers, and efforts of our best citizens have been constantly directed to that object. But politicians now appear who insist that this opinion is erroneous, and that instead of looking for safety and happiness in union, we ought to seek it in the division of the States into distinct sovereignties. However extraordinary this new doctrine may seem, it nevertheless has its advocates." [1] Even from France Jay had urged the necessity of centralization: " I am perfectly convinced that no time is to be lost in raising and maintaining a national spirit in America. *Power to govern the confederacy as to all general purposes should be granted and exercised.*" [2] In his zeal for nationality he was almost extreme. " It is my first wish," he wrote, May 10, 1785, to John Lowell, " to see the United States assume and merit the character of one great na-

[1] *Federalist*, No. 2.
[2] To Gouverneur Morris, September 24, 1783, Jay's *Jay*, ii. 132.

tion, whose territory is divided into different States merely for more convenient government and the more easy and prompt administration of justice, just as our several States are divided into counties and townships for the like purposes."[1] "I am convinced," he wrote to John Adams in 1786, "that a national government as strong as may be compatible with liberty is necessary to give us national security or respectability."[2]

When, therefore, in 1787, the question was put, "What is to be done?" and an answer was demanded, Jay could write to Washington with some definiteness. To increase the power of Congress would be ineffectual, for the same reasons that always make a large committee a dilatory and inconsistent executive. " Let Congress legislate, let others execute, let others judge. Shall we have a king? Not, in my opinion, while other expedients remain untried. Might we not have a governor-general, limited in his prerogatives and duration? Might not Congress be divided into an upper and lower house, the former appointed for life, the latter annually, and let the governor-general (to preserve the balance), with the advice of a council formed, for that only purpose, of the great judicial officers, have a negative on their acts? . . . What powers should be granted to the government, so constituted? . . . I think the more, the better; the States retaining only so much as may be necessary for domestic purposes, and all their

[1] Jay's *Jay*, i. 190.   [2] May 4, *Ibid*. i. 249.

principal officers, civil and military, being commissioned and removable by the national government." [1]

The convention which met at Annapolis in the autumn of 1786, to frame a uniform system of commercial regulations, dissolved without other result than recommending a convention of delegates from the several States to revise the Articles of Confederation. Such a convention Jay thought of doubtful constitutionality, as the legislatures from which the delegates were to derive their authority were themselves not authorized to alter constitutions. He also feared the effects of delay, in case their report was to be purely recommendatory, inoperative till ratified by the people. Instead, he suggested that Congress should recommend the election of state conventions " with the sole and express power of appointing deputies to a general convention," whose conclusions should have the force of law. By this scheme, it has been thought, the bitter partisan dissensions that attended the adoption of the Constitution might have been avoided; [2] but it is doubtful whether the same struggle would not have taken place over the election of the delegates, and whether many States might not have refused on such conditions to elect any delegates at all. [3]

Of the Constitutional Convention, which was

[1] Jay's *Jay*, i. 254, 255.
[2] *Ibid*. i. 255.
[3] J. A. Stevens, *Mag. Am. History*, July, 1878, p. 394.

elected on the recommendation of Congress " to
establish a firm national government," and which
met at Philadelphia in May, 1787, Jay was not a
member ; his appointment was urged by Hamilton,
was carried in the Assembly, but was defeated in
the Senate on the ground only of his well-known
ultra-federal opinions. Of the three delegates from
New York, two left the convention, one of them,
Lansing, declaring that the legislature would
never have sent him had they supposed its powers
extended " to the formation of a national government, to the extinguishment of their independency." [1]

Jay, however, was not idle in the cause of federalism.   Between October, 1787, and June, 1788,
the " Federalist " was published serially in the New
York journals, with the object of recommending
the cardinal principles of the new form of government ; and "no constitution," according to Chancellor Kent, " ever received a more masterly and
successful vindication." [2]   " It was undertaken last
fall," wrote Madison to Jefferson, August 10, 1788,
" by Jay, Hamilton, and myself.   The proposal
came from the two former.   The execution was
thrown, by the sickness of Jay, mostly on the two
others." [3]   Jay was the author of the second, third,
fourth, fifth, and sixty-third numbers.   The first
series of papers was a careful but concise argu-

[1] Elliott, *Debates*, i. 141.
[2] *Commentaries*, i. 241.
[3] Jay's second letter to Dawson, p. 21.

ment to prove that a national government was
essential to avert " dangers from foreign force and
influence." " For all general purposes we have
always been one people; as a nation we have made
peace and war, and formed alliances and compacts
with foreign states. The first and every succeeding Congress were agreed that the prosperity of
America depended on its union. Why should it
be otherwise now? " [1]

The States bordering on Spanish and British
territory " under the impulse of sudden irritations,
and a quick sense of apparent interest or injury,
will be most likely by direct violence to excite war
with those nations; and nothing can so effectually
obviate that danger as a national government,
whose wisdom and prudence will not be diminished
by the passions which actuate the parties immediately interested." [2]   But whatever our situation,
whether united or split into a number of confed-
eracies, foreign nations will know it and act accordingly. Independent and probably discordant
republics, "one inclining to Britain, another to
France, and a third to Spain, and perhaps played
off against each other by the three," would fall an
easy prey to foreign invasion or encroachment.
" How soon would dear-bought experience proclaim, that when a people or family so divide, it
never fails to be against themselves? " In war,
what armies could they raise or pay, and how?
" Who shall settle terms of peace? And in case

[1] *Federalist*, No. 2.   [2] *Federalist*, No. 3.

of disputes, what umpire shall decide between them, and compel acquiescence?" By a national union unreasonable causes of war will be less likely to arise; just causes will seldom be incurred; and it will secure the safety of the States " by placing them in a situation not to invite hostility." With France and Great Britain as our rivals in the fisheries and commerce, with Spain excluding us from the Mississippi, and Britain keeping us from the St. Lawrence, the possibility of war must be considered. " War may arise; will not union tend to discourage it?"[1] With separate States making separate and perhaps inconsistent treaties with foreign nations, will not disunion certainly tend to encourage war?[2] The last number written by Jay, No. 63, was a vindication of the treaty-making power vested in the Senate; and the original draft, which is still preserved, with its frequent alterations and interlineations, shows the extreme care with which these simply written, popular papers were prepared.[3]

The " sickness " that Madison speaks of, which interrupted Jay's work on the " Federalist," was due to a wound he received in that singular riot known as " The Doctors' Mob." In the spring of 1788 there were many complaints in the newspapers of the rifling of graves, one body being taken, it was said, from Trinity Churchyard. These complaints were replied to with ridicule as

[1] *Federalist*, No. 4. [2] *Ibid*. No. 5.
[3] *Hist. Mag.*, May, 1867, p. 267.

showing " a disposition to interrupt the students of physics and surgery in their pursuit of knowledge." On Sunday, April 13, some boys playing by the hospital declared that they saw a limb hanging out of a window; and a mob formed, broke into the building, and destroyed some valuable collections. The next morning the mob, two thousand strong, started to search the houses of the suspected physicians, who had taken refuge in the jail for safety. An attack was made on the jail; the militia was called out, and the mayor and a body of armed citizens marched to its relief. " Among those who interposed their personal influence for the purpose [of restoring peace] was Mr. Jay, the secretary of foreign affairs to Congress. In proceeding to the scene of action he received a severe wound in the head from a stone thrown thro' the glass of his chariot." [1] Gradually the riots subsided, the ringleaders were arrested and indicted, but, in view of the excited state of public feeling, the prosecutions were not pushed.

On February 1, 1788, the legislature of New York resolved to submit the report of the Constitutional Convention to delegates to be chosen by the people; and at the election in the city, late in April, out of 2833 votes cast, Jay received all but 98.[2] With the exception, however, of New York city and one or two adjoining counties, the State

[1] Wm. A. Duer, quoted with the newspaper accounts in *Medical Register of N. Y., N. J., and Conn.* xxii. 265.

[2] Jay's *Jay*, i. 264.

was violently anti-Federalist, and it was calculated
that out of the fifty-seven delegates only eleven
were favorable to the proposed Constitution.   The
crisis was extreme, and Jay, so soon as he recovered
from his wound, published anonymously an " Address to the People of the State of New York." [1]

According to a contemporary, this simply-writ-
ten, logical pamphlet had " a most astonishing influence in converting anti-Federalists to a knowledge
and belief that the new Constitution was their only
salvation." [2]   The author was soon betrayed by
" the well-known style," and Dr. Franklin urged
him to sign his name to it, " to give additional
weight at this awful crisis." [3]   " If the reasoning
in the pamphlet . . . is sound," Jay replied, " it
will have its effect on candid and discerning minds ;
if weak and inconclusive, my name will not render
it otherwise." [4]   The reasoning of the paper was
eminently practical and cogent, and its appeal to
the logic of the situation proved clearly enough the
truth of the remark, that " we were forced into
confederation by external, into union by internal,
necessities." [5]   " Our affairs are daily going from
bad to worse," said Jay, " our distresses are accumulating like compound interest. . . . Let it be
admitted that this plan, like everything else devised

---

[1] Ford, *Pamphlets on the Constitution*, Brooklyn, 1788, p. 67.
[2] S. B. Webb, April 27, 1788.
[3] From J. Vaughan, June 27, 1788, *Jay MSS*.
[4] To J. Vaughan, June 27, 1788, *Ibid*.
[5] H. O. Taylor, *Mag. Am. Hist.*, December, 1878, p. 723.

by man, has its imperfections; that it does not please everybody is certain, and there is little reason to expect one that will. It is a question of grave moment to you, whether the probability of your being able to obtain a better is such as to render it prudent and advisable to reject this, and run the risque." "If this plan is rejected, and a new one fails or is long delayed, as it must be, all government meantime coming to a stop, every band of union would be severed. Then every State would be a little nation, jealous of its neighbors, and anxious to strengthen itself by foreign alliances against its former friends. . . . What in such an event would be your particular case?" The situation was indeed almost absurd, when Jay could report to Washington that "an idea has taken on, that the southern part of the State will at all events adhere to the Union, and, if necessary to that end, seek a separation from the northern." [1]

On June 17 the convention met at Poughkeepsie, the seat of government ever since the destruction of Kingston, and, in spite of the unpromising outlook, Jay was able to foretell with fair accuracy the course of the opposition. "The greater number are, I believe, averse to a vote of rejection; some would be content with recommendatory amendments; others wish for explanatory ones to settle constructions which they think doubtful; others would not be satisfied with less than absolute and previous amendments, and I am mistaken if there

[1] May 29, 1788, *Jay MSS.*

be not a few who prefer a separation from the
union to any national government whatever. They
suggest hints of the importance of this State, of its
capacity to command terms, of the policy of its
taking its own time, and fixing its own price, etc.
They hint that an adjournment may be expedient,
and that it might be best to see the operation of
the new government before they receive it. The
people, however, are gradually coming right, not-
withstanding the singular pains taken to prevent
it." [1] It should be remembered, too, that state
pride had been grievously wounded by the separation of Vermont, and was all the more set against
any further diminution of its power and dignity.

The Constitution was discussed section by section. The question of representation in the House
of Representatives at once awoke the interminable
duel between State Rights and Federalism; and
Alexander Hamilton, the "Colossus" of the convention, was opposed by Melancthon Smith, the
most formidable of the anti-Federalists. The debate was closed by Jay, who, according to a recent
writer, "with extreme tact . . . laid stress on the
point that all sides agreed that a strong, energetic
government was necessary and practicable." [2] The
formation of the Senate then became the theme of
hot discussion for many days, and the anti-Federalists were still urging a shorter term of office for
senators, when news reached Poughkeepsie that

[1] To Washington, June, 1788.
[2] J. A. Stevens, *Mag. of Am. Hist.*, July, 1878.

New Hampshire, the ninth State, had ratified, and the new government was already a fact. The time had come which Jay had anticipated in his Address. "Suppose nine States should . . . adopt it, would you not in that case be obliged either to separate from the Union, or rescind your dissent? The first would not be eligible, nor the latter pleasant." The situation was changed on the instant; it was no longer a question of ratification, but merely of the terms of ratification.

The Fourth of July was spent by the delegates in a general celebration of the day. "Two tables," Jay wrote to his wife, "but in different houses, were spread for the convention, the two parties mingled at each table, and the toasts (of which each had copies) were communicated by the sound of drum, and accompanied by the discharge of cannon." [1] The next day the anti-Federalists returned to their dying struggles. On July 11 Jay moved the ratification of the Constitution and the recommendation of any amendments that should be adopted. After four days' discussion Melancthon Smith moved that the amendments relating to the service of the militia and the laying of direct taxes be conditional to ratification. On the 19th other amendments were moved on similar terms. At length, on the 23d, a test vote was had, under the influence of the news from Virginia; and an expression of "full confidence" that the amendments would be adopted was substituted by a majority of

[1] July 5, 1788, *Jay MSS.*

two for the stipulation of any condition. The reservation of a right to withdraw from the Union if the amendments were not submitted to a general convention was voted down. Instead thereof Jay, in spite of his protest, was directed to prepare and transmit to the several state legislatures a letter recommending another general convention to consider the amendments, " a singular proof," says Stevens, " of the public confidence in the probity and fairness of his judicial mind." [1] Jay and Hamilton had to choose between the evils of a call for a second convention and a rejection of the Constitution by the State, and chose wisely, for the call proved nugatory. " I did not, I confess," wrote Washington to Jay, "see how it could be avoided." [2]

On Saturday, July 26, after forty days of "an ordeal torture," to quote the words of a witness, by a majority of three votes only, the Constitution was ratified. The laurels of the victory were borne by Hamilton, but the work of Jay was such that Washington wrote from Mount Vernon: " With peculiar pleasure I now congratulate you on the success of your labors to obtain an unconditional ratification." [3] In 1815 John Adams bore similar testimony. Writing to James Lloyd about the early Federalists, he said : " I forbore to mention one of more importance than any of the rest, in-

[1] *Mag. of Am. Hist.*, July, 1878, p. 403.
[2] *Writings of Washington*, ix. 408.
[3] August 3, 1788, Jay's *Jay*, ii. 194.

deed of almost as much weight as all the rest. I mean Mr. Jay. That gentleman had as much influence in the preparatory measures in digesting the Constitution, and obtaining its adoption, as any man in the nation. His known familiarity with Madison and Hamilton, his connection with all the members of the old Congress, have given to these writings [the 'Federalist'] more consideration than both the other writers could have given them." [1]

[1] February 6, 1815, John Adams's *Works*, x. 115.

CHAPTER X

JAY continued to act as secretary for foreign affairs till Jefferson's return from France in the spring of 1790, and as such took part in the inauguration of Washington. In forming the new government the President showed his regard and admiration for Jay by offering him the choice of the federal offices. Of the three departments, the executive, the legislative, and the judicial, all theoretically of equal dignity, and each equally independent, that of justice seemed at the moment of most importance. The violent opposition of the anti-Federalists to any strong national government foreboded bitter contests over the construction of the Constitution; and the only safeguard was the organization of a wise and powerful Supreme Court. For almost every other provision of the Constitution there was some precedent either in the theory or practice of the English Constitution, or in the institutions of some colony or province; but the Supreme Court, at least in respect to its original jurisdiction, was apparently the unprecedented result of the requirements of the new system of government with its complex correlation of national and confederate state sovereignties, for its only predecessors were the judiciary committees of the Congress under the Confederation, which acted intermittently as courts of admiralty in cases of prize, and as boards of arbitration in questions of state boundaries. To maintain its theoretical position as "the keystone of our political fabric," in the words of Washington, the court had to claim the dignity and win the popular respect inherited by other courts. Its power as interpreter and guardian of the Constitution, that is to say the conservation and perpetuity of the republic as established by its founders, depended upon the personal respectability and wisdom of the members of its bench. Such thoughts must have been familiar to Jay when, of all the great offices, he chose the chief justiceship. The court was created by the Judiciary Bill, approved on September 24, which provided for the appointment of a chief justice and five associate justices, and on the 26th Jay was nominated and confirmed by the Senate. "In nominating you for the important station which you now fill," wrote Washington, "I not only acted in conformity with my best judgment, but I trust I did a grateful thing to the good citizens of these United States." [1]

During Jay's short tenure of office few causes came before the court, and with one exception the

[1] October 5, 1789, *Writings of Washington*, x. 35.

decisions are preserved only in the brief and dry minutes of the clerk. Yet three great facts were determined once for all: the dignity of the court was vindicated from encroachment by the federal executive and legislative departments; its jurisdiction was established over the state governments; and, incidentally, Jay announced and determined that foreign policy of the United States which has been accepted and followed from that day to this.

On February 1, 1790, in the old Federal Hall in New York, Jay and two associate judges met and adjourned for lack of a quorum. On February 2 the court organized, the letters patent appointing the several justices were read, and a " cryer " was appointed. On the following days a clerk was sworn in, seals for the Supreme Court and the Circuit Courts were chosen, orders were adopted for the admission of attorneys and counselors, and many of the first lawyers in the country were admitted accordingly, — Elias Boudinot, Egbert Benson, Fisher Ames, Robert Morris, Edward Livingston. Twice a year, according to law, Circuit Courts were held, each by two justices of the Supreme Court and a district judge. Jay's circuit included New York and New England, and in New York city, April 4, 1790, he delivered his first charge as a federal judge to the grand jury. " Let it be remembered," he said, " that civil liberty consists not in a right to every man to do just what he pleases; but it consists in an equal right to all the citizens to have, enjoy, and do, in peace, security, and without molestation, whatever the equal and constitutional laws of the country admit to be consistent with the public good." [1]

On adjourning the court in New York, Jay continued on circuit through New England, holding courts in Connecticut April 22, in Massachusetts May 4, and in New Hampshire May 20. At the time of this first circuit, an eye-witness in Boston gives the following account of the personal appearance of the chief justice: " His height was a little less than six feet; his person rather thin, but well formed. His complexion was without color, his eyes black [they were really blue] and penetrating, his nose aquiline, and his chin pointed. His hair came over his forehead, was tied behind, and lightly powdered. His dress black. The expression of his face was exceedingly amiable. When standing, he was a little inclined forward, as is not uncommon with students long accustomed to bend over a table. His manner was very gentle and unassuming." [2] Everywhere, especially in Massachusetts, he was received with enthusiasm. Invitations from friends poured in on him to stay with them while holding court, but with almost supersensitive delicacy he decided that it would be more proper to lodge only at the public inns.[3]

While at Boston he received a degree of Doctor of Laws from Harvard College, an honor he had

[1] Jay's *Jay*, i. 276.
[2] Sullivan, *Letters on Public Characters*, p. 59.
[3] Jay's *Jay*, i. 277.

received also with Adams and Franklin at the close of the peace negotiations from the University of Dublin. He wrote a little later to his wife: " I had two days ago a pleasant ride to Cambridge over the new bridge of which you have often heard. We extended our excursion to some pretty seats not far from the college, and among others Mr. Gerry's. On Wednesday next I purpose, on invitation from Judge Cushing and General Lincoln, to visit them. This will take me thirty miles out of my way to Portsmouth, but having time enough, and my horses in good order, that circumstance is not very important. . . . Cold easterly winds seem to prevail here; I think our climate a better one." [1] In those days a judge must have needed considerable physical endurance to ride in two months through four States, and must have spent far more time in the saddle than on the bench. In the autumn he again rode the circuit and held courts at Boston, Exeter, Providence, Hartford, and Albany. In the winter John Adams at Philadelphia begged for a visit, in characteristic phrase: "As you are a Roman the *jus hospitii* will not be disputed by you." But Jay deferred his visit till the February term, 1791, when the court removed there with the shifting seat of government from New York. Then the first case was entered on the docket, Van Staphorst *v.* The State of Maryland, but was discontinued on agreement by the parties to pay their own costs. In August rules of practice were de-

[1] May 6, 1790, *Jay MSS.*

clared, — substantially the rules of the King's Bench and the Court of Chancery in England.

In April the Circuit Court for the District of New York, with Jay presiding, agreed unanimously to a protest against an act of Congress providing that applications for invalid pensions should be passed on by the judges of the Supreme Court in their respective circuits. The protest declared that Congress could not assign to the judiciary " any duties but such as are properly judicial, and to be performed in a judicial manner. That the duties assigned to the Circuit Courts by this act are not of that description, . . . inasmuch as it subjects the decisions of these courts, made pursuant to those duties, first to the consideration and suspension of the secretary at war, and then to the revision of the legislature; whereas, by the Constitution, neither the secretary at war, nor any other executive officer, nor even the legislature, are authorized to sit as a court of errors on the judicial acts or opinions of this court." [1] Accordingly when the question came before the court on a motion for a mandamus in Hayburn's Case, before a decision was given, the obnoxious act was repealed. Practically the court had declared for the first time an act of Congress unconstitutional.

On February 16, 1792, at a meeting of his friends in New York city, Jay was nominated for governor in opposition to Clinton, who had held that office continuously since June, 1777.[2] He

[1] 2 Dall. 410 note.   [2] *N. Y. Journal*, February 18, 1792.

accepted the nomination, stipulating, however, that he should not be required to take any active part in the campaign. " I made it a rule," he wrote to a friend, " neither to begin correspondence nor conversation upon the subject." The selection of the chief justice as a candidate, and his acceptance, the virulence of the election and its fraudulent conclusion, need a word of explanation ; more especially as those issues were now, for the first time, clearly defined, which a few years later were to give rise to the Republican party.

Before the Revolution the parties in the colonies were practically identical with the Whigs and Tories of the mother country, the Whigs or antiprerogative men supporting ever the cause of the people against arbitrary or illegal acts of the governor or the council. In the early days of the Revolution the ultra Tories were gradually driven into the ranks of the enemy, until for a time it might be said that all Revolutionary America had become Whig; the name Tory, however, was still applied to those who, though opposed to the usurpations of George III., were averse to a final separation from England. The victorious party in a civil war always divides at its close on the question of terms to the vanquished, and so far as concerned American politics the Revolution may be regarded as a civil war. In New York State, where the royalists had been the most united and the most irreconcilable, public feeling against them was intensely vindictive. To the majority of the

people the Revolution meant only the local revolution in the State, the guerrilla warfare in West
Chester County, the Indian raids on the border,
the enemy's occupation and abandonment of the
city; so the return of peace found them excited
by personal resentment, and eager for revenge.
There were few men, even in public life, who had
had experience outside of the State, and it was
chiefly those who had such experience, like Jay
and Hamilton, who could see the necessity of conciliation, the impolicy of alienating any citizens,
however mistaken, who had honestly preserved
their neutrality. Jay would exclude from the
country only those royalists who had shown themselves perfidious or cruel, and was indignant at the
violent acts of confiscation and disfranchisement
which the gust of popular hatred swept through
the legislature during the years immediately preceding and succeeding the treaty of peace. The
infamous Trespass Act, through the fearless oratory of Hamilton, was declared unconstitutional,
and one by one the other proscriptive acts were
repealed in spite of the constant opposition of
Clinton, the war governor of the State, that burly,
magnetic man, of north of Ireland stock, endowed
with all the stubborn prejudices of his race. Pro-
scription of the royalists sprang from unreflecting,
local, personal feelings; it was forbidden also by
the treaty of peace and the recommendation of
Congress. So the Whigs were already dividing
along lines of national and local politics.

The survival of pre-Revolutionary provincial modes of thought and feeling was, perhaps, the basis of anti-Federalism; and as the majority of the people were farmers, slow to change, little moved by argument, the State was naturally anti-Federalist, save so far as it was affected by the excitement and necessities of the Revolution, which made Federalists of the more thoughtful leaders of the war. In 1783 Clinton and his friends brought about the repeal of the act granting the duties of the port of New York to the United States, to be collected by federal officers; and they secured the appointment of the collectors by the State, an impracticable change which soon had to be amended. Before, then, the Federalist party, so called, existed, Clinton and his adherents were virtually anti-Federalists. In the Constitutional Convention two of the three New York delegates left the convention in accordance with the well-known views of the legislature, which desired only the amendment of the Articles of Confederation; and in the Constitutional Convention of the State, Clinton threw his great influence steadily against ratification, until longer resistance became impossible. To the generality of the people, for many years to come, no government seemed legal but the state government, and the Congress at Philadelphia loomed as remote and foreign as a Parliament at London. Of Congress no slander was too gross to be believed, and the cabinet of Washington was represented as "forging the chains of monarchy and

aristocracy." The assumption of state debts by
the national government was a clever device for
enslaving the people; the brilliant financiering of
Hamilton was part of the same dishonest scheme.
The year 1791 was summarized as "the reign of
speculators. A free gift of sixty per cent. added
to the capitals of speculators by means of the
Bank, and other governmental douceurs. Banks,
bubbles, tontines, lotteries, monopolies, usury, gam-
bling, swindling, etc., abound; poverty in the country; luxury in the capitals; corruption and usur-
pation in the national councils." [1] Year after year
was Clinton reëlected without serious opposition;
and in 1789 the Federalists dared attempt no more
than to divide the overwhelming majority by nominating Robert Yates, of the state Supreme Court,
himself an anti-Federalist. Such was the state of
affairs in New York when John Jay was nominated
for the governorship.

From regard to popular prejudice the campaign
was conducted by the Federalists with extraordinary caution. Apparently no appeal was made to
general principles; they simply argued that Clinton had been governor long enough, and urged the
value of Jay's services to the State and the nation.
It was admitted even by the governor's friends
that he had used the patronage of his office "to
strengthen his own popularity and to advance his
own views in regard to questions of public policy." [2] The Federalists, therefore, considered them-

---

[1] *N. Y. Journal*, July 4, 1792.
[2] Jenkins, *Governors of N. Y.* p. 61.

selves civil service reformers, but somewhat curiously contended that rotation in office was in itself desirable, as the best preservative of republicanism and the safeguard against undue influence; [1] while the anti-Federalists, unlike their modern representatives, sensibly replied that change of officers without cause was an absurdity.[2] Clinton, according to the Federalists, had been an admirable "military governor," but his special services had terminated with the war. Troubles with the Iroquois are threatening, was the reply, how can a man of peace deal with them? [3]

As election day drew near, it appeared that the industry of manufacturing what we call "campaign lies" was almost as active, and certainly as ingenious, then as now. The State owned vast tracts of public land towards the Canadian borders, and Clinton was accused of conniving at the sale of a single estate of nearly four million acres to Alexander McComb, with a view to connecting it with British territory. Against Jay stories were circulated equally absurd. New York was then a slaveholding State, and it was asserted that Jay proposed "to rob every Dutchman" of his slaves. Jay was, however, even on the question of slavery, no extremist. As a statesman he considered emancipation, like other political questions, a matter depending on practical rather than abstract considerations. "Every man, of every color and de-

[1] *N. Y. Journal*, March 7, 1792; *Ibid.*, March 24.
[2] *Ibid.*, February 29, 1792.
[3] *Ibid.*, March 7, 1792.

scription," he wrote to a friend, "has a natural right to freedom, and I shall ever acknowledge myself to be an advocate for the manumission of slaves in such a way as may be consistent with the justice due to them, with the justice due to their masters, and with the regard due to the actual state of society. These considerations unite in convincing me that the abolition of slavery must necessarily be gradual." [1] His enemies then published a statement that in conversation with certain gentlemen Jay had said: "There ought to be in America but two sorts of people, the one very rich and the other very poor." The gentlemen mentioned at once signed a card to the public contradicting the ridiculous slander; [2] but so long-lived was it, and so credulous were the people of that day, that it was repeated and had to be again contradicted with affidavits three years later. To the mortification of Jay, his old friend, Chancellor Livingston, and others of his wife's relatives, now deserted the President's party, by reason of some fancied neglect, as it was believed, in the matter of appointments; and the chancellor's enthusiastic zeal of a new convert was skillfully fanned by the publication of satirical letters attributed to Jay. This insinuation was also met by a prompt denial signed by Jay himself. [3]

To the people, Jay and Clinton were sedulously represented as the aristocrat and the republican;

---

[1] February 27, 1792, Jay's *Jay*, i. 285.
[2] April 5, 1792, *Jay MSS.*   [3] Jay's *Jay*, i. 286.

Jay as accustomed to draw a large salary in the "luxury of splendid courts," and now supported by the "powerful landed interest" of the Van Rensselaers, while Clinton was the hardy son of toil. It was said that Jay was the nominee of the President and the secretary of the treasury, and that all the influence of the government was for him. "Do you not tremble for the independence of the State?"[1] "We are rich," thundered "Cato," "our coffers full, while those of the Union are empty, and by no means equal to the exigencies of government. I should not wonder at a proposition from the secretary of the treasury to take on loan at ten per cent. from this State all the unappropriated money in it. . . . Could Mr. Jay discountenance this, as coming from the government, which has been his friend and support?"[2] State love was appealed to by "Cincinnatus," even from another side, to keep Jay where he was: "It is of some importance to have a citizen of your State at the head of the judiciary of the United States."[3]

So the battle raged, but at the election it was soon discovered that the votes for Jay outnumbered those for Clinton. But a returning board, a joint committee of the legislature of whom the majority were Clintonians, found the returns from three counties, which notoriously had gone Federalist, were technically defective. The law provided

[1] *N. Y. Journal*, March 24, 1792.
[2] *Ibid.*, March 31, 1792.   [3] *Ibid.*, April 18, 1792.

that the votes of each town should be transmitted in sealed boxes by the respective county sheriffs to the secretary of state. But the ballots of Otsego County had been delivered by the ex-sheriff, whose term had just expired, the new sheriff not having qualified. Those of Tioga were given by the sheriff to a special deputy, who was taken sick on the road and sent them on by his clerk; and those of Clinton were delivered by the sheriff to one who had no written deputation, but who returned them personally.[1] Aaron Burr and Rufus King were asked for legal opinions; King, the Federalist, advised that the returns from all three counties were legal; Burr, the Republican, held that all were illegal, — a conclusion which he reached, as he said, "not without sensible regret, as no suspicion was entertained of the fairness of these elections."[2] It was generally believed that the Federalist majority in Otsego County alone was sufficient to elect Jay; and on general principles, as the ballots had been delivered to the ex-sheriff by the inspectors before the arrival of his successor,[3] and there was no other acting sheriff in the county on election day, his transfer of the ballots was undoubtedly legal; otherwise the people were disfranchised absolutely without any fault of their own.[4] The Constitution

[1] Davis, *Life of Burr*, i. 333.

[2] *Ibid.* i. 347.

[3] *N. Y. Journal*, July 18, 1792, quoting Smith's own statements in the *Albany Gazette*; *N. Y. Journal*, December 5, testimony of the clerk of Otsego.

[4] Hammond, *Pol. Hist. of N. Y.* i. 62–67.

provided for the annual appointment of sheriffs, but as the Council of Appointment met only when summoned by the governor, it was customary for the sheriffs to hold over till the qualification of their successors. Seventy such instances had occurred since 1777; in one case an ex-sheriff had executed a criminal,[1] and their returns of votes as such had never before been seriously questioned. When it is remembered that the inspectors were required to deliver the ballots to the sheriff without delay, the unsoundness of Burr's decision becomes still more clear. Van Rensselaer, a member of the council, was said to have urged the governor early in the year to appoint a new sheriff in Otsego, and the governor had replied that it was unnecessary to do so, since the old one could hold over. Therefore, however " Brutus " and " Julius Cæsar " might argue it out in the newspapers, the decision of the council was a foregone conclusion, even before June 12, when they announced by a party vote of seven to four the election of Clinton, and ordered the ballots to be burnt, though the custom had always been to preserve them in the office of the secretary of state.[2]

Jay, meanwhile, was leisurely riding his circuit, apparently indifferent to politics. " I learn," he writes to his wife from New Haven, " that we shall have much business to do here, there being about forty actions. . . . On the road I met Mr. Soder-

[1] Jay's *Jay*, i. 288.
[2] *N. Y. Journal*, August 22, 1792.

sheim. . . . He told me Mr. McComb [the unpopular grantee of the McComb patent] was in gaol, and that certain others had ceased to be rich. . . . Mrs. McComb must be greatly distressed. Your friendly attentions to her would be grateful and proper." [1] Once Mrs. Jay made some remark about his having no further use for his official robe as chief justice, — that robe presumably with salmon-colored facings whose origin has excited so much speculation, perhaps a robe he had received as Doctor of Laws, and had adapted to the new purpose. "My robe," he replied, "may become useless or it may not. I am resigned to either event. He who governs all makes no mistakes, and a firm belief of this would save us from many." [2] On the day of the final decision, "People are running in continually," wrote Mrs. Jay, "to vent their vexation. Poor Jacob Morris looks quite disconsolate. King says he thinks Clinton as lawfully governor of Connecticut as of New York, but he knows of no redress." [3] "The reflection that the majority of electors were for me is a pleasing one," was Jay's philosophical answer from Hartford; "that injustice has taken place does not surprise me, and I hope will not affect you very sensibly. The intelligence found me perfectly prepared for it. . . . A few years more will put us all in the dust, and it will then be of more importance to me

[1] To Mrs. Jay, April 24, 1792, *Jay MSS.*
[2] Jay's *Jay*, i. 287.
[3] From Mrs. Jay, June 12, 1792, *Jay MSS.*

to have governed myself, than to have governed the State." [1]

From Vermont the chief justice returned home by way of Albany. As he drew near Lansingburgh, on June 30, the people met him and escorted him to the village, where a committee delivered an address, declaring that : " Though abuse of power may for a time deprive you and the citizens of their right, we trust the sacred flame of liberty is not so far extinguished in the bosoms of Americans as tamely to submit to the shackles of slavery, without at least a struggle to shake them off." [2] Public dinners, addresses, and salvos of artillery were repeated at Albany and Hudson ; and eight miles from New York a body of citizens had assembled and escorted him to his house, and another address followed from a committee of the Sons of Liberty. His answer was eminently conciliatory and conservative : " They who do what they have a right to do, give no just cause of offense; and, therefore, every consideration of propriety forbids that difference of opinion respecting candidates should suspend or interrupt the mutual good-humor and benevolence which harmonize society, and soften the asperities of human life." [3] As the people of Otsego were threatening to march to New York, and there was some actual apprehension of " an appeal to arms," [4] the intensity of public feeling may be imagined. The significance

---

[1] Jay's *Jay*, i. 289.　　[2] *Ibid.* i. 200, 201.
[3] *Ibid.* i. 293.　　[4] *N. Y. Journal*, July 13, 1792.

of these events as regards Jay is, that for the
time the political outrage united the Federalists
and the extreme anti-Federalists, who, before all
things, were lovers of liberty; and so made his
renomination and election sure, in spite of his
opinions. On July 14 the anniversary of the destruction of the Bastille was celebrated by the
Republicans " with nearly the same ardor and sincerity throughout the United States as the 4th." [1]
On that day at a large dinner in New York city
Jay gave the toast: "May the people always respect themselves, and remember what they owe
to posterity;" and after he retired the company
drank: " John Jay, governor by the voice of the
people."   Also among the toasts at Mechanics'
Hall, on the Fourth of July, were these two, in
curious juxtaposition: " The French Revolution,"
and " The Governor (of right) of the State of New
York." [2]

In the United States Supreme Court the question of the conflicting sovereignties of the States
and the nation was gradually brought to an issue.
Several suits were brought by individual States
against citizens of other States, and by individual
citizens against States, but the great question of
the suability of a State remained unargued till
the case of Chisolm, Executor, v. The State of
Georgia came to a hearing.[3]   The State refused
to appear except to demur to the jurisdiction of

[1] *N. Y. Journal*, July 21, 1792.
[2] *Ibid.*, July 14, 1792.   [3] 2 Dall. p. 415.

the court. The chief justice in his opinion, which was in writing, began by asserting that the States had never possessed an independent sovereignty. Before the Revolution "all the people of the country were subjects to the king of Great Britain. . . . They were in strict sense fellow subjects, and in a variety of respects one people." In the establishment of the Constitution " we see the people acting as sovereigns of the whole country; and, in the language of sovereignty, establishing a constitution by which it was their will that the state governments should be bound, and to which the state constitutions should be made to conform. . . . The sovereignty of the nation is in the people of the nation, and the residuary sovereignty of each State is in the people of each State." As one State may sue another State, "suability and state sovereignty are not incompatible." Cases "in which a State shall be a party" are by the Constitution within the jurisdiction of the Supreme Court. "Did it mean here party plaintiff? If that *only* were meant, it would have been easy to find words to express it." The court accordingly gave judgment against the State by default. The legislature of Georgia passed acts condemning to death any one who should attempt to serve the process of execution. But judgment was never executed, for the next year an amendment to the Constitution was passed to counteract the effect of the decision. Jay's logic, however, remained uncontroverted. It established the court as the

supreme interpreter of the Constitution, and his
words were long cited as disproving the extreme
theory of state rights. The importance of the
decision is shown by the fact that it was thought
necessary to argue that it was of no authority " to
determine the political duty of the citizen in a
crisis like that of 1861." [1] It laid down the lines,
indeed, that Marshall followed, in his famous series
of federal decisions, culminating in McCulloch v.
Maryland: " The government proceeds directly
from the people, is ordained and established in the
name of the people." [2] " After this clear and
authoritative declaration of national supremacy,"
said Judge Cooley, " the power of a court to summon a State before it, at the suit of an individual,
might be taken away by the amendment of the
Constitution — as was in fact done — without im-
pairing the general symmetry of the federal struc-
ture, or inflicting upon it any irremediable injury.
. . . The Union could scarcely have had a valuable
existence had it been judicially determined that
powers of sovereignty were exclusively in the States
or in the people of the States severally. . . .
The doctrine of an indissoluble Union, though not
in terms declared, is nevertheless in its elements at
least contained in the decision. The qualified sovereignty, national and State, the subordination of
State to nation, the position of the citizen as at
once a necessary component part of the federal

[1] Hurd, *Theory of our National Existence*, p. 131.
[2] 4 Wheat. p. 316.

and of the state system, are all exhibited. It must logically follow that a nation, as a sovereignty, is possessed of all those powers of independent action and self-protection, which the successors of Jay subsequently demonstrated were by implication conferred upon it." [1]

In the spring of 1793, before Chief Justice Jay and Judges Griffin and Iredell, at Richmond, Patrick Henry made his famous argument in the second trial of Ware's Executors *v.* Hylton, on the question whether British creditors could recover against Virginia debtors by virtue of the treaty of peace, in spite of an act of Virginia to the contrary. Jay told Iredell that Patrick Henry, as he stood there an old decrepit man, was " the greatest of orators." As he spoke " the color began to come and go in the face of the chief justice, while Iredell sat with his mouth and eyes stretched open, in perfect wonder." [2] At the final decision Jay was not present, though doubtless he would have concurred in the judgment of the court in favor of the creditors.

The news of the capture of the Bastille was printed in the papers on the same day as Washington's cabinet nominations, and by this time the eyes of all the world were fixed on the rapidly culminating scenes of the French Revolution. The anti-Federalists, or Republicans, who, in their op-

[1] *Constitutional History of the United States, as seen in the Development of American Law*, 1889, p. 49.

[2] *Historical Mag.*, November, 1873, p. 275.

position to a centralized government, had fallen
back on doctrines of state rights, and finally on the
new theories of the rights of man, were in full
sympathy with the Paris mob, and were forming
throughout the land Democratic clubs, on the
model of the notorious Jacobin Club. The report
that a minister was on his way from France made
it necessary for the government to define its position towards the new republic. "The king has
been decapitated," wrote Hamilton to Jay. "Out
of this will arise a regent, acknowledged and supported by the powers of Europe almost universally;
in capacity to act, and who may himself send an
ambassador to the United States. Should we in
such case receive both? If we receive one from
the republic and refuse the other, shall we stand
on ground perfectly neutral?" And the same day
he wrote again: "Would not a proclamation prohibiting our citizens from taking commissions on
either side be proper? Would it not be well that
it should include a *declaration of neutrality?* If
you think the measure prudent, could you draft such
a thing as you would deem proper? I wish much
you would."[1] Two days later Jay answered the
question about receiving a minister concisely but
in conformity with modern international usage: "I
would not receive any minister from a regent until
he was regent *de facto;*" and he inclosed a draft of
a proclamation. "It is hastily drawn," he added;
"it says nothing about treaties; it speaks of neu-

[1] April 19, 1793, Jay's *Jay*, i. 298, 300.

trality, but avoids the expression, because in this country often associated with others."[1] This was, apparently, the first draft of the still more concise proclamation issued by Washington on April 22, which also avoided using the word "neutrality." "The murmurs and disgust which this measure occasioned," it has been well said, "evinced its necessity and wisdom." The reason for not using the word "neutrality" was, probably, because at that time it was popularly taken to mean "non-intercourse," and so would have caused confusion.[2]

"The duty and interest of the United States," ran the President's proclamation, "require that they should, with sincerity and good faith, adopt and pursue a conduct friendly and impartial towards the belligerent powers. I have, therefore, thought fit . . . to exhort and warn the citizens of the United States carefully to avoid all acts and proceedings whatsoever, which may in any manner tend to contravene such disposition." Very necessary was such a declaration when the friends of France were doing everything that private citizens could do to involve the country in the European war, in which they could see nothing but a coalition of despotisms against republicanism. Events moved rapidly. Genet, the French minister, arrived at Charleston on April 8, and at once began to compromise the neutrality of the country by distributing naval and military commissions, fitting

[1] To Alex. Hamilton, April 11, 1793, Jay's *Jay*, i. 300.
[2] *Historical Mag.*, February, 1871, p. 129, and Ap. p. 137 n.

out privateers in American ports, and organizing
courts of admiralty under the various French consuls for the condemnation of prizes. " The minister
of France," said a Philadelphia newspaper, supposed to be the organ of Jefferson, " the minister
of France, I hope, will act with firmness and spirit.
The *people* are his friends, or the friends of France,
and he will have nothing to apprehend, for, *as
yet*, the people are the sovereign of the United
States." [1] Emboldened by his enthusiastic reception, the minister used language of the gravest in-
discretion; especially on one occasion, when the
government, relying on his word, tried in vain to
prevent the sailing of a privateer. Jay and Rufus
King then thought it necessary to publish their testimony to his words: " A report having reached
this city [New York] from Philadelphia, that Mr.
Genet, the French minister, had said he would
appeal to the people from certain decisions of the
President, we were asked on our return from that
place whether he had made such a declaration; we
answered that *he had*, and we also mentioned it
to others, authorizing them to say that we had so
informed them." [2] This statement provoked the
unmeasured indignation of the Republican press:
" Is the President," asked one paper, " a consecrated
character, that an appeal from his decisions must
be considered criminal? Or are the people in such
a state of degradation, that to speak of consulting
them is an offense as great as if America groaned

[1] Jay's *Jay*, i. 303.   [2] *Ibid*. i. 304.

under a dominion equally tyrannical with the old monarchy of France?"[1]

Washington's proclamation would have been a dead letter, signifying nothing, unless its principles had been sustained by the courts. It fell to Jay to place it upon a legal basis, and to establish what Sir Henry Maine recently asserted to be the distinctively American doctrine: that "international has precedence both of federal and of municipal law, unless in the exceptional case where federal law has deliberately departed from it."[2] In his charge to the grand jury at Richmond, Virginia, May 22, 1793, the chief justice said: "You will recollect that the laws of nations make part of the laws of this and of every other civilized nation. They consist of those rules for regulating the conduct of nations towards each other, which, resulting from right reason, receive their obligations from that principle and from general assent and practice. To this head also belong those rules or laws which, by agreement, become established between nations. . . . We are now a nation, and it equally becomes us to perform our duties as to assert our rights;" and he concluded accordingly that "the United States are in a state of neutrality relative to all the powers at war; . . . that, therefore, they who commit, aid, or abet hostilities against those powers, or either of them, offend against the laws of the United States, and ought to be punished."

[1] Jay's *Jay*, i. 305.   [2] Maine, *International Law*, p. 37.

In accordance with this charge, one Gideon
Henfield, a citizen of the United States, who had
served as officer on a French privateer which
brought a British vessel as a prize into Philadelphia, was indicted, though no jury could be found
to convict him. The importance of the charge,
however, lay in the fact that, independent of statutes, and in the face of violent popular prejudice,
it declared violations of neutrality to be criminally
indictable at common law, and that, with singular
prescience, it defined the duties of neutrals in almost the exact words of the rules which, by desire
of the United States, were afterwards included in
the treaty of Washington. The proclamation of
the President was implicitly held to be simply
declaratory of existing law. This position was
sound, though criminal jurisdiction was assumed
by the Supreme Court at that time rather of necessity than of right; but it was a position which
no one would dare to take without a confident
knowledge of legal principles. International law
is part of the common law;[1] by international law
neutrality is presumed to exist till a tacit or public
declaration of war; and a neutral, except so far
as stipulated by treaty, must grant aid, neither by
arms nor men, to a belligerent.[2] By the treaty
with France no such stipulation is expressed, as
even Jefferson notified Morris at Paris.[3] Finally,

---

[1] Kent, *Commentaries*, 13th ed. i. 1, note *a*.

[2] Levi, *International Law*, p. 294.

[3] August 6, 1793, Waite, *State Papers*, i. 140.

in becoming a nation, the United States became amenable " to that system of rules which reason, morality, and custom had established among the civilized nations of Europe as their public law; " [1] these words of Chancellor Kent, which open his "Commentaries," are little else than a condensation of Jay's charge at Richmond. To a certain extent, the policy then laid down for the United States was a departure from that adopted in the treaties made during the Revolution, which contemplated an active neutrality, so to speak, on behalf of the favored nation when at war. Such a policy, if continued, might, indeed must, have involved the country in European quarrels with which it had no concern. In the civil war the Alabama taught us the practical distinction between active and real neutrality; and the wisdom of Washington and Jay was never more clearly vindicated than by their most virulent critic of recent days, who declared that " France was the first victim, and Poland, and Ireland, and Hungary followed, in the sad procession." [2] The charge was printed by the government for distribution abroad, in order to explain its position; while the Democrats, with at least unconscious misapprehension, demanded loudly, " What law had been offended, and under what was the indictment supported? . . . Were they to be punished for violating a proclamation which had not been published when the offense

[1] Kent, *Commentaries*, i. 1.
[2] Dawson, *Hist. Mag.*, February, 1871, p. 139.

was committed, if, indeed, it could be termed an offense to engage with France, combating for liberty against the combined despots of Europe?"[1]

Similarly, when the case of the sloop Betsey came up for decision, in which the owners, Swedish neutrals, claimed restitution in the District Court after the vessel had been condemned by a French prize court, the chief justice held, "that no foreign power can of right institute, or erect, any court of judicature of any kind within the jurisdiction of the United States, but such only as may be . . . in pursuance of treaties. It is therefore decreed and adjudged that the admiralty jurisdiction, which has been exercised in the United States by the consuls of France, not being so warranted, is not of right."[2]

This April session was the last which Jay attended as chief justice, though it was not till 1795 that he resigned. The causes brought before him were, perhaps, not of a character fully to test his professional ability, though Wharton speaks of his "sound, wary, experienced judgment,"[3] and Story describes him as "equally distinguished as a Revolutionary statesman and a general jurist."[4] So far, however, as circumstances permitted, no opportunity was lost of establishing the authority of the court, and promoting the welfare of the country.

[1] Marshall, *Life of Washington*, ii. 273, 274.
[2] Glass *et al. v.* The Sloop Betsey *et al.* 3 Dall. pp. 6–15.
[3] Wharton, *State Trials*, p. 88.
[4] Story, *Comm. on the Constitution*, i. § 216.

CHAPTER XI

THE daily increasing "love-frenzy for France," and the intemperate language of the Democratic press, naturally emphasized in England that reaction against America which set in with the treaty of peace. On the other hand, the retention of the frontier posts in violation of that treaty was a thorn in the side of the young republic. In the course of the war England had adopted, by successive Orders in Council, a policy ruinous to the commerce of neutral nations, especially of the United States. In the admiralty courts of the various British West India islands hundreds of ships from New England were seized and condemned for carrying French produce or bearing cargoes of provisions chartered to French ports. The New England fishermen and shipowners were vociferous for war, and the Democratic clubs denounced every British insult and celebrated every French victory. On March 26, 1794, an embargo against British ships was proclaimed for thirty days, and then extended for thirty days longer. The day after

the embargo was laid, Dayton of New Jersey
moved in Congress to sequestrate all moneys due
to British creditors, and apply it towards indemni-
fying shipowners for losses incurred through the
Orders in Council; and on April 21 the Republicans moved a resolution to suspend all commercial
intercourse with Great Britain till the western
posts should be given up, and indemnity be paid
for injuries to American commerce in violation of
the rights of neutrals.

The passage of such an act meant war; and for
war the United States was never more unprepared.
The resources of the people had been taxed in recov-
ering from the ruin brought by the Revolution and
in organizing a government. In spite of Jay's recommendation the Confederation had left the country without a navy, and there was no army. The
veterans of the Revolution in their eastern homes,
or in the near western colonies had been pauper-
ized by the depreciation of the currency, and were
among the discontented rioters who rebelled under
Shays in Massachusetts, and had threatened Congress at Philadelphia. Jealousy of military influence had prevented their organization into anything
like the nucleus of an army, and jealousy of federal
power had retarded the formation of a new one.
The union of the States was too new to bear the
strain of a war which to half the people would be
repugnant, and the burden of which would fall
chiefly on a few States. One policy only was open
to a wise government, and that was the policy of

Washington : " Peace," he declared, " ought to be pursued with unremitted zeal before the last resource, which has so often been the scourge of nations, and cannot fail to check the advancing prosperity of the United States, is contemplated."[1]

Peace could be secured only by immediate negotiation and at least a temporary settlement of the causes of mutual irritation, and for such a task the ministers at London and Washington were incompetent or unsuited. Mr. Pinckney, the American minister at London, was, according to John Adams, a man of prejudices and strongly pro-Gallican ; while Hammond, the English minister at Washington, had little prudence or moderation.[2] In this crisis Washington decided to send to England a special envoy. Hamilton was his first choice, but Hamilton had excited bitter enmities ; Monroe warned the President against his nomination so soon as it was suggested, and it would doubtless have failed of confirmation by the Senate.[3] Hamilton then himself proposed the name of Jay : " Of the persons whom you would deem free from any constitutional objections, Mr. Jay is the only man in whose qualifications for success there would be thorough confidence, and him alone it would be advisable to send."[4] Two days later Jay was nomi-

---

[1] *Writings of Washington*, x. 404.

[2] To Christopher Gore, March 5, 1794, *Works of Fisher Ames*, i. 137.

[3] Madison's *Works*, ii. 11.

[4] To Washington, April 14, 1794, Hamilton's *Works*, iv. 536.

nated, and after three days of violent debate was confirmed by the Senate. " You cannot imagine," wrote Adams to his wife the day of the final vote, " what horror some persons are in, lest peace should continue. The prospect of peace throws them into distress. . . . The opposition to Mr. Jay has been quickened by motives which always influence everything in an elective government. . . . If Jay should succeed, it will recommend him to the choice of the people for president, as soon as a vacancy shall happen. This will weaken the hopes of the Southern States for Jefferson. This I believe to be the secret motive of the opposition to him, though other things were alleged as ostensible reasons; such as his monarchical principles, his indifference about the navigation of the Mississippi, his attachment to England, his aversion to France, none of which are well founded, and his holding the office of chief justice." [1]

This month Jay was holding court in Philadelphia. On April 9 he wrote to his wife : " Yesterday I dined with the President. The question of war or peace seems to be as much in suspense here as in New York when I left you."[2] The next day he wrote again : " Peace or war appears to me a question which cannot be solved. Unless things should take a turn in the mean time, I think it will be best on my return to push our affairs at Bedford briskly [where he proposed

[1] To Mrs. Adams, April 19, 1794, Adams's *Letters*, ii. 156.
[2] *Jay MSS.*

building a country-house]. There is much irritation and agitation in this town and in Congress.
Great Britain has acted unwisely and unjustly,
and there is some danger of our acting intemper-
ately." [1] When he heard that he might be sent to
England, the question presented itself to Jay's
conscientious mind merely as one of duty. He
was not for a moment misled as to the effect which
his mission, however successful diplomatically, was
almost sure to have on his reputation. The learned
Dr. Carnahan, who became president of Princeton
College in 1823, in his lectures on moral philosophy used to quote a conversation between Jay and
some friends at this time that was told him by an
ear-witness, as a striking instance of courageous
patriotism: "Before the appointment was made,
the subject was spoken of in the presence of Jay,
and Jay remarked that such were the prejudices of
the American people, that no man could form a
treaty with Great Britain, however advantageous
it might be to the country, who would not by his
agency render himself so unpopular and odious as
to blast all hope of political preferment. It was
suggested to Mr. Jay that he was the person to
whom this odious office was likely to be offered.
'Well,' replied Mr. Jay, 'if Washington shall
think fit to call me to perform this service, I will
go and perform it to the best of my abilities, fore-
seeing as I do the consequences to my personal
popularity. The good of my country I believe

[1] *Jay MSS.*

demands the sacrifice, and I am ready to make it.'" [1] In a similar spirit he wrote to his wife April 15: "The object is so interesting to our country, and the combination of circumstances such, that I find myself in a dilemma between personal and public considerations." And again: "Nothing can be more distant from every wish on my own account. . . . This is not of my seeking; on the contrary I regard it as a measure not to be desired, but to be submitted to." [2] His acceptance he explained a few days later: "No appointment ever operated more unpleasantly upon me; but the public considerations which were urged, and the manner in which it was pressed, strongly impressed me with a conviction that to refuse it would be to desert my duty for the sake of my ease and domestic concerns and comforts." [3]

On May 12 Jay set sail in the ship Ohio, with his son Peter Augustus, and with John Trumbull as secretary. On June 8 he landed at Falmouth. At the moment of his departure the New York Society, in an address to the people, began to fan the embers of that partisan virulence which was to flame into frenzy on his return. "We most firmly believe," it ran, "that he who is an enemy to the French Revolution cannot be a firm republican,

[1] Extract from Lecture VII., communicated from the original MSS. by the kindness of Mr. McDonald, a grandson of Dr. Carnahan.

[2] Jay's *Jay*, i. 310.

[3] To Mrs. Jay, April 19, Jay's *Jay*, i. 311.

and, therefore, though he may be a good citizen in other respects, ought not to be intrusted with the guidance of any part of the machine of government."

"The passage across the Atlantic was pleasant," wrote Trumbull in his "Autobiography," "and on the 1st of June we must have been near, almost within hearing, of the decisive naval battle which was fought on that day, between the British and the French fleet; for on our arrival at Falmouth, a few days after, we found there a sloop of war just arrived with dispatches from Lord Howe, . . . and we met the note of triumph at Bath, on our way to London."[1]   There, soon after his arrival, Jay was introduced to the cabinet ministers at dinner at Lord Grenville's, and a few days later he dined with Lord Chancellor Loughborough and Pitt.[2]

The complaints to be adjusted between the two countries were numerous and complicated.   Great Britain, on the one hand, had retained the western military posts in violation of the treaty of peace, and had made no compensation for the negro slaves carried away by her officers; on the other hand, several of the States had prevented the collection of debts to English merchants contracted before the Revolution.   The boundaries of the United States on the west and northeast were unsettled. Great Britain, finally, complained of damage to her commerce by French privateers fitted out in Amer-

[1] *Autobiography of John Trumbull*, p. 174.
[2] To Alex. Hamilton, July 11, Jay's *Jay*, ii. 228.

ican ports; while the United States complained of
similar damage through irregular captures by British cruisers. To avoid interminable discussion and
hasten an accommodation, Jay, at his first meeting with Lord Grenville, the secretary for foreign
affairs, suggested that they should at first avoid
written communications, and merely meet and con-
verse informally, "until there should appear a
probability of coming to some amicable mutual
understanding;" that they should then exchange
preliminary papers, which still should not be binding, and that in all this they should not employ
secretaries or copyists, in order to escape the influence of public opinion and national feeling as
much as possible. They should always bear in
mind, said Jay, "that this was not a trial of diplomatic fencing, but a solemn question of peace or
war between two peoples, in whose veins flowed
the blood of a common ancestry, and on whose continued good understanding might perhaps depend
the future freedom and happiness of the human
race." On this broad statesmanlike basis was the
negotiation conducted, and the secretaries had a
holiday till the treaty was almost ready for signing.[1] "I will endeavor to accommodate rather
than dispute," were Jay's words to Hamilton.[2]

On August 5 Jay was able to write to Washington: "Our prospects become more and more promising as we advance in the business. . . . A

[1] *Autobiography of John Trumbull*, pp. 176, 177.
[2] July 11, 1794, Jay's *Jay*, ii. 228.

treaty of commerce is on the carpet. . . . The king observed to me the other day, 'Well, sir, I imagine you begin to see that your mission will probably be successful.' 'I am happy, may it please your majesty, to find that you entertain that idea.' 'Well, but don't you perceive that it is like to be so?' 'There are some recent circumstances (the answer to my representation, etc.), which induce me to flatter myself that it will be so.' He nodded with a smile, signifying that it was to those circumstances that he alluded." [1] "If I should be able to conclude the business on admissible terms," Jay wrote to Hamilton, the next month, "I shall do it and risque consequences, rather than, by the delay of waiting for . . . opinions and instructions, hazard a change in the disposition of this court." [2]

On November 19 the treaty was signed: "Further concessions on the part of Great Britain," wrote Jay to Oliver Ellsworth on the same day, "cannot in my opinion be obtained. . . . The minister flatters himself that this treaty will be very acceptable to our country, and that some of the articles in it will be received as unequivocal proofs of good-will. We have industriously united our efforts to remove difficulties, and few men would have persevered in such a dry, perplexing business, with so much patience and temper as he has done." [3] A copy of the treaty was at once dis-

---

[1] Jay's *Jay*, ii. 220.
[2] To Alex. Hamilton, September 11, 1794, *Jay MSS*.
[3] Jay's *Jay*, ii. 235.

patched to Congress by an American sea captain
then in London, David Blaney; but wind and
wave delayed its arrival till the session was over.
" The winds blue continually from the westward,"
is Blaney's own account of the voyage, " from the
time the ship left England until we came on the
course of America. . . . I took a small flask of
rum " [an item, by the way, that the secretary of
the treasury wished afterwards to have explained],
" to encourage the sailors to keep a better watch,
and pay attention to the ship, and promised them
all small rewards if the ship arrived at such a
time; but we could not alter the contrary winds.
. . . I mentioned to you . . . the French cruser
boarding us, and making mention of the treaty
signed by you, he serch'd every part of the ship;
but such care was taken of the treaty it was impossible for it to have been discovered. . . . I landed
at Norfolk at ten o'clock at night, hired horses,
and made all the despatch I could to reach Philadelphia; my first horse founder'd after getting to
Richmond, which I did in one day and part the
night. . . . In seven days from the time I landed
in Norfolk I delivered the despatches to E. Randolph, Esq.; when I reach'd Philadelphia my hand
as well as feet was fros'd. . . . Unfortunately the
Senate had rose as well as Congress three days before I reach'd the Capital." [1]

The main points that Jay had been instructed
to gain were compensation for negroes, surrender

[1] From David Blaney, September 20, 1795, *Jay MSS.*

of the posts, and compensation for spoliations ; in addition, a commercial treaty was desired. When secretary for foreign affairs, Jay had argued that the negroes, some three thousand in number, who, at the time of the evacuation, were within the British lines, relying on proclamations that offered freedom, and who followed the troops to England, came within that clause of the treaty of peace which provided that the army should be withdrawn without " carrying away any negroes or other property."[1] Lord Grenville, however, insisted upon refusing any compensation. Once within the British lines, he said, slaves were free for good and all, and could no longer be regarded as property for which compensation could be claimed ; and these reasons must have appealed strongly to Jay's anti-slavery convictions. From any point of view the matter was too insignificant to wreck the treaty upon it, and Jay waived the claim.

As to the western posts, it was agreed that they should be surrendered by June 12, 1796. But compensation for the detention was denied on the ground that it was due to the breach of the treaty by the United States in permitting the States to prevent the recovery of British debts.

Where the collection of such *bona fide* debts incurred before the Revolution had been barred, or their value impaired by " legal impediments " since the peace, it was provided that " full and complete compensation " should be made by the

[1] *Secret Journals*, iv. 185-287.

United States, to be ascertained by a board of
five commissioners to meet, first, at Philadelphia.
Similarly, the British government agreed to make
"full and complete compensation" to American
citizens for losses sustained "by reason of irregular
or illegal captures or condemnations under color
of authority or commissions from his majesty,"
wherever "adequate compensation" cannot be had
at law, the damages to be ascertained by a board
of five commissioners to sit at London. These
claims should be decided "according to the merits
of the several cases, and to justice, equity, and the
law of nations." The same commissioners were
also to pass on claims of British subjects for losses
by captures within the jurisdiction of the United
States, which agreed to make compensation accordingly.

It must have been a delicate matter to obtain
such a concession from Great Britain, for it practically amounted to an admission that the Orders
in Council were in violation of neutrality, irregular and illegal, though the language was skillfully
adapted to avoid wounding English susceptibilities.
Under this clause American merchants received
$10,345,000. Jay wrote to Pickering: "Perfect
justice to all parties is the object of both the
articles (vi., vii.), and the commissioners are empowered to do it, in terms as explicit and compre-
prehensive as the English language affords."[1]

The disputed questions of boundaries, arising

[1] October 14, 1795, *Jay MSS.*

from the construction of the treaty of peace, were referred to joint commissioners: properly enough, as the confusion was due to ignorance of the geography of the Northwest.

British and American citizens holding lands at the time respectively in the United States and in any of the possessions of Great Britain were secured in their rights; a clause much objected to in America, but which was obviously just. A still more important provision followed, a novelty in international diplomacy, and a distinct advance in civilization: that war between the two countries should never be made the pretext for confiscation of debts or annulment of contracts between individuals. In the war of 1812 the United States happened for the moment to be the creditor nation, and the millions which this provision saved to her citizens it would be difficult to estimate.

"The commercial part of the treaty," wrote Jay to Washington, "may be terminated at the expiration of two years after the war, and in the mean time a state of things more auspicious to negotiation will probably arise, especially if the next session of Congress should not interpose fresh obstacles."[1] It was the commercial articles which excited the most intense hostility in America, and one article was very properly rejected. But it was apparently conveniently forgotten at the time, that there was then no treaty of commerce at all with England; that England, according to the economi-

[1] September 3, 1795, *Jay MSS.*

cal notions of the day, had little to gain and much
to lose by any such treaty; and that what privileges
she did allow were, as Lord Grenville may well
have thought, practically gratuitous. As it was,
reciprocal freedom of commerce was established
between the United States on the one side and
British North America and Great Britain on the
other; American vessels were admitted to trade
between American ports and the East Indies, with
certain restrictions as to exportation in time of
war; and American vessels of not over seventy
tons' burden were admitted to carry to the British
West Indies goods of American growth or man-
ufacture, and to export to American ports only
West Indian products, on condition that "the
United States will prohibit and restrain the carrying away any molasses, sugar, coffee, cocoa, or cotton, in American vessels, either from his majesty's
islands or the United States to any part of the
world except the United States, reasonable sea-
stores excepted." It was this latter clause that
was so bitterly condemned. The explanation of it,
however, is clear. The particular articles mentioned were supposed to be peculiarly the products
of the West Indies, and it was unsuspected by Jay
that cotton was to be one of the great staples of
export from this country. Such lack of foresight
was not surprising, since, only the previous year,
1794, when an American ship entered Liverpool
with eight bags of cotton fibre as part of her cargo,
it was confiscated as an unlawful importation, "on

the assumption that so large a quantity could not have been the produce of the United States." [1] Moreover, it seems that it was but a few years earlier that the cultivation of cotton had been attempted at all, for "a member from South Carolina observed, in the House of Representatives in '89, that the people of the Southern States intended to cultivate cotton, and 'if good seed could be procured, he believed they might succeed.'" [2]

The remaining articles of the treaty dealt with the conduct to be observed by either nation when the other was at war. It was agreed that when a neutral vessel was captured on suspicion of carrying enemy's goods, it should be tried speedily at the nearest port, and only the enemy's goods should be confiscated. "Contraband" was defined. Privateers were required to give security not to injure the commerce of the neutral. Acts of reprisal for alleged injuries should not be permitted until complaint made and compensation refused. Mutual efforts should be made to abolish piracy. Against this final series of articles the two chief objections urged were, that they implied that the flag does not cover enemy's goods, and that provisions might become contraband. But both these positions were part of the international law of the time. As to enemy's goods, the law as stated was: "Les marchandizes neutres chargées par l'enemie sont libres; mais le pavillion neutre

[1] *The First Century of the Republic*, New York, 1876, p. 163.
[2] *Diplomacy of the U. S.* p. 220.

ne neutralize pas la marchandize enemie." [1]   And
as to provisions, the clause in the treaty that concerned them was, that whenever any doubtful articles, " which had become contraband under the
existing law of nations," should be seized, the neutral owners should receive full compensation.   The
principle then maintained by England and denied
by the United States, that in certain cases — for
instance, of imperfect blockade — provisions became contraband, has since been generally abandoned even by England.   But as late as the recent
Franco-Chinese war the French government declared rice, conveyed by neutral vessels to North
China ports, to be contraband of war ; and when
provisions are to be used in warlike operations,
they are unquestionably contraband. [2]   It was
finally provided that nothing in the treaty should
be so construed as to conflict with existing treaties
with other states.   It was, therefore, a false political cry to assert, as was asserted a thousand times,
that the treaty was in violation of the treaties with
France.

It is true that Jay failed to obtain an article
against impressments, which then and the next
year [3] he urged on Lord Grenville as essential to
preserve friendship between the two countries.
But even the war of 1812 failed to secure a

[1] Schoell, iv. 15.

[2] J. R. Soley, "The Effect on American Commerce of an Anglo-
Continental War," *Scribner's Magazine*, November, 1889.

[3] To Lord Grenville, May 1, 1796, *Jay MSS.*

formal renunciation of that evil. That negotiation should have succeeded in effecting what war failed to achieve, was scarcely to be expected.

To unprejudiced eyes after the lapse of a hundred years, considering the mutual exasperation of the two peoples, the pride of England in her successes in the war with France, the weakness and division of the United States, the treaty seems a very fair one. Certainly one far less favorable to America would have been infinitely preferable to a war, and would probably in the course of time have been accepted as being so. The commercial advantages were not very considerable, but they at least served as "an entering wedge," to quote Jay's expression, and they were *pro tanto* a clear gain to America. Some such thoughts may have been in Lord Sheffield's mind when, at the breaking out of the war of 1812, he remarked: "We have now a complete opportunity of getting rid of that most impolitic treaty of 1794, when Lord Grenville was so perfectly duped by Jay." [1] And it is significantly admitted by the latest biographer of the Democratic hero, Andrew Jackson, that "Jay's treaty was a masterpiece of diplomacy, considering the time and the circumstances of this country." [2]

The truth of the whole matter was probably expressed as well as ever by Lord Grenville to Jay, in 1796: "It is a great satisfaction to me, when,

[1] To Mr. Abbott, November 6, 1812, *Correspondence of Lord Colchester*, ii. 409.

[2] Sumner, *Andrew Jackson*, p. 12.

in the course of so many unpleasant discussions as
a public man must necessarily be engaged in, he is
able to look back upon any of them with as much
pleasure as I derived from that which procured me
the advantage of friendship and intercourse with a
man valuable on every account. . . . I, on my part,
should have thought that I very ill consulted the
interests of my country, if I had been desirous of
terminating the points in discussion between us on
any other footing than that of mutual justice and
reciprocal advantage; nor do I conceive that any
just objection can be stated to the great work which
we jointly accomplished, except on the part of those
who believe the interests of Great Britain and the
United States to be in contradiction with each
other, or who wish to make them so." [1]

In England Jay made many friends: the Bishop
of London, whose parents were American born,
Henry Dundas, Sir William Scott, Sir Henry
Newenham, Edmund Burke, to whom he afterwards sent cuttings of apple-trees, Lord Chancellor
Loughborough, who invited him to attend the trial
of the pyx, and sent him a brace of grouse, Sir
John Sinclair, the president of the Board of Agriculture, who invited him to look at his flock of
sheep and various mechanical inventions, of which
he wrote a long account to Judge Hobart, Lord
and Lady Mornington, Jeremy Bentham, Dugald
Stewart, and William Wilberforce, with each of
whom he kept up an occasional but most friendly

[1] From Lord Grenville, March 17, 1796, Jay's *Jay*, ii. 267, 268.

correspondence for the rest of his life. In Wilberforce's diary is the entry: " Dined at Hampstead to meet Jay (the American envoy), his son, etc., — quite American — sensible. I fear there is little spirit of religion in America; something of French, tinctured with more than English simplicity of manners; very pleasing, well-informed men. American Abolition of Foreign Slave Trade." [1]

On May 28 Jay arrived in New York. As during the period of his mission he had continued to hold the position of chief justice, he refused any compensation except for actual expenses. The treaty was not published till July 2, the day after Jay's inauguration as governor, and then only by a breach of senatorial etiquette; yet some mention must be made here of the exciting scenes which followed.

Even before its contents were known, letters, signed " Franklin," appeared abusing the treaty; and in Philadelphia an effigy of Jay was placed in the pillory, and finally taken down, guillotined, the clothes fired, and the body blown up. [2] It was clear, then, that it was not this particular treaty, but any treaty at all with Great Britain, that excited the wrath of the Republicans. On July 4 toasts insulting Jay, or making odious puns on his name, were the fashion. Two days after a copy of the treaty reached Boston, a mass meeting was called, though there had been no time to consider it, and

[1] *Life of William Wilberforce*, ii. 57.
[2] McMaster, *Hist. of the People of U. S.* ii. 213.

condemnatory resolutions were passed. In New
York, on the 18th, similar action was had; Hamilton tried to make himself heard, but was stopped
by a volley of stones; and the treaty and a picture
of Jay were burned on the Bowery. One effigy
represented Jay holding a pair of scales, with the
treaty on one side and a bag of gold on the other,
while from his mouth proceeded this label, " Come
up to my price, and I will sell you my country."
James Savage, once president of the Massachusetts
Historical Society, told his grandson that he remembered seeing these words chalked in large
white letters around the inclosure of Mr. Robert
Treat Paine: —

"Damn John Jay! Damn every one that won't
damn John Jay!! Damn every one that won't
put lights in his windows and sit up all night damning John Jay!!!"[1]

On June 24 the treaty was ratified by the Senate,
with the exception of the article about the West
India trade. On August 15 it was signed, with
the same exception, by Washington. The following spring, March 3, 1796, the treaty was proclaimed the supreme law of the land; yet even then
the Republicans, claiming that the House had an
equal share with the Senate in treaty-making, tried
to defeat it by preventing the passage of laws
necessary to carry it into effect; and the honor of
the nation was saved only by the casting vote of

[1] John Jay, *Second Letter on Dawson's Federalist*, New York,
1864, p. 19.

Muhlenberg, the chairman, in committee of the whole, though he was a member of the Democratic Club, and in the House only by a majority of three. That the essays of Hamilton as "Camillus," and the famous speech of Fisher Ames, contributed as much as anything to this happy issue, is too well known to need more than mention of the fact. One may at least, however, reëcho Ames's prayer: "Lord, send us peace in our day, that the passions of Europe may not inflame the sense of America!"[1]

Throughout the storm of vituperation Jay himself remained calm and philosophical. "As to my negotiation and the treaty," he wrote to Judge Cushing, "I left this country well convinced that it would not receive anti-Federal approbation; besides, I had read the history of Greece, and was apprised of the politics and proceedings of more recent date."[2]   "Calumny," he said again, "is seldom durable, it will in time yield to truth."[3]   He had at least done his duty, though by so doing he very possibly lost the presidency of the United States.[4]

[1] *Works of Fisher Ames*, i. 196.
[2] To Judge Cushing, July 11, 1795, *Jay MSS.*
[3] To John Patterson, November 17, 1795, *Jay MSS.*
[4] Hamilton, "Camillus," July 22, 1795, *Works*, vii. 175.

CHAPTER XII

GOVERNOR OF NEW YORK

1795–1801

BEFORE his return from England, and long before any details of the treaty were published, Jay was nominated for governor of New York by a caucus of the Federalists in the legislature, and in due time was elected. "It had been so decreed from the beginning," [1] wrote Egbert Benson; it had at least been so decreed ever since the infamous counting out in 1792. "God only knows," was Jay's reply, "whether my removal from the bench [2] to my present station will conduce to my comfort or not. The die is cast, and nothing remains for me to consider but how to fulfill in the best manner the duties incumbent on me, without any regard to personal consequences." [3]

One of his first acts as governor showed his conservative adherence to legal customs, even when he had full discretion. To a request from Governor Huntington of Connecticut for the extradition of

[1] June 12, 1795, *Jay MSS.*
[2] Jay resigned the chief justiceship of the United States.
[3] To Egbert Benson, June 27, 1795, *Jay MSS.*

two criminals, in a case where urgency seemed to justify the omission of some of the usual papers, Jay answered: "I do not think myself at liberty to dispense with the precise formalities prescribed." [1]

In the autumn the yellow fever broke out in New York. During the French and English war the price of necessaries had risen enormously, out of all proportion to the rise in wages; house rent had almost doubled; the poorer people, mainly Irish immigrants, lived in damp cellars, and the system of sewerage also was most imperfect, if there could be said to be any system at all. In such conditions everything favored the spread and continuance of epidemic diseases. In the autumn of 1791 there was an outbreak of yellow fever near Peck Slip, among the boating population, while on the west side intermittent fever was common. Occasional cases of the fever occurred during the next few years, till in August and September, 1795, there was a real epidemic. Tar was burned in the streets. The students left Columbia College. A member of the health committee died of the fever, and one of Jay's intimate friends, Mr. Wentworth, also died of it after two days' sickness. On August 14 Jay issued a proclamation forbidding any vessel from the West Indies to approach nearer the city than Governor's Island till she had a health certificate from the health officer of the port. The alarm spread to other cities, and Governor Mifflin of Pennsylvania, on

[1] To Governor Huntington, July, 1795, *Jay MSS.*

August 31, prohibited "all intercourse" between
Philadelphia and New York for a month; and intercourse was not resumed till October 21. The
governor of Virginia also ordered all vessels from
New York to perform quarantine. New York
merchants were greatly inconvenienced, and Jay,
after consulting the Medical Society, the Health
Committee, and the mayor, forwarded their reports
to Governor Mifflin, urging that the disease was
strictly localized and under control, and that such
violent preventive measures were unnecessary; but
the memory of the fever in Philadelphia in 1793
was too vivid for his words to have much effect.[1]
The French consul and his fellow citizens invited
Jay to a "republican entertainment" on September 22, but he declined, saying: "While general
anxiety and alarm" pervaded his native city, it
would not "be in his power to command that
degree of hilarity which becomes such convivial
scenes."[2] Throughout the whole period of danger
he stayed in the city, as a matter of duty; and
refused an invitation to visit for safety a friend
in New Jersey, with the explanation: "Our situation affords us considerable security against the
disorder, and I think it best that my family should
remain here, lest their removal should increase the
alarm which is already too great. If, indeed, the
danger should become very imminent, it would

[1] Davis, *A Brief Account of the Epidemical Fever which lately
prevailed in the city of New York*, New York, 1795.
[2] To the consul, September 19, 1795, *Jay MSS.*

doubtless be right for Mrs. Jay and the children to leave me, and go into the country." [1] With the return of cold weather the plague ceased, and Jay issued a proclamation appointing Thursday, November 26, a day for " his fellow citizens throughout the State to unite in public thanksgiving to that Being through whose Providence the ravages of the yellow fever had been stayed." This was the first Thanksgiving Day in New York, though in other States, on exceptional occasions, days for special thanksgiving had been similarly appointed. But the innovation was thought by Jay's political enemies to be a stretch of executive power, and few acts of his were more bitterly censured than this innocent one of gratitude and reverence. The fever of 1795 is now chiefly noteworthy historically as the immediate cause of the introduction of an underground system of sewerage. [2]

On January 6, 1796, the legislature convened with a Federalist majority in both houses. It was then customary for the governor to open the session by a speech which was answered by an address. In his speech Jay stated that he was determined " to regard all his fellow citizens with an equal eye, and to cherish and advance merit wherever found ; " he recommended that provision be made for the defense of the State in case of war ; that the chancellor and the judges of the Supreme Court should receive pensions on their

[1] To John Blanchard, October 3, 1795, *Jay MSS.*
[2] Schouler, *Hist. of U. S.* i. 238.

superannuation ; that a penitentiary be established
for the employment and reformation of criminals;
and that some plan of internal improvements be
adopted for facilitating travel through the State;
he also requested a settlement of the doubts that
had arisen as to whether the governor had, under
the Constitution, the exclusive right of nomination
in the Council of Appointment. The legislature
returned a most amiable answer: " The evidence,"
they said, " of ability, integrity, and patriotism
which have been *invariably* afforded by your conduct in the discharge of the variety of arduous
and important trusts, authorize us to anticipate an
administration conducive to the welfare of your
constituents." The word " invariably," which
Hammond terms an " instance of legislative syco-
phancy,"[1] was inserted by the Senate, by a vote
of eleven to six, on motion of Ambrose Spencer,
the future chief justice, who was so soon to become a Republican.

No practical result immediately followed the
governor's suggestions; and a bill to abolish slavery, introduced by an intimate friend of his, was
defeated by the casting vote of the chairman in
committee of the whole. In the spring of 1796
Jay thought fit to publish his views on the French
Revolution, in the form of a letter to a friend,
R. G. Harper, who had defended him with rather
undiscriminating zeal, asserting that he always
had expressed " the utmost pleasure in the French

[1] Hammond, *Pol. Hist. of N. Y.* p. 97.

Revolution."[1]   Many politicians would be only
too glad to have their unpopular opinions discreetly explained away or suppressed; but such
was not Jay's feeling. He had from early life,
he said, expressed "strong dislike for the former
arbitrary government of France;" he rejoiced in
the revolution "which put a period to it," "the
one which limited the power of the king, and restored liberty to the people."   "The successors of
that memorable assembly produced another revolution. They abolished the constitutional government which had just been established, and brought
the king to the scaffold."   That revolution did not
give him pleasure, marked as it was by "atrocities
very injurious to the cause of liberty, and offensive
to liberty and morality."   Yet, as its overthrow
by the combined powers would be "an interference not to be submitted to," he wished success to
the revolution so far as it had for its object the
formation of a constitution adapted to the people
of France, and "not the disorganizing and man-
aging of other states, which ought neither to be
attempted nor permitted."   This temperate letter
was violently attacked by "An Enemy of Oppres-
sion,"[2] by "Publius," in a series of articles,[3] and
finally by "Common Sense," the pseudonym of
Thomas Paine.[4]   Paine's argument was limited to

[1] January 19, 1796; *N. Y. Journal*, February 26, 1796.
[2] *N. Y. Journal*, March 8, 1796.
[3] *Ibid.*, March 29, April 1, 5, 1796.
[4] *Ibid.*, April 15, 1796.

asserting that, if John Jay had had his way, America would never have secured independence, and that Jay once said that the senators should have been appointed for life. " These are the disguised traitors," including Washington and Adams, " that call themselves Federalists." [1]   Jay, however, was a revolutionist as true as Paine was, but infinitely wiser. As he wrote to Vaughan: " Liberty and reformation may make men mad, and madness of any kind is no blessing. I nevertheless think that there may be a time for change, as well as for other things ; all that I contend for is, that they be done soberly, by sober and discreet men, and in due manner, measure, and proportion. It may be said that this cannot always be the case. It is true, and we can only regret it. We must take men and things as they are, and act accordingly ; that is, circumspectly." [2]

The governor incurred still further odium by refusing to order the flags to be hoisted on Governor's Island and the Battery on the anniversary of the Tammany Society ; the reason he gave was, that " if such a compliment be paid to the Tammany, it ought not to be refused to any other of the numerous societies in this city and State." [3]

This year, according to Jay's suggestion, a penitentiary was built in New York, on the model of the one of which Philadelphia was at this time so

---

[1] *N. Y. Journal*, October 21, 1796.
[2] To William Vaughan, May 26, 1796, *Jay MSS.*
[3] Letter of May 11, 1796, *Jay MSS.*

proud. He also advised the purchase of Bedloe's Island for a lazaretto. At his suggestion, also, Governor Clinton's recommendation of a revision of the penal code was revived, and the number of offenses punishable by death was greatly diminished. His strictness, however, in exercising the right of pardon was illustrated by his refusal of a request from Governor Wolcott of Connecticut to intervene in behalf of a young gentleman of good family, convicted of forgery: "Justice . . . cannot look with more favorable eye on those who become criminal in spite of a good education and of good examples than of those other offenders who from infancy have lived destitute of those advantages."[1]

The seat of government was now changed to Albany, where the legislature held its first session January 2, 1798. No provision was made for the governor's residence, so Jay lived in lodgings, and was not joined by Mrs. Jay till the following year. Again a bill to abolish slavery was introduced, but was lost in the Senate. A characteristic anecdote of Jay at this time is given by Hammond. When the Council of Appointment voted on the nomination of a successor to the secretary of state, who died in office, Jay's nominations were rejected time after time by a Doctor White and other friends of Major Hale of Albany. At last the governor reluctantly nominated Hale, who was immediately confirmed. "The governor soon became convinced

[1] To Governor Wolcott, October 20, 1797, *Jay MSS.*

that his opposition to the appointment was caused by erroneous impressions, and when so convinced he lost no time in communicating to Doctor White and Major Hale his conviction that he was well satisfied that he was wrong, and that the friends of Major Hale were right." [1]

In April, 1798, Jay was renominated and re-elected by the large majority of 2380 votes, about one twelfth of all the votes cast, over the Republican candidate, Chancellor Livingston; a personal triumph, as the Republicans made great gains in the legislature. Soon the news of the insolent treatment of the American envoys by the French government, and the famous X, Y, Z letters, excited general resentment among the people. War with France was thought to be imminent. In June committees of citizens of New York petitioned the governor to summon a special session of the legislature for the sake of passing measures for the better defense of the city and the port. The mayor and council coöperated with the citizens' committees in raising money for defense. Jay accordingly by proclamation called an extraordinary session of the legislature to meet at Albany in August, giving as his reasons the fear of a war with France and the necessity of raising funds and making preparations for defense. " At this place," wrote Peter A. Jay from New York, " the stream of public opinion continues to run with increasing rapidity in our favor. Several insults lately offered

[1] Hammond, *Pol. Hist. of N. Y.* pp. 112, 113.

to the Cockade,[1] and the song of 'Hail Columbia,' contributed to accelerate it. A few evenings ago I was unluckily one of a company who received much abuse on account of the latter." [2] The legislature, however, was still Federalist, and unanimously voted an address to the President pledging the support of the State in his endeavors to maintain the rights and honor of the nation. Money was also appropriated for the erection of fortifications and the purchase of arms at the discretion of the governor.

The extra session adjourned till January 2, 1799. During this session, in April, emancipation was at last enacted. It was provided that all children born of slave parents after the ensuing 4th of July should be free, subject to apprenticeship, in the case of males till the age of twenty-eight, in the case of females till the age of twenty-five, and the exportation of slaves was forbidden. By this process of gradual emancipation there was avoided that question of compensation which had been the secret of the failure of earlier bills. At that time the number of slaves was only 22,000, small in proportion to the total population of nearly a million.[3] So the change was effected peacefully and without excitement. Jay himself was a slaveholder in a certain sense. " I have three male and

---

[1] The Federalists had adopted a black cockade as a distinctive badge.

[2] From Peter A. Jay, August 1, 1798.

[3] Roberts, " New York," *An. Comm. Series*, ii. 483, 484.

three female slaves," he wrote in a return of his
property to the Albany assessors, November 8,
1798; " five of them are with me in this city, and
one of them is in the city of New York. I purchase slaves and manumit them at proper ages,
and when their faithful services shall have afforded
a reasonable retribution." [1] Perhaps the govern-
or's practice in this respect may have suggested the
practical manner of emancipation.

Though the legislature was still Federalist, and
remained so even after the April elections, there
were a number of members, elected as Federalists,
who acted in all except personal and minor matters
with the Republicans.[2] Accordingly amendments
to the Constitution, proposed by the legislature of
Massachusetts, increasing the disability of aliens,
were rejected in spite of the governor's favor. Also
the House passed a Republican resolution, which
was rejected by the Senate, for dividing the State
into districts for the election, by the people, of
presidential electors.

In the electoral college this year Jay received
nine votes for the presidency of the United States,
viz.: those of New Jersey and Delaware, five out
of Connecticut's nine votes, and one from Rhode
Island.

In his message to the legislature, January, 1800,
the governor delivered " a short but graceful "
eulogy on Washington, who, to the sorrow of the

[1] *Jay MSS.*
[2] Hammond, *Pol. Hist. of N. Y.* ii. 123.

country and the "irreparable loss" of the Federalists as a party, had died in December. He recommended further provision for the public schools, and various amendents of the laws. In March the Republicans renewed the attempt to secure a districting of the State, but without success, the Federalists declaring that such an act would be unconstitutional, and that it was essential that the State should act as a body corporate in the choice of presidential electors.

At the spring elections, contrary to general expectation, through the able political management of Burr, the Republicans triumphed throughout the State, wresting New York city from the Federalists, and returning a majority of twenty-eight to the House, while the Senate was Federalist by only the small majority of eight. As it was admitted that the next election for president would turn on the vote of New York, and New York would certainly return Republican electors if they were chosen by the legislature in joint session, as was then the law, it was now the interest of the Federalists to advocate their election by the people in districts. Accordingly, disregarding the previous record of his party and their assertion of the unconstitutionality of the measure, Hamilton, on May 7, wrote to Governor Jay urging him to call an extra session of the legislature to pass such an act before the expiration of the legislative year on July 1st. Philip Schuyler wrote to the same effect, saying that Marshall was of the same opinion: "Your

friends will justify it," he continued, "as the only
means to save a nation from more disasters, which
it must and probably will experience from the mis-
rule of a man who has given such strong evidence
that he was opposed to the salutary measures of
those who have been heretofore at the helm, and
who is in fact pervaded with the mad French philosophy."[1]　These words well expressed the fears
and frenzy of the Federalists.　As a party, they
had created a nation out of a confederation, and, in
the spirit of latter-day Republicans who felt that
they had saved the country from dismemberment,
they were convinced that on their continuance in
power depended the conservation and prosperity of
the State.　A party which tacitly or openly holds
such a belief will naturally justify any measure to
secure itself in power by the final appeal to national
self-preservation; but such a party in control of the
government is a menace to popular liberty, and in
any healthy state of public opinion is doomed to
swift defeat, and, perhaps, as happened in this
case, to extinction.　Jay, though as "stalwart" a
Federalist as any, nevertheless did not believe that
a good end ever justified bad means; and he contented himself with simply indorsing on Hamilton's
letter the significant words: "Proposing a measure for party purposes which I think it would not
become me to adopt."

On the convening of the new legislature in November the governor, in his speech, deprecated the

[1] *Jay MSS.*

danger of undue political excitement, and urged the suppression of partisan inflammatory feeling. He also recommended the calling of a convention to restrict the number of senators and assemblymen. His appeal, however, was in vain; and for the remainder of his term he was harassed by the partisan attitude of the legislature. Thus that body instantly proceeded to elect a new Council of Appointment, of which only one member was a Federalist; and the new council, from the moment when it first met the governor in the following February, began a controversy which was settled only by an amendment to the Constitution.

Before separating, after adjournment on November 8, the Republicans nominated Clinton as their next candidate for the governorship, and the Federalists, in a complimentary address, urged Jay to consent to be renominated. "The period is now nearly arrived," was Jay's answer, "at which I have for many years intended to retire from the cares of public life, and for which I have been for more than two years preparing; not perceiving, after mature consideration, that my duties require me to postpone it, I shall retire accordingly." [1]

The contest between the governor and a majority of the Council of Appointment must be mentioned, though briefly. On February 11 the governor made a nomination for sheriff of Dutchess County; it was rejected. Seven other nominations by him for the same office were successively re-

[1] Jay's *Jay*, i. 419, 420.

jected. He then nominated a Republican, who was confirmed. On February 24 the governor made several nominations for sheriff of Schoharie and sheriff of Orange, but all were rejected. Finally a member of the council made a nomination, and the governor, instead of putting the question, made another. The issue was now defined, the governor insisting on the sole right of nomination, and the council claiming, for the first time, a concurrent right. The governor never called the council together again. In a special message to the legislature he referred to his first address as governor, when he had requested a settlement of the question, and now he again asked their directions. The legislature declined acting on a constitutional question. He asked the opinion of the judges of the Supreme Court and the chancellor; but they refused to decide the question as extra-judicial. On April 6 an act was passed " recommending a convention " to ascertain the construction of the disputed clause in the Constitution, and to consider the question of diminishing the number of senators and assemblymen. The convention, which met after the election of Clinton as governor, upheld the position of the council. In the later Constitutional Convention of 1821 Governor Tompkins, who had voted against his party in the earlier body, declared that it was " assembled to sanction a violent construction of the Constitution. Then, the maxim was to strip the governor of as much power as possible. Now, gentlemen are for giving him more power." [1] It was, indeed, the allowing members of the council, among whom were various senators, to exercise the power of nomination as well as confirmation, that made the council a byword for political corruption and favoritism until popular contempt achieved its abolition.

In his first address to the legislature, as we have seen, Jay had announced that he would seek out and advance merit, wherever found; and there is no reason to doubt that, so far as the political complexion of the council and the exigencies of the times permitted, he endeavored to do so. For appointments, however, he was not solely responsible; and for removals he was not necessarily responsible at all, as a person might be removed from office on motion of any member of the council by a majority vote. His son, Judge William Jay, says: —

"During the six years of Governor Jay's administration, not one individual was dismissed by him from office on account of his politics. So long as an officer discharged his duties with fidelity and ability, he was certain of being continued, and hence his devotion to the public became identified with his personal interest. It is related that in the council a member was urging in behalf of a candidate his zeal and usefulness as a Federalist, when he was interrupted by the governor with: 'That, sir, is not the question; is he fit for the office?'" [2]

[1] Hammond, *Pol. Hist. of N. Y.* ii. 155, 156, 166, 167.
[2] Jay's *Jay*, i. 392.

And it is significant that, in answer to this statement, Hammond, the Republican historian of New York, could only point to two cases where the causes of removal might possibly have been political, but were not certainly so. Mr. Flanders corroborates Judge Jay, saying : —

" The practice of removing officers on a change of administration had not yet been introduced. Governor Jay dismissed no officer during the six years of his administration on account of his political opinions. On one occasion he was urged to remove a member of his own party who had little or no influence, to make room for one of the opposite party who possessed a great deal, and would, if appointed, use it in favor of his new connections. ' And do you, sir,' replied the governor to this unusual application, ' advise me to sell a friend that I may buy an enemy ? ' " [1]

In respect to the whole question under consideration Jay was sensitively conscientious. Thus, when Gouverneur Morris asked him to recommend a nephew of Morris's to the President for an appointment, the refusal, which Morris said he had anticipated, was prompt: " It appears to me," said Jay, "that the President of the United States and the governors of individual States should forbear to interpose their official or personal influence with each other in the appointment of officers. It would open a door for reciprocal recommendations which would frequently prove embarrassing from the diffi-

[1] Flanders, *Chief Justices*, i. 416.

culty of always reconciling them to local circumstances and public considerations." [1]

Jay's determination to retire from public life was absolute and final. He was unmoved even by the complimentary letter of President Adams announcing his unsolicited nomination and confirmation, a second time, as chief justice of the United States. "I had no permission from you," said President Adams, "to take this step, but it appeared to me that Providence had thrown in my way an opportunity, not only of marking to the public the spot where, in my opinion, the greatest mass of worth remained collected in one individual, but of furnishing my country with the best security its inhabitants afforded against its increasing dissolution of morals." [2] "I left the bench," Jay replied, "perfectly convinced that under a system so defective it would not obtain the energy, weight, and dignity which was essential to its affording due support to the national government; nor acquire the public confidence and respect which, as the last resort of the justice of the nation, it should possess. Hence I am induced to doubt both the propriety and the expediency of my returning to the bench under the present system. . . . Independently of these considerations, the state of my health removes every doubt." [3]

On January 13 the Federal Freeholders of New

---

[1] To G. Morris, November 26, 1799, *Jay MSS.*

[2] John Adams to Jay, December 18, 1800, Jay's *Jay*, ii. 421.

[3] To President Adams, January 2, 1801, *Jay MSS.*

York passed resolutions commending his public services and regretting his retirement; and his answer showed how far removed he was from the violent partisanship of the day : " I take the liberty of suggesting whether the patriotic principles on which we profess to act do not call upon us to give (as far as may depend upon us) fair and full effect to the known sense and intention of a majority of the people, in every constitutional exercise of their will, and to support every administration of the government of our country, which may prove to be intelligent and upright, of whatever party the persons composing it may be." [1] These certainly are not the words of a disappointed and embittered politician. In May the corporation of Albany presented him with the freedom of the city, " as a further testimony of the high sense the common council entertain of your excellency's exalted character." [2]

Thus ends the public life of John Jay. For twenty-eight years he had been continuously in office, his appointments not infrequently overlapping one another. But public office had always been to him a public trust, or rather a public duty, and he cared for neither its reputation nor its emoluments.

[1] *Jay MSS.*   [2] *Jay MSS.*

CHAPTER XIII

IN RETIREMENT

1801–1829

THE time had come at last to which Jay had for years looked forward with so much eagerness, when, relieved from public cares, he might devote himself to those quiet country pursuits which he loved, to the society of his wife, and the education of his children. He had inherited a property of some eight hundred acres at Bedford, Westchester County, forty miles from New York, which had fallen to his mother's share on the partition of the old Van Cortlandt estate. To this he had added by purchases from his brothers: here for some years he had been repairing and building additions to the dwelling-house, and now with his family he retired to this new home, where he lived continuously for the remaining twenty-eight years of his life.

No sooner, however, was the cup of happiness at his lips than it was dashed to the ground; for within a year he had to mourn the death of his dearly beloved wife. Since their marriage they had been pained by constant separations, but their

love for each other had ever been so great as to
provoke the gentle raillery of their friends, and to
the day of her death Jay had not come to sink the
lover in the husband. "Tell me," he wrote to her
not many years before, referring to her eyes that
he had not gazed on for months, "tell me, are they
as bright as ever?" and her letters to him were
always what she was fond of calling them, "little
messengers of love."

His loneliness, fortunately, was lightened by the
presence of his children: Ann, who never married
and in disposition was extremely like her father,
now just growing into womanhood; William, a
serious, studious lad of thirteen years; and Sarah,
a pretty little girl, who was to die unmarried when
only twenty-six years of age. In 1806 an older
daughter, Maria Banyer, joined the family group
on her husband's death, bringing with her a
charming little child, who also soon passed away.
Mrs. Banyer and Miss Jay lived afterwards a long,
gentle life of quiet benevolence in New York;
there were few works of charity in which they had
not a part; and they were the fairy godmothers of
countless young nephews and nieces.

For a time the household at Bedford must have
been a somewhat sad one, but gradually Jay found
content and happiness in the simple country life,
with its regular and early hours, with experiments
in farming and horticulture, with a little reading,
frequent correspondence with Wilberforce in England, Lafayette and Vaughan in France, and Judge

Peters in Philadelphia, and occasional visits from old friends who lived within a few days' drive. " My expectations from retirement," he was soon able to say, " have not been disappointed, and had Mrs. Jay continued with me, I should deem this the most agreeable part of my life. The post, once a week, brings me our newspapers, which furnish a history of the times." . . . " Attention to little improvements, occasional visits, the history which my recollections furnish, and frequent conversation with the 'mighty dead,' who, in a certain sense, live in their works, together with the succession of ordinary occurrences, preserve me from *ennui*. . . . Party feuds give me concern; but they seldom obtrude upon me."

"My farm," he wrote to Judge Peters, "was from its first settlement occupied by tenants. They have left no trees fit for rails; nor can I obtain a supply in this neighborhood. The stones they could not destroy, and they are the only materials I have for fence. With some expense I had collected and formed a flock [of sheep] which pleased me, but the unceasing care and trouble of keeping them, induced me to sell them and to buy what are here called otter sheep. They have short, crooked legs, and are no beauties, . . . but they are orderly and stay at home, and that is more than can be said of most beauties."[1] To Washington, at Mount Vernon, he had written about the wisdom of introducing a breed of mules. With

[1] November 21, 1810.

others he discussed a new kind of rye, and the
novel use of plaster for manuring. " A frost took
my watermelons when they were about as large as
a marble," he wrote to Judge Peters, who, though
still occupying the bench at an advanced age,
shared Jay's interest in agriculture. " They turned
black, and dropped off. The ends of the vines began to die, and continued to do so for some days.
I then had the vines cut below the mortified part,
and the whole well sprinkled with plaster. They
recovered, and brought some, though not much,
fruit to perfection. I believe," he continued, " that
you and I derive more real satisfaction from attending to our vines and fruit-trees than most con-
querors from cultivating their favorite laurels." [1]

Many trees, elms and maples, he planted about
Bedford; indeed, several years earlier, in sending
some mulberry-trees to his son Peter, he became
almost enthusiastic over what he called this " innocent and rational amusement." " It always gives
me pleasure to see trees which I have reared and
planted," he said, " and therefore I recommend it
to you to do the same. . . . My father planted
many trees, and I never walk in their shade without deriving additional pleasure from that circumstance. The time will probably come when you
will experience similar emotions." [2]

He was always fond of animals, and unusually
kind to them. In 1783, amid the cares and anxi-

[1] February 26, 1810, Jay's *Jay*, ii. 323.
[2] April 25, 1792, *Jay MSS.*

eties of the negotiations, he was mindful to write to his son : "If my old mare is alive, I must beg of you and my brother to take very good care of her. I mean that she should be well fed and live idle, unless my brother Peter should choose to use her. If it should be necessary to advance money to recover her, I am content you should do it even to the amount of double her value." It was probably of another mare that he wrote to Judge Peters in 1811: "There was a mare belonging to my father, which I rode as soon as I could ride. She was a favorite, and often carried me to and from school. Of her stock I have always had saddle horses. Those which I selected for that purpose remained mine as long as they lived; and the remembrance of them recalls that of agreeable days and incidents. The one I now have is above twenty years old, and, though of little real value, has more of my particular care and attention than any of the others of whatever price. This kind of favoritism or predilection may not be philosophical, but it is innocent and pleasing, and I indulge it. . . . It is a rainy afternoon, I have written a long letter, and should probably continue to amuse myself in writing on to the next page, but it is now so dark that I can hardly read what I write." [1]

He was frequently written to for advice on public or semi-public questions, and always responded with habitual frankness and common sense. William Wilberforce requested his views about the

[1] October 16, 1811, *Jay MSS.*

Reform Bill, which he was agitating in Parliament. "Wise and good borough-holders, like wise and good kings," replied Jay, "doubtless wish and endeavor to make the best appointments; but ought either borough-holders or kings to appoint representatives for the nation?"[1]

A company at Mamaroneck applied to the legislature for authority to increase its water supply by overflowing adjacent land compulsorily on payment of damages. Jay indignantly asserted legal principles, which, perhaps, have been too little considered by subsequent legislatures. "When a piece of ground is wanted for a use important to the state, I know," he said, "the state has a right to take it from the owner on paying the full value of it; but certainly the legislature has no right to *compel* a freeholder to part with his land to any of his fellow citizens, nor to deprive him of the use of it, in order to accommodate one or more of his neigh-bors in the prosecution of their particular trade or business. Such an act, by violating the rights of property, would be a most dangerous precedent."[2]

The governor of Ohio submitted to him some plans for taxation: "However extensive the constitutional power of a government to impose taxes may be," was Jay's reply, "I think it should not be so exercised as to impede or discourage the lawful and *useful* industry and exertions of individuals. Hence, the prudence of taxing the products

[1] October 25, 1810, Jay's *Jay*, ii. 331.
[2] To Peter Jay Munroe, March 2, 1812, *Jay MSS.*

of beneficial labor, either mental or manual, appears to be at least questionable. . . . Whether taxation should extend only to property, or only to income, are points on which opinions have not been uniform. I am inclined to think that both should not be taxed." [1]

A pamphlet was sent him on "The Missouri Question," in 1819, and in acknowledging it he expressed his own very decided opinion: "The obvious dictates both of morality and policy teach us, that our free nation cannot encourage the extension of slavery, nor the multiplication of slaves, without doing violence to their principles, and without depressing their power and prosperity." [2]

In politics Jay studiously avoided taking any active part, though he performed his duties as a citizen with unostentatious punctuality, and continued as ever to take keen interest in affairs. "He read the papers constantly," said Judge William Jay, contradicting a report to the contrary, "and at times took papers of opposite politics, that he might obtain more full information of passing events." [3] "The proprieties attached to a situation like mine," wrote Jay to Pickering in 1808, "assign certain limits to active interferences in political concerns. I attend every election, even for town officers, and, having delivered my ballots, return

[1] To E. A. Brown, governor of Ohio, April 30, 1821, Jay's *Jay*, ii. 420, 421.

[2] To Daniel Raymond, December 21, 1819, Jay's *Jay*, ii. 406.

[3] Hammond, *Pol. Hist. of N. Y.* i. 155 n.

home, without having mingled in the crowd or
participated in their altercations."[1]

To Jay, as to most of the older Federalists, the
war of 1812 seemed ill-advised. He said: "In
my opinion, the declaration of war was neither
necessary, nor expedient, nor reasonable; and I
think that they who entertain this opinion do
well in expressing it, both individually and collec-
tively;" but he added this important qualification:
"As the war has been *constitutionally* declared,
the people are evidently bound to support it in
the manner which constitutional laws do or shall
prescribe."[2] He accordingly for the time joined
that section of the Federalists known as the Peace
Party; but he was no partisan, and when the
party nominated for assemblyman, from Westchester County, a man of objectionable private
character, Jay and his friends promptly joined in
defeating him. In vindicating his action, he laid
down the ethical rules that should determine obligation to one's party, rules of general application,
but which in these days would be stigmatized as
the unpractical notions of a *doctrinaire* or "Mug-
wump." "We approve," he said, "of the customary mode of nominating candidates, and have
uniformly concurred in it; that concurrence certainly involved our tacit assent to be bound by the
nominations which should be so made. But it is
equally certain that such consent did, does, and ever

[1] December 24, 1808, *Jay MSS.*
[2] July 28, 1812, Jay's *Jay*, i. 445.

will rest on the condition, trust, and confidence that such nominations only be made as we could or can support, without transgressing the obligations we are under to preserve our characters and our minds free from humiliation and reproach. . . . Adherence to party has its limits, and they are prescribed and marked by that Supreme Wisdom which has united and associated true policy with rectitude, and honor, and self-respect." [1]

In 1815 Jay became president of the Westchester Bible Society; the next year, on the organization of the American Bible Society, he was appointed one of its vice-presidents, and, on the death of Elias Boudinot in 1821, its president. He was also a member of the Tract and Sunday-school societies, and of that for educating pious youth for the ministry. In 1814 he was elected a member of the American Antiquarian Society.

Jay's health had always been delicate: now, in his later years, he was seldom free from attacks of rheumatism, or some disorder of the liver, but the most serious ailment of all was what he termed "the incurable" one of old age. In 1813 Gouverneur Morris asked him to become godfather to his son: "True it is that you may not be able to perform the duties of that office; but, my friend, should you be mingled with the dust, he shall learn from the history of your life, that a man must be truly pious to be truly great." [2]   But Jay felt

[1] Jay's *Jay*, i. 449.
[2] February 15, 1813, Jay's *Jay*, ii. 355.

bound to decline on the ground of old age; "as I expect," he said, "to remove at a more early period to a distant country, where I shall not be in a capacity to attend to persons or things here." [1]

In 1814 he was invited by Rufus King to join their friends in the city "in the proposed celebration of the overthrow and repulsion of Bonaparte;" but he regretted that his health prevented his presence on "so joyful an occasion." [2] In 1821 a note in the third volume of Franklin's Works, then just published, that the editor had consulted journals kept by Jay and Adams concerning the peace negotiations, led the two old friends once more to exchange letters. The note was of course erroneous. There was, however, something touching in the greeting of these aged men. "I too am feeble and confined to the house the greater part of the winter," wrote Adams, "but I hope to crawl out like a turtle in the spring; your chirography gives me full assurance that you will be on horseback before that time." [3] "For twelve years past," wrote Jay, "I have not had one well day. . . . It rarely happens that the maladies and infirmities which generally accompany old age will yield to medical skill; but happily for us patience and resignation are excellent palliatives." [4] "I hope," replied Adams, "you will be a member of the convention in New York [for the revision of the Constitution]. It will want some such heart-of-oak pillar to sup-

---

[1] Jay's *Jay*, ii. p. 356.   [2] June 23, 1814, *Jay MSS.*
[3] March 6, 1821.   [4] May 7, 1821.

port the temple." [1]   But the old statesman was not called on to attend the convention, though his son, Peter Augustus, was a delegate.

Occasional visits from friends to Bedford cheered Jay's declining years. Then, as he smoked his long clay pipe, he used to delight in telling anecdotes of the Revolution, the true history of which he often said never had been and never would be written. Of such conversations, unfortunately, there is but scanty record.   His opinion of the second Continental Congress, expressed to Gouverneur Morris, has been already quoted ; and Fenimore Cooper was so impressed by hearing from his lips a story of his own experience as to make it the groundwork of "The Spy." Jay was speaking of the heroism and patriotism shown during the Revolution by men in humble life and of little learning. When on a secret committee to prevent the enlistment of troops in Westchester County by the British, he had occasion to employ a poor man, "but cool, shrewd, and fearless," to act the part of a spy.   "It was his office to learn in what part of the country the agents of the crown were making their efforts to embody men, to repair to the place, enlist, appear zealous in the cause he affected to serve, and otherwise to get possession of as many of the secrets of the enemy as possible." He ran the risk not only of discovery by the English, but of falling into the hands of his fellow countrymen. Frequently he was arrested by the local authorities,

[1] May 13, 1821.

and once he was condemned to the gallows, and
was saved only just in time by private orders to
his jailer. "By the Americans in his little sphere
he was denounced as a bold and inveterate Tory."
Thus he continued to serve his country in secret
during the early years of the Revolution. Jay, on
being appointed to Spain, reported an outline of
the facts to Congress and obtained an appropria-
tion for his agent, without revealing his name; and
undertook to deliver the money personally. They
met in a wood at midnight. Jay praised his companion for his fidelity and adroitness, and finally
tendered the money; but the man drew back and
refused to receive it. "The country has need of
all its means," he said; "as for myself, I can work,
or gain a livelihood in various ways." [1]

In the spring of 1818 Peter Van Schaack and
Judge Egbert Benson "went from Kinderhook to
Bedford, in the judge's one-horse wagon, . . . to
visit their mutual and bosom friend, Mr. Jay.
They were both, at this time, upwards of seventy." [2]
"A happy new year," wrote Van Schaack, at the
dawn of 1826. "You have passed fourscore, and
I am but a few months from it. Benson is between
us, and I shall soon be followed by Harrison,
Watts, and Rutgers. These I believe are all that
survive of our college contemporaries. *Nos turba
sumus.*" [3] Two years later, in an address before

[1] J. Fenimore Cooper, Introduction to *The Spy*.
[2] *Life of Peter Van Schaack*, p. 451.
[3] *Ibid.* p. 458.

the New York Historical Society, Judge Kent referred to Jay as the sole survivor of those who sat in the first Continental Congress. The next year Jay joined the rest of that "memorable convention."

"For many months before his death he was unable to walk without assistance. During the day he passed much of the time in his own room; the evenings were spent with his children and guests, partly in conversation, and partly in listening to books which were read aloud by one of the family. Unable to attend church, he occasionally had the Lord's Supper administered to him in his chamber." In the night of May 14, 1829, he had an attack of palsy, and on the 17th he died. In his will he remembered his servants, and gave his gold watch to his special attendant; he directed that there should be "no scarfs, no rings," provided at the funeral; "instead thereof I give two hundred dollars to any one poor deserving widow or orphan of this town, whom my children shall select." The funeral services were held at Bedford, but he was buried in the family graveyard at Rye. In New York the courts were in session, and brief eulogies were delivered by the presiding judges on news of the decease of the late chief justice. "Few men in any country, perhaps scarce one in this," said Chief Justice Jones at the opening of the Superior Court, "have filled a larger space, and few ever passed through life with such perfect purity, integrity, and honor." [1]

[1] *Mirror*, May 30, 1829.

Jay's principles of conduct were so unvarying, and his actions so consistent with them and with one another, that the most careless reader of his life, if it has been fairly presented, must be already familiar with the dignified and simple character of the man. Everything he did seems to have been inspired by a keen sense of impersonal moral duty. He might for a time be uncertain as to what this duty was, but the moment it was clear to him, he acted accordingly, promptly, fearlessly, without regard to personal considerations, undeterred by the consequences to his friends or his family. It was this singleness and uprightness of purpose, and the firmness with which he adhered to it, that made Adams call him ;" a Roman." In disposition he was more like an ancient hero, such as Cato, than he was like any of his contemporaries ; but where the Roman found moral inspiration in philosophy, Jay found both inspiration and great comfort and happiness in religion. It was one of his favorite remarks, that if men would never forget that the world was under the guidance of a Providence which never erred, it would save much useless anxiety, and prevent a great many mistakes. This optimistic fatalism, if one may so term it, produced in Jay a singular serenity of temper. When he had done what he conceived to be his duty, he was satisfied that all was for the best, and was undistracted by popular applause or condemnation.

Such complete self-dependence and self-control

are generally held by the world at large to be somewhat unamiable qualities ; and many have doubtless deemed Jay, in consequence, a cold, austere man, with all the classic virtues, but also with much of classic remoteness from ordinary humanity. Such, however, is very far from truth.   No man in his day had warmer, truer, or more constant friends. There were few who were nearer to the heart of Washington.   Hamilton from early youth admired and trusted him.   He won even the affection of those who, like Alexander McDougall and John Adams, began by misunderstanding him.   His friendship with Franklin was unaffected by their differences at the negotiation of the peace; and his friendship with Peter Van Schaack seemed to be only strengthened by the sternness of his judgment in the secret committee.   Even Captain Paul Jones wrote from Paris : " As there is no man who inspires me with more esteem than yourself, I beg you to accept my bust as a mark of my affection ; " [1] and it must have been a lovable character, indeed, to whom Gouverneur Morris would have sent this brief note across the sea : —

DEAR SIR, — It is now within a few minutes of the time when the mail is made up and sent off.   I cannot therefore do more than just to assure you of the continuance of my love.   Adieu.   Yours,

GOUV. MORRIS.[2]

" To see things as they are, to estimate them

[1] February 8, 1787, *Jay MSS.*
[2] November 7, 1783, *Jay MSS.*

aright, and to act accordingly, is to be wise," Jay once wrote to Wilberforce;[1] and this saying he repeated again, with the addition: "to do this effectually, self-command is absolutely indispensable. To look at objects through our passions is like seeing through *colored* glass, which always paints what we view in its own and not in the true color."[2] "To avoid mistakes," he said again, "it is necessary to see things as they really are. Minutiæ are often omitted, or imperfectly drawn in representations. Great part of the good within our reach depends on minutiæ; they merit more attention than many apprehend."[3] Here is to be found the secret of Jay's great success as a compromiser and negotiator. Without prejudice, he would proceed carefully to examine all the facts, and then it would seldom happen that they would not suggest a course of action at once obvious and mutually satisfactory.

He was eminently prudent, discreet, wary, and, though conscientiously truthful, averse to saying more than was necessary. Prudence was a virtue inherited from his father, and he handed on the tradition to his children. "The longer we live, and observe what passes in the world," he said, "the more we become sensible of the value and of the necessity of prudence."[4] The lesson was veri-

[1] November 3, 1809, Jay's *Jay*, ii. 320.
[2] Jay's *Jay*, ii. 429.
[3] To B. Vaughan, March 21, 1784, *Jay MSS.*
[4] From letters to his children, Jay's *Jay*, ii. 428.

fied by the misunderstandings of the factions at
the beginning of the Revolution, by the false
constructions put on language by the anti-Federalist and Democratic demagogues and newspapers.
As he became old the habit of reticence grew
upon him; but it had always been a personal characteristic, as is shown by an anecdote that Colonel Troup used to tell. "'Let us ride over,' said
General Gates to Troup, soon after the surrender
of Burgoyne, 'and see the chief justice' [who was
then at Fishkill]; 'I wish to learn his opinion of
our late Saratoga convention.' They went; and
during a two hours' visit Gates labored in vain to
draw from Mr. Jay some favorable opinion of that
military mistake. Finding himself ever baffled,
he at length ventured upon the direct question:
"Pray, Mr. chief justice, do you not think the
Saratoga convention a good convention?' 'Unquestionably, my dear general,' was the ready
reply, '*provided* you could not have made a better.' 'Come,' said the general to his companion,
'it is time for us to go.'"[1] Professor McVickar,
of Columbia College, whose sister had married
William Jay, and who was ever a welcome visitor
at Bedford, relates a similar experience with Jay
in his later years. Once, with some pertinacity,
he pressed the old gentleman for an opinion on the
authenticity of Washington's Farewell Address.
The discovery of a copy of it among Hamilton's
papers in his handwriting had raised the question

[1] Professor John McVickar, in *N. Y. Review*, October, 1841.

of its authorship, which, as a matter of fact, was settled by Jay's statement that the address had been submitted to him and Hamilton for suggestions and amendments, and, not wishing to spoil Washington's fair manuscript, they had made their notes on a copy.[1] "When," said McVickar, "the slow-puffing pipe and the deaf ear turned were no longer an apology for not hearing, the answer came out with a quiet smile: 'My opinion, my dear sir, you shall freely have. I have always thought General Washington competent to write his own addresses.'"[2]

With such a disposition Jay was inevitably a moderate man, choosing, whenever possible, the middle way between extremes, selecting the course that his judgment commended, independent of the dogmas of creed or party, even in religious questions. "In forming and settling my belief relative to the doctrines of Christianity," he wrote to a clergyman, "I adopted no articles from creeds, but such only as, on careful examination, I found to be confirmed by the Bible."[3] Towards religious views different from his own he was very tolerant, but he had no toleration for atheists. At a party in Paris once the conversation fell on religion. "In the course of it," said Jay, "one of them asked me if I believed in Christ? I answered that I did, and that I thanked God that

[1] Professor John McVickar, in *N. Y. Review*, October, 1841.
[2] To Judge Peters, March 29, 1811, Jay's *Jay*, ii. 345.
[3] To Rev. Samuel Miller, February 10, 1822, *Jay MSS.*

I did. Nothing further passed between me and them, or any of them, on that subject." Some time afterward an English physician, attending one of the family, " during one of his visits very abruptly remarked, that there was no God, and he hoped the time would come when there would be no religion in the world. I very concisely remarked that if there was no God, there could be no moral obligations, and I did not see how society could exist without them. He did not hesitate to admit that, if there was no God, there could be no moral obligations, but insisted that they were not necessary, for that society would find a substitute for them in enlightened self-interest. I soon turned the conversation to another topic, and he, probably perceiving that his sentiments met with a cold reception, did not afterward resume the subject." [1]

In politics, as has been noted, Jay preserved his independence of action; but his own declaration may be worth quoting : " In the course of my public life I have endeavored to be uniform and independent, having, from the beginning of it in 1774, never asked for an office or a vote, nor declined expressing my sentiments respecting such important public measures as, in my opinion, tended to promote or retard the welfare of our country." [2] Frequently such outspoken opinions required no little courage ; but he did not hesitate to condemn

[1] To John Bristed, April 23, 1811, Jay's *Jay*, ii. 346, 347.
[2] Jay's *Jay*, ii. 419.

the popular confiscation acts, to urge the abolition
of slavery, and to declare his honest opinion about
the French Revolution ; and yet, as has been seen,
his opinions on all these questions were in no
sense extreme. The experiences that usually blind
men's eyes and prejudice their judgment left him
clear-sighted and fair-minded. Even the throes of
the Revolution did not make him unjust to England. " I view a return to the domination of Britain with horror," he wrote in 1778, "and would
risk all for independence ; but that point ceded, I
would give them advantageous commercial terms.
The destruction of Old England would hurt me ;
I wish it well ; it afforded my ancestors an asylum
from persecution." [1]

His integrity, strength of character, and fairness
made Jay admirably suited to a judicial career.
How painstaking he was to keep himself wholly
free from improper influence is well seen in his
letter to Trumbull, who had just been appointed
a commissioner under the treaty of 1794. " Firmness, . . . as well as integrity and caution, will be
requisite to explore and persevere in the path of
justice. They who, in following her footsteps,
tread on popular prejudices, or crush the schemes
of individuals, must expect clamor and resentment. The best way to prevent being perplexed
by considerations of that kind is to dismiss them
all, and never to permit the mind to dwell upon
them for a moment. . . . Although a judge may

[1] To Gouverneur Morris, April 29, 1778, Jay's *Jay*, ii. 24.

possess the best talents and the purest intentions, yet let him keep a jealous eye over his sensibilities and attachments, lest they imperceptibly give to error too near a resemblance to truth. Nay, let him even watch over that jealousy, for the apprehension of being thought partial to one side has a tendency to incline a delicate mind towards the other." [1]

Jay was frequently accused of being an aristocrat, of not being in full sympathy with democratic institutions. The same charge was brought against Washington, Adams, and the Federalists generally, as a party. In the strict meaning of the words, perhaps, it may be admitted that Jay was a republican but not a democrat; but in this he was in agreement with the majority of the thoughtful men of his generation. To the statesmen of the eighteenth century an absolutely democratic government, with manhood suffrage, and with all power in the hands of the majority, was something unknown. What precedents there were in the histories of Greece and Rome seemed to show that any approximation to such a government was full of danger to society, and never permanent for any length of time; and contemporary events in France were not more reassuring. They were practical men, not theorists, and distrusted any principle, however pleasing, which had not been long tried and tested. It is from this point of view that many of Jay's opinions should

[1] To John Trumbull, October 20, 1796, *Jay MSS.*

be considered. " As to the position that ' the people always mean well,' or, in other words, that they always mean to say and do what they believe to be right and just, — it may be popular, but it cannot be true. The word *people* . . . applies to all the individual inhabitants of a country. . . . That portion of them who individually mean well never was, nor until the millennium will be, considerable." [1] " Pure democracy, like pure rum, easily produces intoxication, and with it a thousand mad pranks and fooleries." [2] Such remarks, however, are misleading, unless they are taken in connection with Jay's policy as a whole. Fortunately, he stated this concisely but comprehensively in a letter to Vaughan in 1797. " To me it appears important that the American government be preserved as it is, until mature experience shall very plainly point out very useful amendments to our Constitution ; that we steadily repel all foreign influence and interference, and with good faith and liberality treat all nations as friends in peace, and as enemies in war ; neither meddling with their affairs, nor permitting them to meddle with ours. These are the primary objects of my policy. The secondary ones are more numerous, such as to be always prepared for war, to cultivate peace, to promote religion, industry, tranquillity, and useful knowledge, and to secure to all the quiet enjoyment of their rights by wise and equal

[1] To Judge Peters, March 14, 1815, Jay's *Jay*, ii. 370.
[2] To Judge Peters, July 24, 1809, *Jay MSS.*

laws irresistibly executed. I do not expect that mankind will, before the millennium, be what they ought to be; and therefore, in my opinion, every political theory which does not regard them *as being what they are* will prove abortive."[1] Such a policy is certainly neither narrow nor illiberal, and when there is added to it the following declaration, it can hardly be termed aristocratic in any proper meaning of the word : "I wish to see all unjust and unnecessary discriminations everywhere abolished, and that the time may come when all our inhabitants of every color and discrimination shall be free and equal partakers of our political liberty."[2]

The type of man that is now regarded as distinctively American, and the watchwords, glittering and unscientific generalities for the most part, which are often upheld as comprehending the whole doctrine of American policy, originated rather in the ferment of the French Revolution than of that in which Jay was a leader. It is then, perhaps, not without interest to recall the simple, practical, sturdy, common-sense principles, based on fact and history, which animated that earlier generation, and made their work permanent in a sense almost unexampled among the works of men.

Once, for instance, in ordering a watch and chain for Mrs. Jay, through a friend, he remarked : "In these as in most things we must be guided

---

[1] Jay's *Jay*, ii. 232.
[2] To Dr. Rush, March 24, 1785.

by the rules of propriety which one's situation and circumstances dictate. Neatness and utility is all I ought or wish to aim at in dress or equipage, and perhaps every citizen of a republic would do well to forbear going farther." [1]

[1] To William Franklin, April 1, 1781, *Jay MSS.*

INDEX

INDEX

ADAMS, ABIGAIL, thanks Mrs. Jay for hospitality, 218.

Adams, Charles Francis, on causes of corruption in Continental Congress, 140; gives true explanation of Franklin's attitude toward France, 186.

Adams, John, first comments of, on Jay, 31 ; on Jay's reasons for objecting to opening Congress with prayer, 33; comments on Jay's various addresses for Congress, 41 ; on reluctance of America for independence, 42; says that his letter to Wythe furnished Jay with model for New York Constitution, 69 : satisfied with New York Constitution, 81; appointed minister to treat with Great Britain, 113 ; candidate of New England, 113, 144; says Jay's quarrel with Gérard made him distrust all Frenchmen, 115; his instructions dictated by Luzerne, 141; disliked in France, 144; complained of by Franklin, 144; endeavors of Vergennes to have him instructed to follow French directions, 144–146; believes Vergennes to have inspired Rayneval, 167; arrives in Paris, 182; describes Jay's position, 182, 183; consults with Jay and Franklin, 183, 184; his comments on Franklin's attitude exaggerated, 186; tells Franklin of his determination to support Jay, 187; suggests separating British debts and Tory claims, 188; convinces Strachey regarding northeastern boundary, 188; discusses fisheries, 189; tells Vergennes of difficulties over Tories and Penobscot, 190; reports to Livingston unanimity among commissioners, 191; suspects ideas of cabinet concerning fisheries inspired from Versailles, 193; explains fisheries and draws up clause, 193, 194; insists on " right " of fisheries, 194; on necessity of signing treaty, 195; says credit for treaty is Jay's, 200; complained of by Vergennes as unmanageable, 200; his appointment as minister to England urged by Jay, 203; compliments Jay in letter to Barclay, 204; protests against British retention of western posts, 214 ; letter of Jay to, on this subject, 215; his request for a favor declined by Jay, 216; letters of Jay to, on collapse of Confederacy, 221, 223; on importance of Jay in adoption of Constitution, 233, 234; receives degree of LL. D. from Dublin, 239; invites Jay to visit him, 239; considers Pinckney pro-Gallican, 265; on grounds of opposition to Jay for special envoy to England, 266; nominates Jay for chief justice, 301; late correspondence of Jay with, 312; wishes Jay to be member of New York Convention, 312; calls Jay "a Roman," 316; his friendship with Jay, 317.

Adams, John Quincy, his explanation of Franklin's conduct, 186.

Adams, Samuel, on committees with Jay, 40, 44; his absence enables Luzerne to manage Congress, 145; opposes any terms of peace which do not preserve fisheries, 169.

Allen, Ethan, writes pamphlet vindicating independence of Vermont, 94.

Alsop, John, chosen delegate to Continental Congress, 29; reëlected, 39; urged by Hamilton to frustrate Tory scheme, 47.

Maryland, State of, McCulloch v., 254.

Maryland, State of, v. Van Staphorst, 239.

Masserana, Prince, introduced by Jay to Franklin, 121; his kindness to Jay, 121.

Maurepas, Count, opposes France giving aid to colonies, 132.

Mechanics, of New York, their share in Revolutionary organization, 29, 30; approve action of New York delegates to Continental Congress, 36; coöperate in enforcing non-importation, 37.

Merchants, of New York, oppose non-importation, 24–26; value of their conservative action, 27; first to demand common action of colonies, 27; gain control of movement, 30; consider Jay their representative, 50; their influence in forming Constitution of 1777, 68.

Mifflin, Governor Thomas, prohibits intercourse with New York during yellow fever, 285, 286.

Mirales, Spanish envoy, discusses western boundaries with Jay, Gérard, and others, 110; pleased at Jay's appointment to Madrid, 114.

Mississippi navigation, desired by colonies, 110; efforts of France to induce United States to abandon, 111, 112, 123, 142; Jay instructed to retain, 114; desire of Spain for, prevents a treaty, 117, 118, 123; instructions of Jay regarding, modified, 123; demanded by Southern States, 142; effort of Gardoqui to prevent, by offer of commercial treaty, 208, 209; proposal of Jay to surrender for thirty years, 209; opposition to, in Congress, 210; causes of Jay's error, 210, 211; its evil effects, 211.

"Mohawks," of New York, guard tea-ships, 22.

Monroe, James, letter of Jay to, on territorial government, 217; warns Washington that Senate will reject Hamilton as special envoy to England, 265.

Montmorin, Count de, French minister at Madrid, tries to get Spanish alliance, 108; describes Spanish attitude to Vergennes, 109; describes character of Florida Blanca, 116; induces Jay to promise to inform him of course of negotiations with Spain, 117; urges Jay to come to agreement with Spain over Mississippi, 122; dissuades Jay from demanding a categorical answer, 124; puzzles Jay by his silence concerning French relations to Spain, 125; makes vain attempts to influence Spain, 125, 126; on Jay's departure from Spain, 127; letter of Vergennes to, on Spanish interests, 132; letter of Jay to, on French politeness, 152; letter of Vergennes to, on Oswald's commission, 160; tells Vergennes of Spanish position, 161, 167, 168; astonished at De Grasse's communications, 172.

Moore, William, on Revolutionary committees, 28.

"Moot," club of lawyers in New York, 17; its membership and importance, 17, 18; its decision said to have been followed by Superior Court, 18.

Mornington, Lord and Lady, friendly with Jay, 280.

Morris, Gouverneur, opposes Jay in contested election case, 16; member of the "Moot," 18; dreads mob rule in New York, 31; moves committee to form plan of government for New York, 58; on secret committee to examine Tories, 60; warned by Jay to avoid suspicion on account of Tory relatives, 66; opposes vote by ballot in Constitution of New York, 75; invited by Jay to write criticisms on Constitution, 80; confers with Washington on defenses of Hudson, 85; letter of Jay to, on court duties, 87; on Vermont revolters, 95; defends Deane, 96; on low character of Continental Congress, 140; notified by Jefferson of absence of neutrality stipulations in French treaty, 260; asks Jay to recommend a nephew to the President for appointment, 300; asks Jay to be god-

father to his son, 311; his affection
for Jay, 317.

Morris, Jacob, disconsolate over Jay's
defeat for governor, 250.

Morris, Lewis, letter of Jay to, on
independence, 54.

Morris, Robert, thinks Deane unjustly accused, 97; admitted to
practice in Supreme Court, 237.

Muhlenberg, Peter, saves Jay treaty
in House, 283.

Munro, Peter Jay, supported by his
uncle John Jay, 104; accompanies
him to Spain, 115.

Murray, George, prepares Jay for college, 8.

Murray, Lindley, in law office with
Jay, comments on his ability, 14.

NECKER, JACQUES, opposes proposed
French aid to colonies, 132; a liberal in politics, 132.

New England, approves New York
Constitution, 81; demands fisheries
in treaty of peace, 143, 144, 169;
approves treaty of peace, 199, 200;
condemns English Orders in Council,
263; condemns Jay treaty, 281, 282.

Newenham, Sir Henry, friendly with
Jay, 280.

New Hampshire, Tories sent to, 62;
connection with Vermont question,
94.

New York, Assembly of. See Legislature.

New York, Huguenots and Dutch in,
1, 2, 8; merchants of, 2; feeling
in, against Stamp Act, 4, 5; law
practice in, 15, 16; opposition to tea-
tax in, 22, 23; debate in, over non-
importation, 24-30; elects delegates to Continental Congress, 29,
30; to second Congress, 38, 39;
Revolutionary committees in, 37,
39; prepares to resist, 40; occupied
by British, 54, 55; measures of defense suggested by Jay, 57; condition of society and parties in, 58,
59; suppression of Tories in, 59–
66; voting population in, 71; government in, organized after new
Constitution, 79; Clinton elected
governor, 82; growth of parties in,

among Whigs, 83; invaded by Burgoyne, 83, 84, 86; demoralization
in, 87, 88; boundary troubles in,
94; difficulties with Vermont, 94–
96, 102, 103; advised by Jay and
Congress to submit Vermont matter to arbitration, 102; hard times
in, 104; welcomes Jay on return
from Europe, 205; growth of conservative and radical parties in, 206;
appoints Jay agent to settle boundary controversy, 217; riot in,
against medical students, 227, 228;
election of state convention, 228,
229; debate in, over ratification of
Constitution, 230-233; ratifies, 233;
campaign of Jay for governor
against Clinton, 240, 244-247; divisions of parties in, 242, 243; campaign
lies, 245, 246; defeat of Federalists through legal technicalitiy, 247–
249; popular feeling in, turns toward Jay, 251, 252; mobs in, against
Jay treaty, 282; Jay elected governor of, 284; yellow fever in, 285-
287; Jay's governorship, 285-299;
reëlects Jay, 292; carried by Democrats, 295; struggle of Council of
Appointment with Jay, 297, 298;
convention in, upholds Council
against Jay, 298.

Non-importation, advocated by Sons
of Liberty, 22; committees formed
to execute, 22, 24, 27; unpopular
with New York merchants, 24; left
for Congress to settle, 29; adopted
by Congress, 34, 35; enforced in
New York, 37.

North, Lord, driven out of office, 149.

O'REILLY, COUNT, entertains Jay in
Andalusia, 116.

Osborne, Sir Danvers, governor of
New York, commits suicide, 4.

Oswald, Richard, begins unofficial negotiations with Franklin, 149, 155;
thinks Franklin means to negotiate
without regard to France, 156; instructed by Shelburne to promise
independence, 156; receives his
commission, 157; describes Jay's
objections to commission, 157, 158,
159; dreads Jay's influence in nego-

An author and lawyer, GEORGE PELLEW (1859-1892) was the nephew of Jay's grandson, John Jay II. As a member of the family, Pellew had access to private papers and enriched his biography with the memories and personal anecdotes of Jay's immediate relatives to create an intimate portrait of the statesman and first Chief Justice. In addition to the Jay biography, he wrote *Women and the Commonwealth* and *In Cabin and Castle* before his untimely death at the age of thirty-three.

RICHARD B. MORRIS, Gouverneur Morris Professor Emeritus of History at Columbia University, is co-chairman of Project '87, an interdisciplinary study of the Constitution sponsored jointly by the American Historical Association and the American Political Science Association. He is currently editing a four-volume edition of the unpublished papers of John Jay. Past President of the American Historical Association, he has published extensively; his volume *The Peace-makers: The Great Powers and American Independence* was awarded the Bancroft Prize in 1966.